INTRODUCING THE
TEN TERRAINS
OF CONSCIOUSNESS

UNDERSTAND YOURSELF
OTHER PEOPLE AND
OUR WORLD

Tahnee Woolf ~ Allen David Reed

SOCIETY FOR COLLECTIVE AWAKENING

First Print Edition, April 2016. Correlates to Fourth Kindle Edition, April 2016.

Published by Society For Collective Awakening, Hilo, Hawaii.

The author(s) of this publication do not dispense medical advice or prescribe the use of any technique as a form of treatment for physical, emotional, or medical problems without the advice of a physician, either directly or indirectly. The intent of the author(s) is only to offer information of a general nature to help you in your quest for emotional and spiritual well-being. The author(s) and publisher do not assume and hereby disclaim any liability to any party for any loss, damage, or disruption caused by errors or omissions, whether such errors or omissions result from negligence, accident, or any other cause. In the event you use any of the information in this publication for yourself, which is your right, the author(s) or the publisher assume no responsibility for your actions.

Ten Terrains™, Terrain Mapping™, Terrain Mapper™, Beinghood™ and the Ten Terrains continuum of icons are trademarks and service marks of Beinghood Education Project (BEP) and/or Society for Collective Awakening and is/are protected under applicable International laws. Other names appearing herein may be trademarks and service marks of BEP and/or Society for Collective Awakening or trademarks and service marks of their respective owners.

Ordering Information: Quantity sales. Special discounts are available on quantity purchases by corporations, associations, and others. For details, contact the publisher at the address above. Orders by U.S. trade bookstores and wholesalers. Please contact Ingram Distribution: Tel: (800) 937-8000 (US); (615) 793-5000, ext. 27652 (Outside US) or visit www.ingramcontent.com.

Publisher's Cataloging-in-Publication Data

Reed, Allen D. and Woolf, Tahnee J.

Introducing the ten terrains of consciousness : understand yourself, other people, and our world / Allen D. Reed, Tahnee J. Woolf. – Hilo, HI : Soc. Coll. Awakening, c2015.

p.; cm.

Includes bibliographical references and index.

ISBN 978-0-9966625-5-0 (hardcover : alk paper) ISBN 978-0-9966625-6-7 (pbk.)

1. Consciousness. 2. Philosophy of mind. 3. Mind and body. 4. Extra-sensory perception. 5. Awareness. 6. Attention. 7. Conflict management. I. Woolf, Tahnee. II. Reed, Allen. III. Title.

B808.9 .R44 2015

128.2 – dc23

Tradepaper ISBN: 978-0-9966625-6-7
Hardcover ISBN: 978-0-9966625-5-0
Digital ISBN: 978-0-9966625-7-4

Cover design by Allen David Reed and Tahnee Woolf.

Printed in the United States of America.

To The Reader

*"This information is offered to you
from a place of humility and service.
We are grateful to have been
the messengers
to bring this Model to you.
May it awaken in you a wonder
at the richness of human existence.
May it give you understanding
of yourself and others,
and compassion for our world.
And may it help you
on your evolutionary journey."*

Tahnee Woolf ~ Allen David Reed

Table Of Contents

List Of Figures

Acknowledgments

*We thank each other for all the love, friendship, support,
companionship, partnership, inspiration, playfulness,
passion and commitment we have given each other
throughout this journey of co-creation.*

*We thank every person and every experience that
has been our teacher or mentor,
has expanded our minds and
has challenged us to grow.*

*We thank Diana and Ernie Woolf,
who have believed in us from day one and
have been the most loving and generous supporters
a pair of visionaries could ever wish for.*

*We thank all our dear friends who have shared our vision,
championed our gifts, pointed out our blind spots,
encouraged us in our vulnerable moments
and nourished our hearts with friendship and love.*

*We thank everyone around the world who has
supported the Ten Terrains Of Consciousness.*

1

INTRODUCTION

the
matter
based
terrain

PARTICLE

the
connection
based
terrain

CIRCLE

the
faith
based
terrain

RADIAL

the
coherence
based
terrain

SPIRAL

the
will
based
terrain

PYRAMID

the
fractal
based
terrain

TOROID

the
order
based
terrain

SQUARE

the
unity
based
terrain

INFINITY

the
reflection
based
terrain

DIAMOND

the
void
based
terrain

NO-THING

CHAPTER ONE

WELCOME

WELCOME TO a groundbreaking new Model that explains what is truly going on beneath the surface of human behavior and human civilization. This Model sets out the ten different fundamental paradigms that are playing out in our world. We call this new Model 'The Ten Terrains Of Consciousness'.

Your Terrain Of Consciousness is the *perceptual lens* through which you view the world. It governs the fundamental way you interface with life and therefore creates the way you think, your worldview, your beliefs, your values, your behavior and all your actions. It is your core operating system.

This Model of the Ten Terrains Of Consciousness will help you understand yourself better: why you make the choices you make, face the challenges you face and live the life you live. It will help you better understand your relationships with other people: why you get along with some, can't seem to see eye to eye with others and end up in conflict with others still. It will help you better understand why our world is in the state it is in: why we live in the culture we do, why we have the political systems we have, and why the people in power make the decisions they make.

By coming to understand this Model of the Ten Terrains Of Consciousness well, you will have both a *tool* to make sense of what is happening in your own life and in the world around you, and a *language* with which to describe it. In addition, beyond even explaining human behavior and the state of the world, the Ten Terrains Model provides a *map* of humanity's spiritual journey of evolution. As we will see later in this book, the 10 Terrains lie upon an evolutionary Continuum, and every person alive is moving along this Continuum, at their own pace; as is every human civilization.

Therefore the Ten Terrains Model is truly groundbreaking because it explains everything that is happening on this planet, at both a macro and micro level. It explains human nature and human behavior. It explains social, political and cultural phenomena. And it explains the evolutionary spiritual journey of humanity. It is a complete system for understanding our world.

WHAT LIES AHEAD

This book, *Introducing The Ten Terrains Of Consciousness*, is our introductory book. It sets out the basics of the Ten Terrains Model. This book is designed for people who are new to the Ten Terrains of Consciousness, to give you a simple overview of this powerful Model. In this book, we are going to provide you with a brief synopsis of the key points about the Ten Terrains Of Consciousness, so that you will have enough of an understanding to be able to observe the interplay of the Terrains in the world around you.

At the back of the book, we have provided you with a Glossary of the key language that we use in this book, some of which is entirely new vocabulary and some which is existing terminology that we are using in new ways. We encourage you to dip into this Glossary as you read the book, whenever you come upon a term you are not familiar with. You may even wish to read through the Glossary now, to orient yourself in the key language of this book, before you get started.

Part 1 of this book—'Introduction'—is a short section, giving you a quick introduction to the Ten Terrains and some background to the Model. In this section, we will describe some of the incredible benefits you can get from having a deep understanding of the Ten Terrains.

Then we will give you some simple examples of what a person's life might look like at each Terrain, so that you can get an initial impression of each Terrain. Then we will share the background and historical foundations of this Model, and explain the fundamental spiritual assumptions that underlie it.

In Part 2 of this book—'Explaining Terrains'—we will explain to you all about Terrains Of Consciousness, what they are and how they affect your life. We will describe how and when a person shifts from one Terrain to another. We will explain the mechanics of your spiritual evolution across the Continuum of the Ten Terrains. We strongly recommend that you *carefully read this section*. Do not skip it and race ahead to read about the individual Terrains. This section contains crucial information that you will need in order to be able to understand the material we cover in Part 3.

In Part 3 of this book—'Meet The Ten Terrains'—we will go through each of the 10 Terrains individually, devoting a chapter to each. Here is where you will start to learn about the different Terrains and how they are playing out in our world. We will explain the mindset that underlies each Terrain and its unique relationship with reality. We will give you a summary of the core features of each Terrain with enough examples of how it is expressed in human behavior that you will have a good sense of it.

In Part 4 of this book—'Collective Terrains'—we will discuss how the Terrains are also playing out at a collective level in nations and civilizations. We will share the kinds of systems, both social and political, that tend to emerge at each Terrain.

By the end of this book, you will be able to go out into the world and start to recognize the different Terrains as they play out around you, in your social circles, in the public sphere and in your own life.

If you are excited by what you read in this introductory book, you can study the Ten Terrains Of Consciousness in more depth. This entire Model is set out in full in our deeper body of work called *Mastering The Ten Terrains Of Consciousness*. That is the core material you need to study in order to fully understand the Ten

Terrains Model. It explains everything we will be touching on in this introductory book in far more detail, covering more than 1000 pages of content. It provides a much more complete grounding in the Ten Terrains Model and will give you the essential knowledge you need to both understand your own Terrain and to navigate the Terrains in the world around you—in both your personal and professional life. You can find out more about *Mastering The Ten Terrains Of Consciousness* at www.tenterrains.com.

Please note, in this introductory book you are reading now, we are attempting to summarize simply and briefly some very deep and complex topics that we cover at great length in *Mastering The Ten Terrains Of Consciousness*. We are merely scratching the surface here, and the nature of this book requires us to simplify concepts. So bear that in mind as you are reading this. There is a much deeper pool awaiting for you to dive into...

CHAPTER TWO

HOW THIS MODEL CAN HELP YOU

W<small>E ARE EXCITED</small> that you are reading this book, because understanding the Ten Terrains Of Consciousness Model is far more than just another interesting 'idea'. It can actually have a *huge* impact on your life.

UNDERSTAND YOURSELF

By understanding which of the 10 Terrains Of Consciousness is YOUR Terrain and coming to really understand that Terrain, you can better understand yourself. You can come to understand the core perception of reality that is creating the specific operating system that is running you. You can understand what is driving your beliefs, your values, your actions and your choices.

By discovering which Terrain you are at, you can begin to understand why you live in the house you do, why you do the job you do, why you have the kind of lifestyle you do, and why the things that matter to you do so. You can come to understand why your values are so important to you, why you relate to the world in the way you do, and why you make the choices that you do. All these things arise out of your specific Terrain.

By finding out your Terrain, you can begin to understand why you resonate better with some people than with others and why you have chosen the friends, lovers and partners you have. They most likely share the same Terrain as you do, or at least they probably did at the point when you were first drawn to them. You can also start to understand why certain people push your buttons so much, and why you always find yourself arguing with others. They are most likely at a completely different Terrain to you.

By knowing your Terrain, you can come to understand why some ways of living seem wrong to you and why some things happening in the world really upset you. These actions may seem foreign to you because they are coming from a radically different Terrain Of Consciousness to yours.

By finding out your Terrain, you can come to understand where you are at on *your* unique spiritual journey. You can get a sense of where you've been and where you are going next. You can look back at your journey so far and understand the challenges you have faced, the struggles you have endured and the great moments of shift you have experienced.

If you have recently experienced a 'Terrain Shift', discovering which Terrain you have shifted to will help you understand why your life no longer seems to fit and will enable you to find the resources to help you adjust to your new Terrain. Even more importantly, you will be able to look ahead to see what the next stage of your spiritual learning is and start to prepare for it.

MAKE BETTER CHOICES

Another wonderful benefit of knowing your Terrain is that you can start to consciously make *choices* based on your Terrain.

Health & Healing

For example, if you suffer from a major health problem, you can go and find a healing modality that is coming from the same Terrain that you are at, which is much more likely to heal you than a modality that is coming from a Terrain different to your own.

Relationships

With this knowledge of your Terrain, you can choose to enter into relationships—whether romantic or business-related—with people who are at the same Terrain as you are, which will mean that your values will be aligned and your actions will be synergistic. You will be on the same page with these people beyond merely common interests or compatible personality type. You will be on the same page in the deepest and most profound sense: your relationship with reality. This is a very strong basis for any kind of relationship.

Personal Development & Spiritual Growth

If you know your Terrain, when wanting to work on your personal growth, you can choose teachers, workshops and courses that are coming from the same Terrain that you are. You can choose spiritual processes and practices that are designed for your Terrain. If you are moving towards a new Terrain, you can choose mentors and coaches who are at that new Terrain, to help prepare you for your jump. Once you shift into a new Terrain, you can find new friends, teachers and modalities at that new Terrain to help you settle in there.

Career & Projects

If you understand your Terrain, when you are thinking of starting a new career or a business project, you will be able to choose one that resonates with your Terrain. You will be able to match yourself with audiences, markets and clients who are at your Terrain, so that you will be the perfect person to solve their problem and they will choose your product over that of someone coming from a different Terrain to them.

And more!

Basically, once you know your Terrain, you will have a profoundly accurate basis for making many of your life choices, that will set you up for the maximum flow, ease and success in your life.

IMPROVE COMMUNICATION

One of the greatest benefits to understanding the Ten Terrains is how it improves your communication with people, both people at the same Terrain as you and at different Terrains.

You will find yourself able to communicate your needs and desires much more clearly to people who used to misunderstand you, once you understand the Terrain filter through which they are listening to you. In love relationships and family interactions, you will be able to share your feelings and needs in language that your partner or family members can actually hear, once you know their Terrain.

If you are a parent, you will be able to use the Ten Terrain Model to discover the Terrains of each of your children. Once you know their Terrain you can give them the kind of nurturing that they specifically need at their stage of evolution, communicate with them in ways that they actually understand, and allow them the spiritual growth that their Infinite Self[1] is yearning for. You will be able to develop a much healthier relationship with them, based on mutual understanding rather than misunderstanding.

If you are a businessperson or health practitioner, you will be able to speak to your clients in language that they understand, even if they are not at the same Terrain as you. If you are a storyteller or in the media, once you understand the Terrain of your audience, you will be able to present stories in a way that deeply resonates with your audience. If you are an artist, you will be able to more powerfully convey your artistic point of view. If you are a marketer, you will be able to craft your marketing message to meet the Terrain of the people you are targeting, with integrity and precision.

If you are a service provider, you will be able to go much further than 'find a need and fill it'. By knowing your Terrain and being able to speak specifically in the language of that Terrain, you will be able to draw to you clients and purchasers who are at the same Terrain as you are or who are moving towards your Terrain. This way, you will be able to build an audience of like-minded people who truly resonate with you, are in genuine need of your services and see you as the answer to their prayers.

All of this comes from having a deeper understanding of where other people are coming from. You will get this once you understand their Terrain Of Consciousness.

RESOLVE CONFLICT

As you start to study the Ten Terrains Model, you will come to see that clashes of Terrain are at the heart of many of the conflicts on our planet. Consider the kinds of disagreements that take place between family members around issues of money, health, food, sexuality and lifestyle. Many of these arguments are the result of two different Terrains colliding with each other.

Consider the kinds of political clashes happening about issues such as logging, climate change, fluoridation, GMO foods, vaccinations, etc. Think of people arguing over different kinds of political systems, money systems, and social systems. The people on each sides of these arguments tend to be at very different Terrains.

Once you truly understand not only your own Terrain, but also the other 9 Terrains, you will be able to start navigating the Terrains in the world around you consciously in a way that reduces such conflicts and creates harmony.

You will be able to see immediately when you are interacting with people coming from a different Terrain to yourself and will be able to adjust your communication style so they can understand you better. You will know what is really driving their fears and will be able to come up with solutions that meet their needs. Once you understand about Terrain differences, you will be able to develop internal tools to get along with all people better, to resolve conflict and to bring a higher level of compassion and empathy to every interaction.

Once you are familiar with the 10 Terrains, you will come to understand what is causing the inter-generational conflicts in your family. You will understand why your grandfather sees the world so differently from your mother, and why your father sees the world so differently from your son. You will be able to observe and diffuse the tension that inevitably arises at family gatherings such as Christmas. You will be able to untangle long standing family conflicts and get along much better with the people around you.

As you become more familiar with the Ten Terrains Model, you will also come to understand what is causing the conflicts between other people in your work environment, in your community and globally between nations. If you are interested in peacemaking or conflict resolution, you will be able to mediate, counsel and negotiate between others more effectively, understanding where both parties are truly coming from.

Therefore, both in the personal realm and the broader political realm, the Ten Terrains is an incredibly powerful tool to help all of us live our lives in greater peace and harmony.

FIND KINDRED SPIRITS

Many of you reading this may be surrounded by friends and family at a very different Terrain Of Consciousness to you. Some of you may find it hard to meet people who truly see the world the way you do. You may spend much of your life feeling misunderstood and alone.

In addition, you may be at a Terrain that is very different from the Terrain of the mainstream culture. This can cause you to feel out of sync with society and out of place in your world.

One of the most life-changing benefits of discovering your Terrain is that once you have this knowledge you can then go out into the world and find people at the *same Terrain* as you. These are people whose fundamental relationship with reality is the same as yours, who see the world just like you do. Imagine how much happier you would be if you were surrounded by people who really *got* you, who were like-minded and like-hearted!

One of our primary goals in releasing this information into the world is to enable people at the same Terrain to *find each other*. We are setting up many different groups and networks to facilitate this. When you complete your 'Terrain Analysis Questionnaire'—the online test designed to pinpoint your Terrain—you will be given the opportunity to connect with others at your Terrain, both in your own country and around the world.

UNDERSTAND OUR WORLD

It is not just in your personal, professional and social life that knowledge of the Terrains is helpful. Once you understand the 10 Terrains Of Consciousness, you will start to see them playing out EVERYWHERE. In your own family, on the streets, on television and in the political sphere.

Movies and television shows will suddenly reveal a powerful subtext that you had never seen before, as you come to recognize the Terrains of the characters and what is really driving their behavior. Books and novels will take on a whole new level of meaning, once you realize the Terrain that the author is coming from. Even works of art will start to reveal the Terrain of their creator to you, as will songs and music that you hear on the radio.

You will start to look at the political, economic and social systems around you in a new way, as you come to understand the Terrains that are creating them. Historical events will take on new meaning for you, as you realize the Terrains of the players involved. Social changes, market trends and global phenomena will start to make sense, as you understand the Terrains Of Consciousness driving these shifts.

By coming to fully understand the Ten Terrains Model, you will have a unique understanding of the dynamics of our world that most people do not have.

This kind of understanding is not just helpful intellectually. If you are engaged in any kind of activism, social change or global transformation, you will be able to work towards that change and transformation without getting angry at the state of the world, without feeling helpless or being driven by attachment to outcomes. Instead, with the understanding you have of Terrains, you will be able to understand WHY the things are happening that you are trying to change, and you will be able to more easily feel compassion and acceptance, which allows you to create truly empowered transformation in the world.

UNDERSTAND EVOLUTION

By becoming learned in the Ten Terrains Model, you will also develop a profound understanding of the Journey of Spiritual Evolution that every single person on this planet is on, and that every single civilization on this planet is on too.

You will understand where we have all come from in our spiritual evolution and where we are moving to, both as individuals and as collectives. You will understand the specific lessons that each person and group is here to learn, the specific challenges we face and the specific gifts we bring, arising out of our specific Terrain Of Consciousness.

Furthermore, you will understand where humanity as a species is at on its collective Spiritual Journey. This is powerful knowledge, indeed.

Essentially, by knowing your own Terrain and coming to understand the interplay of all the 10 Terrains Of Consciousness, you will no longer be walking through your life or this world blindly, buffeted by the invisible forces of these ten parallel universes— instead you will be able to step through them with confidence, awareness and mastery.

HOW TO FIND OUT YOUR TERRAIN

Now that we have explained all the incredible benefits you will get from knowing your Terrain, you are probably wondering how to find out which of the 10 Terrains is yours.

The simplest way to discover your Terrain is to complete the 'Terrain Analysis Questionnaire', available at www.tenterrains.com. This comprehensive tool has been designed very carefully to reveal your true Terrain. The questions in it are very deep and wide-ranging and will help reveal the core way you see the world and the specific way you interface with reality. After you complete the questionnaire, you will be sent an analysis that will tell you your Terrain.

Once you know your Terrain, there are several resources available that will be very helpful for you. Firstly, we have a series of *Terrain Guidebooks* that are targeted to each specific Terrain. Reading the *Guidebook* for YOUR Terrain will give you priceless tools to help you navigate life at your Terrain, overcome the challenges of your Terrain, more fully learn the lessons of your Terrain and truly enjoy the gifts and blessings of your Terrain. The *Guidebook* will also help you understand how people at other Terrains see you and give you strategies to get along with them better.

In the near future we will also be offering *Terrain Mapping Pamphlets*, where we will list the Terrains of different life tools such as health and medical modalities, relationship and sexuality approaches, personal growth processes, exercise and body movement systems, nutritional and diet approaches, popular song genres and music styles, etc. These practical pamphlets will help you find products, services, approaches and modalities at *your* Terrain so that they will be right for you at this point in your life.

Further information about both the *Terrain Guidebooks* and *Terrain Mapping Pamphlets* can be found at www.tenterrains.com.

CHAPTER THREE

A GLIMPSE AHEAD

W E KNOW that many of you are excited to find out what the 10 Terrains are and may not want to wait until Part 3 of this book when we go through each Terrain in detail. So to satisfy your curiosity right now, before we even get into the background of this Model or any introductory points about Terrains, we are going to give you a simple example of a person at each Terrain. Hopefully this will ensure that you don't skip ahead, as there is much crucial information in the first two parts of the book, that you will need to read first if you are to completely understand the 10 Terrains.

TEN EXAMPLES

Obviously each Terrain can play out in an infinite variety of ways, so the following examples are *very simplistic*, but they will at least give you a feel for the 10 different Terrains. In Part 3 of this book, we will explore each Terrain in detail, illustrating many different variations of each Terrain, beyond the simple stereotypes we are presenting here.

The Matter-Based Terrain (Particle)

Imagine a person who has grown up in a famine-stricken war zone, who lives in a constant state of danger and starvation, always having to stay alert in every moment to ensure his immediate survival. He believes life is a constant struggle for survival. He does not have the luxury of thinking about friendships, career, relationships, society, politics, religion or personal growth. Life for him is about dodging gunfire, scrounging for food, finding shelter, avoiding danger and staying alive.

The Faith-Based Terrain (Radial)

Imagine someone who is a member of a fundamentalist religious group. She prays every night and lives a strict religious life, fearful that if she does not, her God will punish her. When something good happens to her, she believes she must have pleased her God. When something bad happens, she blames herself for having sinned. She believes her God has full power over her life, her death and her immortal soul. She is highly superstitious, devout and fully devoted to the God she worships. She will do anything a representative of her God tells her to do, as she believes they are speaking God's will.

The Will-Based Terrain (Pyramid)

Imagine a charismatic mafia leader who rules his territory by fear and threat. He seeks power and domination, wanting to gain as much wealth and territory as he can. He extorts people in the local area where his crime syndicate is based, demanding 'protection money'. He loves his family passionately, seeing them as an extension of himself. He sees the other mafia families as enemies to be defeated. His followers are scared of him, yet also look up to him for his heroic charisma. He is emotionally volatile, insatiable and seeks to satisfy his every whim and desire. He lives in a dog-eat-dog world and is always on his guard against potential enemies.

The Order-Based Terrain (Square)

Imagine a civil servant or bureaucrat working for the government. She is traditional, conservative, well-meaning and dedicated to duty. She likes things to be done as they have always been done, and has little interest in new fangled gadgets and trends. She has done this same job her entire adult life and is very proud of the role she plays in 'the system'. She believes in the nuclear family and traditional family values. She carefully saves for her retirement and has several different types of insurance policies. She believes what she reads in the newspapers, trusts what she was taught in high school, happily pays her taxes and puts her health in the hands of mainstream doctors. She tries to be a model citizen in every way.

The Reflection-Based Terrain (Diamond)

Imagine a free thinking, radical activist for social justice. He wants to change the world and leave his mark. He loves the latest technology and uses the internet to organize protests around the world. He loves to study the most brilliant new political thinkers. He has his own unique 'look', and keeps himself fit and healthy by drawing on the latest alternative fitness and health information. He does not believe the 'lies' that the media is telling him, and he questions everything that is accepted by the status quo. He considers himself to be pretty 'awake' and prides himself on the personal development he has done. He loves to talk about 'consciousness'. He admires people who are innovative, original and have made a big impact on our world.

The Circle-Based Terrain (Circle)

Imagine a young woman who lives in an alternative community, enjoying a simple life close to nature. She is deeply connected to her community, to the ancestors and to future generations. She wears clothing made from natural fibers, and does not shave her body hair or wear makeup. She eats whole, living foods and regularly does cleanses. She participates regularly in body-centered processes like tantra, ecstatic dance, drumming circles and yoga. She is a member of a women's circle and loves to work through her emotions. She enjoys eye-gazing and other heart-connecting practices. She lives in tune with the seasons, in harmony with animals and plants. She feels deep sadness at what is happening to Mother Earth and fights to save the planet in every way she can. She is passionate about Love and Oneness.

The Coherence-Based Terrain (Spiral)

Imagine an energy worker who teaches vibrational healing techniques. He has no interest in changing the people around him or saving the world, but instead spends his days focusing on transforming himself. He spends most of his time working on his own inner development, and practices non-judgment, deep forgiveness and compassion. He is continually developing his ability to perceive subtle energies and connect to the multidimensional realms. He hears messages in songs that play on the radio, and sees signs and guideposts for how to live his life everywhere around him. He checks in with his 'higher Self' regularly and works with spirit guides. When something happens in his life, he immediately asks what is the lesson here for him to learn and how did he create this situation. He sees that this 3D world is an illusion and that we are all One.

The Fractal-Based Terrain (Toroid)

Imagine a woman who intuitively understands the deepest principles of the Universe. She is able to access Truth directly from Infinite Consciousness, simply by asking the right questions. She allows her higher knowing to guide her at all times and knows how to cooperate with the collective Field in a way that generates true Power. She lives in a state of complete trust that life will provide everything she needs. She doesn't worry about money or about the future; she simply gives her gifts freely to the world, knowing that she will be taken care of. She often speaks in metaphors and parables, and sees things in archetypal terms. She is considered a wise woman and great spiritual teacher, yet she is deeply humble.

The Unity-Based Terrain (Infinity)

Imagine a man who knows that he IS every thing in existence. He seeks to hold all things with compassion and unconditional Love; and when he finds himself unable to do so, he goes within and clears the charge force that is keeping him in separation. When challenges happen in his life, he accepts that everything is perfect as it is and has no desire to change anything. He does not get attached to the dramas of life, for he sees everything as an expression of Infinite Consciousness, and he therefore has no judgments. He has instant and direct Knowing in every moment, without needing to ask questions. His ego is completely surrendered to Infinite Consciousness and he exists in pure Service. Regardless of what is happening around him, he experiences inner peace.

The Void-Based Terrain (No-Thing)

Imagine a Being who is immortal, and who is not subject to any of the basic 'beliefs' the rest of humanity subscribes to, such as gravity, time or space. This Being can effortlessly do feats such as levitation, translocation and walking through walls, for to them all matter is an illusion. This Being is beyond gender, race or age. This Being is simply Presence, without any Self or body. This Being is beyond even Unity or light and is beyond Infinite Consciousness. This Being simply IS.

BEAR IN MIND

The above examples merely show one way each of the Terrains can play out in our world. Obviously, as human beings are infinitely varied in their personality, interests and life purpose, there are infinite expressions of each Terrain. For example, you may meet someone at the Connection-Based Terrain (Circle), who is *nothing* like the example of Circle we just gave above. They may have completely different interests and be living a completely different kind of lifestyle. Yet if you were to look deeper, into the way they see the world, you would find much in common with the person in the example above.

This is because *the Ten Terrains are NOT ten different kinds of behaviors*. They are ten fundamentally different ways of relating with reality, ten dramatically different ways of seeing the world. As you read the rest of this book you will start to realize what is really *under* the ten sets of behaviors we described above, and you will come to be able to recognize the Terrains playing out around you even when they take a less expected form than in the stereotypical examples we gave above.

CHAPTER FOUR

BACKGROUND

PEOPLE OFTEN ASK US where this revolutionary new Model came from. It is difficult to answer precisely, as it has grown from our own personal learnings and experiences in this great classroom of life, gained on a daily basis over a combined total of over 95 years. Everything we have ever seen, heard, read, observed, experienced, felt and intuited, has been grist for the mill of our understanding of the world and has enabled us to bring forth this highly accurate framework of human nature. It is almost impossible to separate out the individual threads of insight and influence that have gone into our perception, for once we have integrated an awareness, idea, observation, or experience into ourselves, it becomes part of us. Therefore the source of this work is truly Life itself, as experienced by us.

In essence, the Ten Terrains Of Consciousness Model came from the All-Knowing of Infinite Consciousness, delivered via two humble human beings, Allen David Reed and Tahnee Woolf, who took the initiative to ask some big questions:

> "What is it that is truly driving human behavior?"
> "Why do people see the world so differently from each other?"
> "What is really underlying the problems we are facing on
>   this planet?"
> "What has really caused human history to unfold the way it has?"
> "Where are we heading to as individuals and as a species?"

The impetus for us to ask these big questions came in response to the combined experiences of both our lives. Co-writer Tahnee Woolf has spent her life seeking to understand the dynamics of interpersonal relationships and co-writer Allen David Reed has spent his life seeking to understand the dynamics of global systems and politics. Since coming together in 2011 as a couple, we have been in a process of deep inquiry into what is at the root of everything unfolding on this planet. Our combined focus on the personal and the political has led to a rich investigation into the fundamental dynamics that make up our world, and has given rise to this Model of the Ten Terrains of Consciousness that we are presenting here.

In retrospect, it is now clear that Infinite Consciousness has prepared both of us over the course of this lifetime—and many previous lifetimes—to receive this Model of awareness so as to be able to bring it to a world thirsting for true wisdom for the healing of our planet. It was the double helix of our life experiences that led to our synthesis of this Model. Neither of us could have developed it by ourselves—as we each needed the input from the other in order to complete the picture.

OUR FOUNDATIONS

The 'Ten Terrains Of Consciousness' Model emerged after decades of close empirical observation of the world, cross-checked using ancient methodologies of intuition to access our all knowing Field of Consciousness, and by systematically corroborating all of these concepts across numerous related schools of thought on Consciousness to check their veracity. The cross-correlation of the many lineages of wisdom confirms and verifies the integrity of these Ten Terrains of Consciousness as an accurate perceptual framework of human reality.

The Ten Terrains of Consciousness is a highly original work. However, its foundations go very deep—to the very core of Humanity's collective wisdom gained over tens of thousands of years.

We could not have created this new Model without the aeons of deep thought and investigation that so many people before us have put into understanding what makes people and our world tick.

In developing this Model, we have built upon humanity's esoteric history, including many pieces of the puzzle from previous bodies of work that also seek to identify different human modes in our world. These are bodies of work that we consider to be 'on fractal' to some degree or other with what we have ourselves observed and understood. They include modern systems such as the 'Map of Consciousness' set out by the late Dr. David R. Hawkins MD. Ph.D. in his seminal work 'Power vs Force'[2], which is coming from the Fractal-Based Terrain (Toroid), and the 'Levels of Human Existence' theory set out by psychologist Clare W. Graves[3], which is coming from the Reflection-Based Terrain (Diamond).

More ancient maps of knowledge have also provided keen insights for us, such as the foundational principles of the oriental and occidental mystery traditions. Between us, we have undertaken decades long research into many ancient systems including the I Ching, the Tao Te Ching, the Kabbalah, the Mayan Calendar of human conscious evolution, the Indian and Shamanic chakra systems, the Shamanic Medicine Wheel, Astrology, Feng Shui and more. These ancient wisdom systems come from the innate knowing gained at the Fractal-Based (Toroid) and Unity-Based (Infinity) Terrains and they see the patterns of Universal Truth, Universal Law and Infinite Singularity. Therefore these ancient systems all have a very expanded perspective that sheds great light on the fractal patterns known as 'reality' and on human behavior. We are very grateful to these ancient systems, as it is our steeping in these traditions that has enabled us to make sense of the information that has come through us while writing this book, and to present it to you in a way that is coherent.

In addition, in preparing this research, we have both for decades gained wisdom from teachers and Masters of many walks of life at many different Terrains, who have combined to give us a very clear pattern of Being in our world. We have also both taken in the wisdom from many luminaries, mystics, sages and great thinkers throughout history—many names of whom are included throughout our writings—all of whom have provided insights and influence in shaping the map and model of the Ten Terrains of Consciousness.

In the Additional Resources section at the back of this book, we provide a list of many of the key philosophical, mystical, psychological and scientific texts that have informed our thinking over the years. We highly encourage you to read these books, as they will provide you with a deeper understanding of many of the core ideas and assumptions that underlie this Model. We also include a list of organizations and other resources that you may find helpful in your further studies.

In addition to the esoteric studies we have undertaken, we are both highly trained in many secular areas. Californian co-writer Allen David Reed has done graduate studies in Civil Engineering, Landscape Architecture, Architecture, Regional and Urban Planning, Ecosystems and Environmental Design and has worked as an architect, builder, urban planner and environmental landscape designer. Allen was also a pioneer in the field of virtual reality in Silicon Valley in the 1990s. In addition, he has extensive training in applied and quantum physics and all branches of science; is a historian, political analyst and philosopher deeply schooled and studied in divination science and the esoteric gnostic arts; and is also a master dowser and shamanic intuitive.

Australian co-writer Tahnee Woolf has a Masters in Law from Oxford University, a graduate degree in literature and politics, and significant training in screenwriting. She has worked as a corporate lawyer, screenwriter, radio show host, personal development coach, workshop facilitator, spiritual channel, high level writer, inspirational speaker, emcee and public speaking mentor. She is also a trained Feldenkrais Practitioner and has worked as a somatic bodyworker and healer. Tahnee speaks multiple languages and has lived and travelled extensively around the world, giving her great insight into the human condition.

As a result of Allen and Tahnee's combined knowledge, life experience, immersion in the wisdom traditions and engagement in fields of academic study, The Ten Terrains model brings to balance the secret teachings of all ages together with our modern scientific world's latest understandings of our universe.

THE INFINITE AUTHOR

From the very earliest years of conceiving and discussing the ideas in this book we found that in our sessions spent together examining and pondering all the learnings we had gained from our walks through esoteric history, academic study and direct observation of human dynamics, our combined energy field in collaboration always opened up a kind of portal into the instant Knowing of Infinity. Original ideas and revelations would pour through prolifically from both of our mouths, giving rise to continual 'A-ha' moments. In these sessions together, we came to realize that these revelations were coming *through* us, but were not coming *from* us. This was confirmed when we had a Human Design reading of us as a couple that showed that when we are together our minds are wide open to receive expanded perception.

So in essence, the Author of this book is Infinite Consciousness. Both of us, Tahnee and Allen, each have the kind of brains that are able to take in vast amounts of information from a multitude of areas, see patterns in them and see the widest, largest possible picture, so we were well able to understand the ideas that were coming through us. Nevertheless the information did not come *from* us. It came from the Infinite Knowing of Consciousness, not from our limited human brains. Our job was to quickly scribble down everything that we were receiving and then to come up with intelligent questions that would trigger the next batch of information that came through. Our next job was to test the awareness that had come through us by scientific dowsing, academic research and direct observation of the world around us, at a personal, interpersonal, political and historical level. Our final job was to find a way to write down all these ideas so that they would make sense to others!

NO-THING

In writing any book such as this, sharing a map or model of human patterns, one will be heavily influenced by one's own Terrain Of Consciousness. Indeed, one's map will take the shape of one's Terrain, whether one chooses that or not. Therefore it is important that we declare that this book is written from the perspective of the ninth Terrain, the Unity-Based Terrain of Consciousness (Infinity), and therefore the ideas set out here are shaped by the Infinity perspective of Infinite Consciousness.

Co-Writer Allen David Reed is at the Unity-Based Terrain (Infinity); and, at the time of publication of this book, co-writer Tahnee Woolf has just made the jump from the Coherence-Based Terrain (Spiral) to the Fractal-Based Terrain (Toroid). The Prevailing Terrain in our relationship at this time is at Toroid moving to Infinity. Therefore, the widest possible perception we have between us is that of Infinity, and this provides the ultimate container of our work.

As a result of this, we wish to acknowledge that our ideas about the tenth Terrain, the Void-Based Terrain (No-Thing) are less confirmed than the understanding about the first nine Terrains, for neither of us are living at that Terrain and it is therefore outside the realm of awareness of our own rings in the Continuum of Terrains. That being said, we have had brief glimpses of seeing reality from the Void-Based Terrain in expansive spiritual experiences, and have sought intuitive guidance from Masters at the Void-Based Terrain.

We have observed that the things we have been shown about the Void-Based Terrain appear to follow the pattern and trajectory set out by the previous nine Terrains and therefore seem to be 'On Fractal'. They also reflect the spiritual writings of sages throughout the ages who have attained the Siddhic state of No-Thing. We have also dowsed every point that has come through us about No-Thing to check that it is correct, and have asked the same questions from as many different angles as possible to try to get past our own filters. We can confirm that the principles and precepts put forward in this book for the Void-Based Terrain fit with the overall patterns of existence and the many mystery traditions of the world. Therefore, they have a very high (90+%) probability of accuracy.

OUR APPROACH

It should be pointed out that in developing the Ten Terrains Model we did not use the kind of mainstream approach of deductive research and statistical analysis that you might find in a university text on Psychology, coming from academics at the Order-Based Terrain (Square). We are not at Square and we do not think that way.

As we have said above, this book is coming from the Unity-Based Terrain (Infinity). It is not coming from deductive materialism, but from inductive intuition, from a deep Body-Mind-Heart-Self knowing. Not from 'reason' but from the truth of what is. Instead of statistical analysis, we used an approach of openness to wisdom coming through us, allowing our intuition to guide our questions and listening in stillness and humility to the answers that came through. However, we have used deductive techniques such as reasoning and observation extensively to analyze and interpret the information coming through us and as a cross-check in our evaluation of the Model.

In this book, we will not be providing you with statistical studies of the 10 Terrains or citations of papers published in academic journals nor with a list of resources from proven scientists to back up our assertions. The accuracy of this Model is self evident to anyone who objectively observes the world and it is backed up by aeons of mystical wisdom and by both ancient and modern sciences. Furthermore, we know that those of you reading this book who are at the more expanded Terrains will want to make up your own minds about the truth of this Model, regardless of what is said in any scientific journals or academic studies.

What we are sharing here is the Truth as we know it and we offer it to you to feel into for yourself to decide if it is truthful for you. We trust that you will take the information we are sharing with you and *try it on*. Once you have read it and fully understand it, we encourage you start applying it to your life. Apply it to the people you know: see if it explains their behavior. Apply it to the world around you: see if it explains the things that are happening. See if is it true FOR YOU. As the great shamanic sages ask, "Does it grow corn for you, in your heart?"

We are fully aware that some people, particularly those at the Order-Based Terrain (Square), will be unable to accept that true knowledge can come through a person from the non-physical realms, without the need for scientific experiments, statistical data, lists of research papers and peer review. That is okay. For those people, there are plenty of texts found in university libraries that will give them great insight into the human condition. However, for those of you who have felt the tingle of Truth in your own body, who have experienced the clarity of intuition yourself, or who have heard great wisdom coming out of people's mouths who are deeply tapped into their higher knowing, you know that there is much wisdom to be found outside the narrow domain of scientific studies.

Indeed, most of the great works of religion and mysticism throughout the ages have come from received wisdom. This Ten Terrains Model follows in that tradition. Therefore, anyone who reads this book with an open mind and open Heart, who sits quietly in meditation and FEELS for the resonance of the ideas laid out here, will come to a personal experience of the truth of it as all the greatest enlightened mystics and sages have come to know truth, down through the ages.

OUR CORE ASSUMPTIONS

Before we delve into the 10 Terrains themselves, we would like to share with you the two major philosophical assumptions that are underlying this Model. These two assumptions are implicit in everything we write.

If you don't agree with either of these two assumptions, you may find this book very challenging to read and difficult to understand. If you do agree with these two assumptions, then we are on the same page!

So what are the two assumptions?

(i) *This is an intelligent, conscious, self-aware universe.*

(ii) *We are all expressions of the One infinite and immortal Consciousness.*

In Appendix A at the end of this book we include an explanation of these two assumptions. They are both very deep concepts, coming from the oldest, most profound wisdom traditions, yet we have done our best to explain them simply for you. You do not need to understand them in order to understand the Ten Terrains Model, which is why we have included them as an Appendix to this book rather than in the body. Yet we feel we need to bring them to your attention, as they are core assumptions that underlie the entire Model. We highly recommend that you read Appendix A in order to familiarize yourself with these two fundamental concepts.

CLARIFICATIONS

Finally, before we go into the Ten Terrains Model in detail, we wish to address the two main objections we hear to this work, both of which come from a misunderstanding of the Model. It is helpful to address these concerns right at the outset.

1. YOU ARE JUDGING PEOPLE AND CREATING SEPARATION

When first hearing about the Ten Terrains Of Consciousness, some people assume that it is ten different 'levels' of consciousness, like steps on a ladder. They think that we are judging some people as being 'better than' or 'ahead of' or 'more evolved than' others. If they are at the Coherence-Based Terrain (Spiral) they find this particularly alarming, as they know that everyone's spiritual journey is equally valuable and that everyone is exactly where they are meant to be.

However, to think that the 10 Terrains are ten 'levels' of consciousness reflects a misunderstanding of the Ten Terrains Model.

The idea of 'levels' of consciousness comes from the Reflection-Based Terrain (Diamond), which is an externally-focused Terrain where people evaluate themselves in comparison with others. The Diamond view of spirituality necessarily and inherently includes judgment-based ideas such as 'enlightenment', 'ascension', 'awakening' and 'levels'. Such a framework is perfectly fine and is to be expected at that Terrain.

However, this Model is not coming from that Terrain. As has been explained, it is coming from the Unity-Based Terrain (Infinity), and as such we are perceiving each Terrain as being a sum total of the charge force a Being has given to the infinite pool of possibilities in creating their own hologram. However, this is not an easy concept to explain, and it can get drowned out with all the popular talk of 'levels of consciousness' that fills the spiritual airwaves in our modern Diamond world. Given the Diamond era we are living in, it is understandable that a person hearing about the Ten Terrains Model for the first time, without knowing much about it, would assume that we are holding the Ten Terrains as 'levels', which we are not.

Because the human mind from the perspective of the ego can only perceive in time, the Continuum of Terrains appears to be linear from one end to the other, much like 'train stops' along a journey. Indeed, in order to make it easy for people to understand the Ten Terrains

Model, we often use this train metaphor to explain it. And for ease of understanding, we often use a simplified form of our Continuum graphic to represent the Ten Terrains, which sets the 10 Terrains out in a horizontal line.

However, from the perspective of the Infinite Self there is no journey at all, there is only ever this one 'Now' moment, and everything we are experiencing is a holographic projection created by the sum total of all our charge forces holding infinite dimensions in place, much like a water molecule holds infinite snowflakes. This is how we, the writers, view the 10 Terrains. The use of linear metaphors and diagrams in this book is simply to meet our readers where they are largely at, in a time-based linear thinking, so that they will be able to grasp the basics of the model and start to utilize it in their life.

Do not lump this Ten Terrains Model in with all the popular spiritual teachings out there which champion 'enlightenment', 'awakening', 'ascension' and 'levels of consciousness'. This body of work is not coming from that place and does not see spiritual evolution in those terms.

For those of you at Spiral, we applaud your vigilance in championing non-judgment, and we assure you that you can set aside your worries. We are not judging people or implying that anyone is ahead of anyone else. The more you come to understand this Model and its incredible depth, the more you will come to see how holographic and non-judgmental it is. When understood and applied accurately, this framework of the Ten Terrains creates harmony and coherence, not separation. Indeed, having knowledge of this Model will cause you to do the opposite of judge people: it will enable you to have much greater compassion and empathy for them.

As you study this Model, you will learn that from the perspective of Infinity no one Terrain is better than any other. To put it in the simplest terms, just like it is no better or worse to be 98 years old than 4, it is no better or worse to be at the Void-Based Terrain (No-Thing) than at the Matter-Based Terrain (Particle). The Terrains are just 10 different stages of a person's development, offering 10 different ways to see the world.

The Terrain you are at right now is exactly where you are meant to be. It is indeed *your* creation. Each Terrain has unique gifts, challenges and lessons. You have chosen to create this as your reality in this moment in time to experience those things.

There is no goal here in this spiritual journey. No 'enlightenment' to attain. No 'ascension' to reach. This moment is all there is and all Terrains are equally valuable choices for how to create this moment.

2. You Are Putting People In A Box

Some people, upon first hearing of the Ten Terrains Model, get quite outraged that someone could dare pigeonhole them at one Terrain of Consciousness. This reaction is particularly common from people at the Reflection-Based Terrain (Diamond), who prefer to think that they are at multiple Terrains, or that they can choose which Terrain they are at, or that they can choose to shift to a different Terrain at will. They dislike being told that they are at one Terrain now and that they will only shift from that Terrain if and when their Infinite Self decides to.

These objections come from a very healthy place. They come from the natural human urge towards freedom. No one likes to be put in a box. This is particularly true of people at Diamond, who treasure freedom in all its aspects, like to be in mental control of their own evolution, want to be able to decide for themselves who they are and where they are at, and as a result, tend to be the quickest to misunderstand this Model. It is also somewhat true of people at Pyramid, Square and Circle.

We can assure you that being at a particular Terrain of Consciousness is not a threat to your ability to design your own life. It is not putting you in a box. As you will read later in this book, you are a unique being with your own unique talents, skills, personality, life purpose, genetic lineage, body type, soul family, past life dimensions, etc., etc. However you do have certain things in common with some people. For example, you have a cultural background in common with people who grew up in your country in your era. You have hair color in common with people who have the same pigmenting as you. You have beliefs in common with people who share the same conditioning as you. You have your Terrain of Consciousness in common with people who see the world through the same perceptual filter as you do. That is all.

Recognizing that you are at a particular Terrain does not put you in a box any more than recognizing that you have a particular hair color does. It connects you with people who share your view of the world and gives you the tools to be able to understand how other people see it.

One of the other reasons why people often resist the idea that they are at a particular Terrain is that they cannot see their own Terrain. Without a deep and true understanding of the Ten Terrains Model it is hard to see your own relationship with reality. Just as it is hard to see your hair color without a mirror. However, just because you can't see it doesn't mean it is not there.

Indeed, every time someone has said to us "I don't have a single Terrain. I'm at multiple Terrains", within five minutes of talking to them it has become apparent which Terrain they are at. It is oozing out of them. It is evident in their every word, their every reaction. It underlies their every thought. It is their core operating system and it is evident to anyone who truly understands the Ten Terrains Model. Once *you* truly come to understand this Model (which may take years of study) you too will be able to see someone's Terrain within minutes.

Yet the person themselves cannot see their Terrain, for it is the water they are swimming in. It is the colored glasses that they do not know they are wearing, that color all their perceptions. So they try to convince us (and themselves) that they are at a more expanded Terrain than they are really at. They say things like, *"But I've experienced Oneness in an Ayahuasca journey, so I must be at Infinity."* Or they believe that they are at multiple Terrains at the same time, saying things like *"Some days I have tantrums at Pyramid and other days I'm totally zen at Toroid"*, or *"When I'm around my family, I become more Square"* etc., etc. All of this reflects a misunderstanding of Terrains.

Your Terrain is not the same thing as your behaviors, it is not the same things as your mental understandings and it is not the same thing as your experiences. Your Terrain is your fundamental relationship with reality, and this does *not* change moment to moment. Even if you are triggered by circumstances to revert to less mature behavior, your fundamental relationship to Infinite Consciousness does not regress. So too if you are temporarily expanded in your awareness by a spiritual or ecstatic experience, when you return from that experience you will analyze it and interpret it through the filter of your current Terrain (unless it was a dramatic enough experience to expand you to the next Terrain).

Some people like to think that they are at multiple Terrains because they feel that they can tune into other Terrains at will. It is true that if you have lived at a more contracted Terrain earlier in your life, you know what it is like to be at that Terrain. But other than that, you can only truly know what life is like at your own current Terrain; you cannot truly know what life is like at the expanded Terrains beyond your own.

Yes, of course, if we have a good imagination we can tune into different Terrains to imagine what they are like. If we are empathetic, we can feel into different Terrains to have a kind of feel for what life at that Terrain is like. If we are intelligent, we can read books and understand ideas from more expanded Terrains. In the right expansive circumstances, we can have glimpses of experiences of more expanded Terrains. But if we have not yet shifted to a Terrain, we cannot truly know what it is like to live there. All we can ever have is hunches, mental ideas, empathetic feelings and glimpses of experience. If we were ever to actually shift to that Terrain in the future, we would look back on our fleeting approximations and smile, realizing that we didn't really get it back then.

Just like if we're 11 years old, we cannot truly know what it feels like to be 21. We only really know this once we pass our 21st birthday.

For those of you who are resisting the idea of having one Terrain, the more you come to understand the Ten Terrains Model, the more easily you will be able to see your own Terrain playing out in your choices, your actions, your reactions, your behaviors and your words. The less you will worry about being put in a box, and the more you will celebrate this tool of self-knowledge which is explaining so much in your life.

The good news is that as you start to truly embrace being at your Terrain, you will allow yourself to more fully learn the lessons of that Terrain and to give the world its unique gifts. And you will be able to connect with like-minded people at the same Terrain as you. Your life will being to flourish in ways you cannot even imagine.

So we encourage you, as you read this book, to be open to the possibility that you are currently at one specific Terrain Of Consciousness. As you read the chapters ahead, try to keep an open mind about which Terrain that is. It will eventually become clear. Once it does, you will see it playing out in every single aspect of your life.

2

EXPLAINING TERRAINS

WHAT ARE TERRAINS?

NOW THAT we have shared with you the benefits of understanding the Ten Terrains Model, given you some simple examples of each Terrain, provided you with a glimpse into the background of this Model and shared the major assumptions that underpin it, it is time to get started on explaining the Model itself! We will start by looking at what exactly is a 'Terrain' and how people shift from one Terrain to another.

WE ALL HAVE A TERRAIN

Everyone has a Terrain Of Consciousness. You do. Your family members do. So do your friends, your favorite celebrities and your political leaders. Every single person alive has a Terrain Of Consciousness. And every single person who has ever lived had a Terrain.

YOUR TERRAIN IS YOUR CORE OPERATING SYSTEM

Your Terrain Of Consciousness is your core way of relating with reality. It creates the fundamental way you SEE the world.

Think of your Terrain Of Consciousness as being like the core operating system of a computer. It is underneath all your programs.

It is running you. It creates your thoughts, your beliefs and your values. It drives your choices, your actions and your behavior. It underlies your worldview and your entire paradigm.

Just like a geological terrain creates the conditions upon which all plant and animal life in an area grows, your Terrain Of Consciousness *creates the conditions upon which everything in your life manifests.*

All your life circumstances arise from your Terrain. For example, your choice of work and hobbies arises from your Terrain. Your relationship with money arises from your Terrain. Your relationships with other people arise from your Terrain.

Your Terrain Of Consciousness is the foundation beneath your entire life. A simple way to understand your Terrain is to imagine that it is a unique pair of colored glasses that you are wearing; a pair of glasses that you never take off. Your Terrain colors, informs and influences everything you experience. You see the world through the specific lens of your Terrain. Your Terrain shapes your entire perception of reality.

THERE ARE TEN TERRAINS

There are 10 Terrains in total. The Matter-Based Terrain (Particle), the Faith-Based Terrain (Radial), the Will-Based Terrain (Pyramid), the Order-Based Terrain (Square), the Reflection-Based Terrain (Diamond), the Connection-Based Terrain (Circle), the Coherence-Based Terrain (Spiral), the Fractal-Based Terrain (Toroid), the Unity-Based Terrain (Infinity) and the Void-Based Terrain (No-Thing).

We will be going through each of these 10 Terrains, one at a time, in Part 3 of this book. There we will describe the unique perceptions and traits of each Terrain, and give examples of the different kinds of behaviors and choices each Terrain creates, so that you can learn to recognize them in the world around you. But for now, we are going to continue explaining exactly what Terrains are and how they work.

EVERY TERRAIN IS COMPLETELY DIFFERENT

Because of your Terrain, you see the world in a fundamentally different way than do people at the other nine Terrains. You share your perception of reality with other people at your Terrain, yet the behaviors of people at different Terrains will seem strange to you.

It is as if there were ten different groups of people on this planet. These groups live side by side with each other. Often in the same house. They talk to each other yet usually do not truly understand each other. They interact with each other but do not really connect. They often argue with each other and try to convince each other to change. They can feel and sense that they are different from each other, yet they don't quite understand why...

These ten groups of people are different from each other not because of their culture, their heritage or their skin color; not because of their thinking style, their values or their beliefs; and not because of their personality type, their body type or their astrological sign; *they are different because of their Terrain Of Consciousness*. It is as if these ten groups are living in completely different realities, or in parallel universes, right next to each other on planet Earth.

This is because each Terrain has its own unique awareness of Infinite Consciousness, an awareness that creates an entirely different relationship with reality. Each distinct relationship with reality gives rise to its own distinct perceptions, values, beliefs, behaviors and systems. This goes far beyond simply having a different worldview or coming from a different paradigm – each Terrain is a radically different meta-paradigm, a dramatically different prism through which you are seeing and experiencing your world.

YOU CAN ONLY BE AT ONE TERRAIN

It is important to understand right at the outset that—at any given stage in your life, and at any one time—you can only be at ONE Terrain Of Consciousness.

Being at a Terrain Of Consciousness is like being at a chronological age. Just like you cannot simultaneously be both 15 years old and 16 years old, you cannot simultaneously be at more than one Terrain. Right now, you are either at Particle or Radial or Pyramid or Square or Diamond or Circle or Spiral or Toroid or Infinity or No-Thing.

When first introduced to the Ten Terrains, many people say things like: "*I think I'm a mix of Circle and Spiral, because I love community but I'm also really committed to Self-responsibility and personal growth*"; or "*I'm a mixture of Square and Diamond because I believe in my government and in the Church, but I have a very scientific rational mind*"; or "*I understand everything about sacred geometry and free energy and I'm passionate about social justice, so I must be part Toroid, part Diamond.*" This reflects a misunderstanding of the concept of Terrains.

We are not talking about tastes or interests or passions here. Neither are we talking about personality types or thinking styles. Nor are we talking about intellectual understanding or areas of study either. We are not even talking about behaviors or beliefs. What we are talking about is something that lies beneath all these things: a person's relative awareness of and relationship to Infinite Consciousness that underlies their entire perception of the world.

It is this fundamental relationship with reality that creates all your thoughts, habits, choices, values, actions and behaviors. They are all coming from your ONE Terrain.

As we will see in the next chapter, a person can be in the process of moving from one Terrain to another, which is a journey of evolution that can take weeks, months, years or even lifetimes. Yet even while a person is moving in this way, they are still only at ONE Terrain Of Consciousness.

So while you are reading this introductory book, remember that you are at *one* specific Terrain Of Consciousness and that all the people around you are at *one* specific Terrain Of Consciousness, even if they appear to have elements of the traits of multiple Terrains.

If you would like to find out YOUR Terrain, make sure to complete your Terrain Analysis Questionnaire and then you will know which of the 10 Terrains is creating every aspect of your life.

YOUR TERRAIN IS NOT YOUR IDENTITY

Another point that is important to understand is that your Terrain is not *who* you are, it is *where* you are in your evolutionary journey at this moment in time. You are not 'a' Square or 'a' Diamond or 'a' Circle; you are 'at' Square or 'at' Diamond or 'at' Circle. Your Terrain is not your identity, it is simply a stage you are passing through during your spiritual journey of evolution in this lifetime. While you are at this stage, you see the world through the lens of this Terrain. It is your current relationship with reality that creates all your current values and behaviors.

It is also necessary to explain that your Terrain Of Consciousness is not the thing that makes you unique. You are unique because of your personality, your talents, your way of thinking, your worldview, your body, your upbringing, your conditioning, your essence, your energetic frequency, your life purpose, your accumulated experiences, your genetic lineage, your past life history, your birth time, and all the other elements that make up your unique 'Geometry' in this lifetime.

You are different from every human being who has ever lived and will ever live. That being said, at this moment in time you share a *perception* that is common to all other people at your Terrain. Regardless of their own talents, personality type, background, genetic lineage, interest, hobbies, Astrology sign, Enneagram type, childhood traumas, etc., and anything else unique to them, if they are at the same Terrain as you, then your core way of interfacing with reality is the same as theirs. You are still all individuals, yet you are at the same Terrain Of Consciousness.

This shared Terrain is a common bridge that runs much deeper than shared interests, similar personality type, or common cultural background. When you come together with others at the same Terrain Of Consciousness with you, there will be a profound affinity there, that runs deeper than many other aspects of human connection.

Another interesting point to understand is that although your unique Geometry in this lifetime is mostly fixed—such as your body type, star sign, personality type, human design, innate talents, energetic signature, life purpose, etc.—your Terrain is not. As you grow and expand and your awareness broadens, your Terrain will shift.

You will take your unique Geometry with you as you evolve through the Continuum of Terrains. For example, if you are a tall, broad shouldered, creative, poetic, Myers Briggs ENFP, Enneagram 7, Manifesting Generator, Gemini, with a life purpose to make beautiful sculptures, then you will remain that same person whether you are at Square, Diamond, Circle, Spiral, Toroid, etc. However, at each Terrain, the way you see and relate to the world will dramatically change, and therefore the way you embody your gifts will be radically different as you move through the Continuum.

So remember, your Terrain is not who you are, it is an evolutionary stage you are at right now.

CAN YOUR TERRAIN CHANGE?

YOU WILL NOT necessarily stay at the same Terrain you are at now for the rest of your life. Your Terrain Of Consciousness can change as you grow and evolve.

TERRAIN SHIFTS

As your awareness expands throughout your life and you learn all the lessons and have all the adventures inherent in your current Terrain, you can reach a point where you pass an evolutionary threshold (we call this an 'Event Horizon of Perception') and suddenly shift to a whole new Terrain Of Consciousness.

Such a Terrain Shift is *monumental*! It changes everything in your life: the way you see the world, the choices you make, the people you are drawn to, the work you do, the way you are living and your very relationship to reality. In *Mastering The Ten Terrains Of Consciousness* we describe the impact of a Terrain Shift on all aspects of a person's life, including their career, friendships, lifestyle, values, beliefs and behaviors. We also discuss the psychological and emotional repercussions of such a vast and sudden jump in awareness.

A person can shift Terrain once, multiple times, or not at all. Essentially, how much a person shifts in their life depends on the 'Evolutionary Role' that they are here to play in our collective Field.

Many people will not have a Terrain Shift in their lifetime; they will remain at the Terrain they are at now for the rest of their life.

These are people whose Evolutionary Role in this lifetime is to hold the collective Field stable. For others whose Evolutionary Role in this lifetime is to *lift* the collective Field, they are likely to grow so much that they jump to the next Terrain and may even expand through several Terrains throughout their life.

It is even possible for a person to expand through the entire Continuum in one lifetime, if that is the Evolutionary Role they are here to play. However, that is extremely rare. Usually, a person will either remain at the same Terrain their entire life, or will shift one or two Terrains. If you meet someone at the Unity-Based Terrain, it is likely that they have shifted four or five Terrains, which is quite unusual.

It is important to understand that your Evolutionary Role can change from lifetime to lifetime; therefore you may move through the Continuum of Terrains at an entirely different speed and to a greater or lesser degree in your next life than you do in this one.

Whether you undergo a Terrain Shift once, twice or more in your life, *you will notice it if you have one*. It is an unmissable event that rocks the very foundation of your entire life. Indeed, for some people, a Terrain Shift can cause their entire life to fall apart, as nothing seems to fit them any longer—not their work, their friends or their lifestyle.

If YOU feel that you have been through a Terrain Shift and would like some support adjusting to your new Terrain, we strongly suggest you complete your Terrain Analysis Questionnaire to determine which Terrain you are at *now* and find others who are already settled at that Terrain to mentor you and guide you.

THE CONTINUUM OF TERRAINS

It is important to understand that the Ten Terrains are NOT ten different levels like steps on a ladder: rather they function in a fractal relationship with each other, more like *a progression of increasingly expanding concentric rings*. At each more expanded ring, a person has a vastly greater perception of Consciousness than do people at the ring inside it.

These expanding rings of perception are 'The Continuum Of The Ten Terrains Of Consciousness'. It is along this Continuum that a person is moving as they expand and shift from one Terrain to the next.

THE CONTINUUM
OF THE TEN TERRAINS
OF CONSCIOUSNESS

The Ten Terrains Of Consciousness span this Continuum from the emptiness of the Void at the outer edge to the fullest resistance of matter at the inner-most ring at Particle.

The Continuum Of The Ten Terrains Of Consciousness is essentially a spectrum of 'awareness'. With each more expanded ring, you have a vastly greater perception of the whole of Consciousness than when you were at the Terrain before. The more expanded a person's awareness is, the lesser is their illusion of separation; and, conversely, the more contracted a person's awareness is, the greater is their illusion of separation. As a person expands along the concentric Continuum from the inside to the outside, their perception slowly expands by degree from fear to Love, from referencing the outer to referencing the inner, from victimhood to Self-responsibility, and from separation to Unity.

It is important to understand that these concentric rings are each bounded by an 'Event Horizon of Perception' that cannot be crossed. Your awareness of Consciousness is orbiting the ring you are at, just like electrons orbiting an atom. You orbit around the ring of your current Terrain, learning the life lessons you need to learn, sharing with the world the gifts you are here to give, and having the experiences you need to have at that Terrain, building the momentum for transformation, until your Infinite Self is ready to make the next leap in your evolution. Only at that point can you pass through the Event Horizon and jump into the next ring. As we will explain in the next section, once you have made that big leap, there is no going back (at least not during this lifetime).

In our writings and presentations, we generally use a much simpler diagram to represent the Continuum of Terrains, taken from a cross-section of the concentric rings:

This simple linear representation of the Continuum powerfully illustrates the spectrum of Terrains, with the least expanded awareness at one end (Particle) and the most expanded awareness at the other (No-Thing). However, always remember that this simple linear diagram is simply a *shorthand* for the full Continuum of concentric rings, ranging from the the most constrained inner ring with the narrowest perception to the most expanded outer ring with the broadest perception.

A BROADER AWARENESS

Another way to describe your Terrain Of Consciousness is to say that it is *the extent of your perception*. You can see everything within the ring that you are orbiting around, but you cannot see beyond it.

For example, if someone is living at The Order-Based Terrain (Square), their perception is expanded out to the edges of the Square ring. Therefore they also have an awareness of the core perceptions of Pyramid, Radial and Particle, as these are both within the larger ring of Square. However they do not have any awareness of the core perceptions of the other Terrains beyond their own.

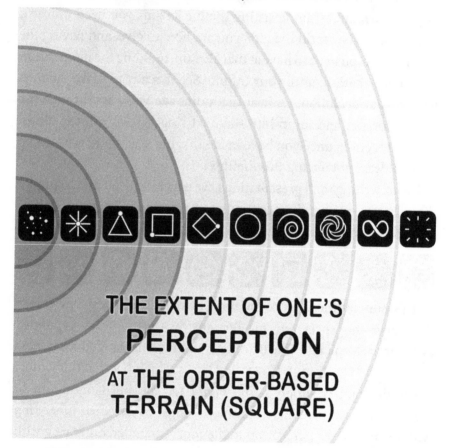

THE EXTENT OF ONE'S
PERCEPTION
AT THE ORDER-BASED TERRAIN (SQUARE)

The fact that a person can only understand their own ring and the ones inside it means that someone living at one Terrain quite simply cannot fully comprehend what it is like to live at the more expanded Terrains. They may read about a more expanded Terrain, they may study it, talk as if they are living it, even try to mimic some of its behaviors and act as if they are living it, but they are not living it... yet.

Indeed, some people simply will not believe the things that come out of the mouths of people at a more expanded Terrain to them. It will sound to them like gobbledegook or madness. Claims of levitation, bi-location, transmutation, telepathy and other things that are perfectly obvious and sensible at the more expanded Terrains appear like science fiction to those in the inner rings.

A simple way to understand this is to think of the hearing range of dogs. A human being cannot hear the sounds that a dog hears. This does not mean that those sounds don't exist. It just means that the frequencies are too high for the human ear and the sounds are therefore out of our range. So too, the truths told to us by those at a more expanded Terrain are real, we simply cannot know them ourselves as they are beyond the present range of our perception.

The caveat to this, that we must always remember, is that *our larger Infinite Self does know Truth.* Even if we have been made to believe it does not exist or have forgotten it in this human incarnation and are living inside the orbit of a very narrow Terrain Of Consciousness, the larger part of us does know it. Even at the most contracted Terrains, there can be peak moments in our life when we can actually remember Truth, even if just for a split second, such as during the stillness of an especially deep meditation session, the profound intimacy of lovemaking, the primal ecstasy of giving birth, the blissful melding of repetitive chanting, a moment of profound peace sitting in nature, the expansion of an ayahuasca journey, etc....

In fact, many people around the world have experienced moments—sometimes only a split second, sometimes whole hours— where they were experiencing life at the Unity-Based Terrain or even glimpsed the Void at No-Thing. But these are mere glimpses; the person's core Terrain Of Consciousness still remains where it is.

To understand this, imagine someone living in the United States who is magically teleported to Australia for a few minutes and then instantly snapped back. They have seen Australia, they have heard the sounds and breathed the air, but they are no longer there. They cannot return there at will. They do not live there. It is simply a place they once experienced for a moment. This is what many people have experienced in their transcendent experiences—glimpses of Terrains more expanded than their own, not an actual Terrain Shift.

THE EVOLUTIONARY DIRECTION

A person's Terrain Of Consciousness can expand over the course of their lifetime, as they move along the Continuum of Terrains from the Particle end to the No-Thing end. However, it is important to note that a person's awareness cannot 'contract' during their current lifetime. That is, *you cannot regress in your evolution.*

For example, just like a person cannot go from 18 years old to 17 years old, a person cannot contract from Circle to Diamond, or from Diamond to Square. They can only expand, e.g. from Square to Diamond or from Diamond to Circle. This is because, as the wise saying goes, *"Once you become aware, you can't become un-aware".*

To understand this, imagine a person who always thought the Earth was flat, who is one day taken up in a spaceship and sees the true roundness of planet Earth. They can never go back to thinking that the Earth is flat. It is the same with your Terrain Of Consciousness. Once you shift across an Event Horizon Of Perception into a more expanded Terrain, your entire perception of reality has changed. You can never go back to the perception you had before, as you now know how much more there is to reality.

Of course, there are situations and times when people can exhibit *behaviors* from a more limited Terrain, but that does not mean they have in fact contracted back to that Terrain in an evolutionary sense. Even while such a person is doing the more contracted behaviors, their perception and their awareness still remain expanded at their current Terrain. *WE do not devolve, merely our behavior does.*

For example, imagine a child at the Connection-Based Terrain (Circle) who is going through a period of rebellion while establishing their independence from their mother. The child's behavior may be temporarily a little willful and ego-centered like a person at the Will-Based Terrain (Pyramid), but the child herself still remains connected to the Web Of Life and aware of the natural world, as all people at the Connection-Based Terrain do. What we are looking at here is our core perception, not our transitory behaviors.

In summary, our awareness can expand along the Continuum of Terrains, but it cannot contract. Our behavior might temporarily regress (although this happens less and less at the more expanded Terrains) yet our true, internal, core nature is always expanding. Consciousness—being Self-organizing and thus Self-healing—always moves towards Unity, and it is always pulling us back there so that we can return home.

STATIONARY OR ON THE MOVE

Moving from one Terrain to the next can take years, or even lifetimes. However, it is important to understand that the journey gets *exponentially faster* once someone is On The Move to the next Terrain. This is because the evolutionary energy required to start shifting someone who is Stationary at their Terrain is much greater than that required to shift someone who is already moving towards the next one, for momentum is at play in the latter case.

Mountain Climbing

To explain this, we often use the metaphor of climbing a mountain. Imagine a big mountain that lies between one valley and the next. It takes a great deal of energy and resources for a person to leave their familiar, comfortable valley and set off on an expedition up this mountain. It is hard work indeed to hike up the steep incline of the first side of the mountain, and can take a long time. However, once a person has reached the summit of the mountain, they can rest there and survey the new valley that awaits them at the end of their climb. Freshly rested and motivated, it is much easier and faster to come down the other side which is downhill now, and they often arrive into the next valley at a run.

The journey from Terrain to Terrain is very much like an experience of hiking up a series of mountains between ten different valleys. In this analogy, the valleys are the 10 Terrains and the mountains are the journey our Infinite Self takes us on in preparation for the move to the next Terrain, allowing us to learn all the lessons we need to learn before we can move on. As we are moving up the mountain from one Terrain valley to the next, at first the going will be very slow, with incremental changes happening in our life, often taking many years, just like a long slow trek up the steep side of a mountain.

At a certain point when we reach the top of our mountain, halfway between the Terrain we are at and the next one, we can now see the valley ahead of us, with its wondrous foreign city. As we can now glimpse the next Terrain, we start to learn a little about it in anticipation of our arrival there. Perhaps some people from that foreign Terrain start to show up in our lives, or we are exposed to teachings or processes from that Terrain. We may even start to act a little as if we are already at that Terrain, almost as if trying it on.

As we move down the second side of the mountain towards this next Terrain, gravity helps us to speed up, for we are on the downhill section now and momentum is taking over. Our Infinite Self is orchestrating more and more things to happen in our lives to bring us closer to the moment where we will jump across the Event Horizon into it.

As we approach the valley below, time starts to feel as if it is speeding up, and more and more synchronicities start to show up in our life. More and more things change around us, and it seems as if fate itself is orchestrating something big to happen to us that we cannot quite put our finger on.

Then as we cross the Event Horizon into the next Terrain, we touch down into the valley below, kissing the ground with relief after our long journey, and we find ourselves in a strange new world, where the landscape is different, the customs are different, and the people are different. Our world will never be the same again.

Evolutionary Phase

The way a person's Terrain influences their life depends to quite a large degree on which part of this journey of mountain climbing they are on. We call this their 'Evolutionary Phase'. There are two different Evolutionary Phases: 'Stationary' and 'On The Move'.

10 CIRCLE
EVOLUTIONARY PHASE: STATIONARY

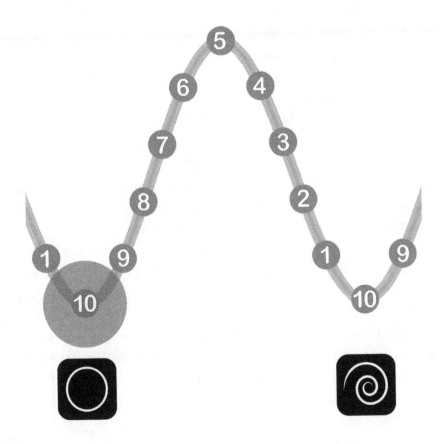

Stationary

In the diagram on the previous page we can see an example of a person who is currently Stationary at the Connection-Based Terrain (Circle) who is therefore 10 out of 10 at that Terrain and has not yet started to move to the Coherence-Based Terrain (Spiral).

A person whose Evolutionary Phase is 'Stationary' has a very different energy than someone whose Evolutionary Phase is 'On The Move', whether the latter is just starting to slog their way up the mountain, is already running down the other side of the mountain towards the next Terrain or has only just arrived into their new land and is trying to learn the ropes.

A person who is Stationary at their Terrain is well settled in their valley and is fully embodying all its customs and practices. We affectionately call such a person a 'Poster Child' of that Terrain. These are the people who most clearly fit the description of each Terrain, as we describe them later in this book. Their behavior tends to be the most stereotypical of a person at that Terrain, as they are not being influenced by either the previous Terrain or the next Terrain on the Continuum. If you are trying to identify the Terrains of the people in your life, these people will be the easiest to pinpoint.

People who are Stationary are not yet on the evolutionary move to the next Terrain. This is neither a good thing or a bad thing, it simply means that their Infinite Self wishes them to spend more time at this Terrain, in order to learn its lessons fully and have the full range of experiences and adventures afforded by this Terrain.

Some Stationary people are those who have only recently arrived at their Terrain after having had a Terrain Shift. Their Infinite Self is giving them time to fully arrive and settle into their new Terrain, allowing them to really immerse themselves in it, before heading off on their evolutionary journey once again. Such people may spend several years settled at their new Terrain, learning the lay of the land, having archetypal experiences of that Terrain, studying its teachings, and exploring what it has to offer, before starting to move again.

Other Stationary people may have been at their Terrain for years, decades and, for some people, their whole life. Such people are so settled at their Terrain that they are actually entrenched there and are unlikely to move. These tend to be people whose life work requires them to profoundly master this one Terrain Of Consciousness. They are here to offer the world the greatest gifts of this Terrain. This is their chosen playground for this incarnation and they are very at ease here.

Whether temporarily settled or permanently entrenched at their current Terrain, all Stationary people are very different from people whose Evolutionary Phase is 'On The Move'. They are so fully embodying their Terrain that it is generally fairly easy to pinpoint which Terrain they are at if you are very familiar with the Ten Terrains Model.

On The Move

In the diagram on the following page you can see someone who is currently at 6 Circle, part way up the mountain on the journey towards Spiral.

People who are moving towards the next Terrain—whether in the slow early stages of hiking up the steep side of the mountain, or in the later stage of running faster and faster down the other side—have a much more open energy than those who are Stationary. They are in a state of growth, and are often searching and questing and trying new things.

They have already learned and integrated many of the lessons of their current Terrain and their Self is now starting to orchestrate events and situations to move them gradually towards the next Terrain. Perhaps a crisis is unfolding in their life, or they are being deeply shaken up in some way or another.

Such people who are 'On The Move' are most likely starting to encounter ideas, people, modalities and systems from the next Terrain, as part of their preparation to enter it. However, these people are still interpreting these new ideas through the filtering lens of their current Terrain. *They have not actually shifted yet*, for until the moment they cross the Event Horizon of Perception, they are still at the same Terrain they have always been at. Nevertheless, when you meet such people, you can sense that they are on the evolutionary move.

6 CIRCLE
EVOLUTIONARY PHASE: ON THE MOVE

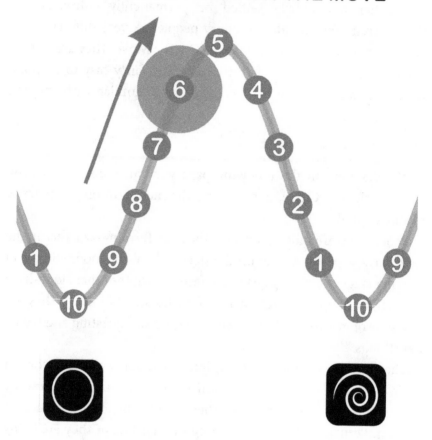

It is not as easy to pinpoint the Terrain of people On The Move as it is in the case of Stationary people, for they are often already being influenced by the Terrain to which they are moving. They themselves will usually feel very different within themselves than they did when they were Stationary at their Terrain, for the shift from being

Stationary to being On The Move is actually a very big shift, almost as big as a Terrain shift itself. People who are On The Move will see people who are Stationary at their Terrain as being quite different from them. In fact, when reading through the Terrain descriptions later in this book, when they read the description of their Terrain, they will most likely think *"Wow, that's how I used to be"* and they may even mistakenly think that they have crossed the Event Horizon to the next Terrain, simply because they have changed so much since being Stationary.

Nevertheless, they are still at the same Terrain. When they do eventually cross the Event Horizon into the next Terrain and feel the even bigger shift within themselves that this brings, then they will realize that what was a huge change before was still all taking place within their scope of perception of their old Terrain Of Consciousness.

Running Down The Mountain

The diagram on the following page shows someone at 2 Circle, who is currently running down the evolutionary mountain towards Spiral, quickly approaching their next Terrain Shift.

With those who are rapidly approaching the jump to the next Terrain, running down the mountain towards it, it can be even harder to pinpoint their Terrain, as they will most likely already be adopting ideas and approaches from the next Terrain and be living some of its behaviors. Indeed, if someone at this point in their evolution were to read this book, they would be quite likely to identify with the Terrain that they are moving towards rather than the Terrain that they are truly at. However, the person's true Terrain will still be picked up when they complete their Terrain Analysis Questionnaire.

For it doesn't matter how fast a person is moving or how much new information they are absorbing, until they actually cross the Event Horizon Of Perception into the next Terrain, they are still at the previous Terrain, and it is that operating system that is still running them. To continue with our mountain climbing metaphor, it is not until you enter the next valley and clear customs there that you are actually considered to have 'arrived' there. Until then, your Terrain is still the same; you are simply in the process of traveling.

2 CIRCLE
EVOLUTIONARY PHASE: ON THE MOVE

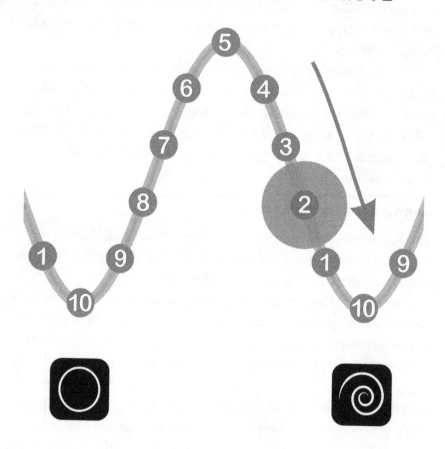

EXPOSURE

When a person who is 'on the move' is traveling down the mountain towards the next Terrain, their Infinite Self will start to put them in contact with ideas and input from the approaching Terrain, to help prepare them for the jump. That being said, it is *not* only those people who are running down the mountain towards a particular Terrain who can be exposed to ideas, practices and teachings from that Terrain. A person can be exposed to ideas and experiences from a more expanded Terrain when they are still several jumps away from it.

However, these ideas and experiences of the more expanded Terrain will have a different effect on someone several jumps away from the new Terrain than they will have on someone who is about to jump to that Terrain. A simple way to explain this is to use the analogy of tourists. If someone visits a foreign city for a few days as a tourist, they will usually have a much more superficial exposure to the city than will a person who is visiting there because he is planning to move there permanently. The tourist will probably travel around in a tour bus, eat at touristy restaurants and see mainly touristy landmarks. The person who is about to move there permanently will most likely spend time with the locals, eat in the places where the inhabitants eat and explore the back streets where people really live. They will have a much deeper, more fully embodied experience there than the tourist will.

This same contrast applies when comparing people who are exposed to ideas and practices from a Terrain while they are still living several valleys away and people exposed to that Terrain who are about to shift into it. The first category of people are exposed to the new information from a much more conceptual or mental place, and will usually simply fit their new knowledge into their pre-existing way of seeing the world. The second category of people are relating very deeply to the new information; it is landing with them viscerally and preparing them on a deep level for their arrival into their forthcoming Terrain.

Therefore, just because someone speaks about 'deep ecology' and 'heart-connection' does not mean they are about to shift into the Connection-Based Terrain (Circle). Just because someone talks about 'energy' and 'telepathy' does not mean they are about to shift into the Coherence-Based Terrain (Spiral). Just because someone speaks about 'the harmonic code' and 'holographic reality', does not mean they are about to shift into the Fractal-Based Terrain (Toroid). These people may simply be tourists with a mental understandings of principles from future Terrains that they are not yet fully embodying.

And there is nothing wrong with that. Such people are not being false or trying to deceive you. Their mental understanding is simply ahead of their Terrain. Indeed, such mental understanding can be a great asset in a person's spiritual journey. By exposing a person to expanded ideas so far in advance, their Infinite Self is preparing them, on some level, for a jump they will make at some distant point in their future.

SPIRIT NOT WILLPOWER

This brings us to one of the most important (and for some people, difficult to accept) points in this book: *you cannot simply decide to shift Terrain.* Just like a child cannot simply decide to be 11 years old when they are 10, a shift in Terrain is not something that can be achieved through mere mental intention or will power.

You can only shift Terrain when your Infinite Self is ready to do so. And your Infinite Self will only be ready to do so when you have had all the experiences you need to have and learned all the lessons you need to learn at your current Terrain.

This may take a day, a week, a year, a lifetime, or multiple lifetimes. It will take as long as it takes. Until your Infinite Self is ready for you to shift, no amount of studying or practicing or training or wishing or praying or setting intentions will work. Our conscious mind is not in control of this journey, and we cannot steer this path by ego or willpower.

This idea is most difficult to accept for those at the Reflection-Based Terrain (Diamond), for as we will see later in this book, the very sense of safety for people at Diamond comes from their belief that they can influence their world with their mind. The Diamond personal growth / spiritual world teaches that we can 'manifest' our own reality merely by setting an 'intention'—and this is a perfectly reasonable view for those at the Reflection-Based Terrain. However, those who have expanded to the Terrains beyond Diamond soon learn that it is not human intellect that is directing the evolution of life on this planet, it is the wiser knowing of Infinite Consciousness as personified in one's Self.

If a person tries, by ego or willpower, to shift Terrain before they are ready to shift, they are likely to suffer a major life lesson to show them what they have yet to learn. This may be even more extreme in those cases where a person tries to skip Terrains or jump to a Terrain far beyond their own. They may suffer a serious illness, experience financial collapse, have a marriage breakup, lose a loved one or find that some other crisis situation arises that causes them to look closely at themselves and at their life. This happens in order to snap them back to the path of learning they were meant to be on, to make sure that they do indeed learn the lessons that they need to learn, rather than jumping ahead to a place they are not yet ready to be at.

Many people find themselves drawn to study ideas or implement practices from Terrains ahead of their own. This is a fine thing to do. While studying about Terrains ahead of where you are presently at will not cause you to jump ahead on the Continuum before your Self is ready to shift, there are still great benefits to doing such study. Studying the more expanded Terrains and learning from teachers who are at those Terrains will be a great help in your preparation toward your eventual evolution across the Continuum of Terrains and will make it much easier for you to land comfortably in your new Terrain if and when you do eventually shift there. In addition, having a deep knowledge of the more expanded Terrains will make it much easier for you to relate to and accept people at those Terrains.

Another thing to understand is that although we cannot simply choose to jump Terrain and then instantly be there, a moment may come when we feel within ourselves that we are *ready* to jump Terrain. The more expanded our Terrain is, the easier this moment will be to feel. So start listening deeply to your Self. Where are YOU at right now on your evolutionary journey? Have you been at your current Terrain for a while? Did you just arrive there recently? Are you feeling the stirring of evolutionary movement within you? Are the changes in your life speeding up? Do you feel yourself gathering energy for another shift?

You cannot rush this shift or alter its course, but you can *track* it as it is happening.

CHANGING OTHERS

Just as we cannot shift our own Terrain by willpower or conscious intention, we also cannot shift the Terrain of another person. No amount of compelling or convincing or forcing or 'educating' someone can cause them to make that quantum leap across the Event Horizon Of Perception to the next Terrain.

This is why it is completely fruitless and a waste of energy to ever try to change others or try to make someone else jump to a 'new paradigm'. Not only is it a complete invasion of their rights as an autonomous Being (and extremely arrogant to assume that you know better than their Infinite Self), but it simply will not work. A person's awareness can only expand if and when their Infinite Self feels that they are ready to.

So much energy is currently being wasted on our planet by people trying to make other people shift before they are ready to do so. This approach happens throughout the first six Terrains on the Continuum, those that we call the 'single-frame' Terrains. For example, people at Square put great effort into trying to convince people at Pyramid to knuckle down, be responsible and do their duty. People at Diamond exert tremendous influence trying to convince people at Square to innovate and think outside the box. People at Circle strain to convince people at Diamond to move into their Heart and to work collaboratively to care for Mother Earth. Indeed, this is the approach of much of the so called 'transformation movement', who are desperate to bring about a 'quantum shift' or a 'paradigm shift' or a 'great turning'. The irony is that this need to change others is fundamentally rooted in the same fear and control as is held by those who are resisting shifting.

Rather than trying to get others to change, the most effective thing you can do is be a model of your own Terrain and develop educational materials and support systems to help those people whose Infinite Self is ready for them to shift into it. Hold their hand as they cross the threshold and welcome them into your Terrain when they arrive there. Going after people who are still living in a different Terrain to you and harrying them to shift is pointless and will lead to great frustration for both them and you.

However, when someone is at one of the first six Terrains Of Consciousness (Particle to Circle), the urge to try to change others is overwhelming. So we must remember that and have compassion for each Being's process. If you feel the need to try to change others, to 'shift' them or 'awaken' them, that may just be where you are at in your evolutionary journey. Do not fight this; it is part of what you are here to experience. Know, however, that the frustration you are experiencing is not because you are bad at convincing people to change, or because the people you are trying to shift are impossibly stuck, it is because it is simply not possible to shift the Terrain of another. Only a person's own Infinite Self can cause them to shift, and this will only happen when they are ready to shift at all levels of their Being.

CASE STUDY: LUKE SKYWALKER

We have covered a lot of points so far in this chapter about how a person's Terrain can change as they move along the Continuum Of Terrains. To help pull all these points together, we are now going to look at an example of a well-loved and iconic fictional character who moves a long way along the Continuum of Terrains over the course of one lifetime: Luke Skywalker, in the 'Star Wars' movie trilogy.

Luke's Journey

Over the course of the three original Star Wars movies—'Star Wars: A New Hope' (historically the first movie, but technically the 4th episode in the Series), 'The Empire Strikes Back' and 'Return Of The Jedi'—Luke Skywalker expands in his relationship to Consciousness all the way from the Order-Based Terrain (Square) to the Fractal-Based Terrain (Toroid).

While several of the other characters in these movies do expand across a single Event Horizon—such as Han Solo, who shifts from Pyramid to Square—Luke Skywalker expands across four Event Horizons. This is an epic evolutionary journey!

Movie 1: Star Wars

At the start of the first movie, 'Star Wars: A New Hope', Luke is a loyal farm boy wanting to join the Imperial Academy and be part of the great military machine. At that time, he is at the Order-Based Terrain (Square), the Terrain of social order and mainstream thinking. However, Luke is fast approaching the Event Horizon into the Reflection-Based Terrain (Diamond), the Terrain of progress and innovation and of questioning the system. This is evidenced by his interest in droids and his dreams of adventure.

When Luke returns home to find that his family have all been killed by Imperial troops, his faith in the Empire shatters and he experiences a massive quantum shift into the Reflection-Based Terrain, transforming from well behaved Square citizen into angry Diamond rebel. Once this Event Horizon of Perception has been crossed by Luke, there is no going back.

Luke then starts traveling around with his first mentor, Obi-Wan Kenobi, a 'Jedi Master' who is at The Unity-Based Terrain (Infinity), the Terrain of total surrender. The Jedi philosophy is from the Fractal-Based Terrain (Toroid), the Terrain of trust and Universal Truth. Therefore Luke is now exposed for the first time to various Toroid ideas, such as 'the Force'. (The Force is in essence the Quantum Field;

and once the Jedi masters complete their training and reach Toroid, they are able to tap into it, which is the source of their Power).

However, because Luke is at Diamond at this time, he is exposed to these very expanded Toroid ideas as a 'tourist', rather than in the fully embodied way of someone at Spiral who is moving towards Toroid in their evolutionary journey. Luke therefore goes about his Jedi training in a very Diamond way. He dreams of fame and glory as a Jedi Master, wanting to excel and be the best, in true Diamond style.

During the rest of this first movie, Luke starts to slowly move up the mountain towards the Connection-Based Terrain (Circle). At the end of the film, Luke has a dramatic experience of tuning into his feelings—a very Circle practice—in order to allow the Force to guide him to fire the critical shot that destroys the Death Star, instead of using his ship's computerized targeting system, as would be advisable at Diamond. In that moment of trusting his feelings rather than technology, Luke glimpses the interconnectedness that runs through every living thing, and he jumps across the Event Horizon of Perception into Circle.

Movie 2: The Empire Strikes Back

At the start of the second movie, 'The Empire Strikes Back', set three years later, Luke is at Circle already on the move towards Spiral, the Terrain of inner truth and multidimensionality. He is starting to glimpse the invisible realms, in preparation for his shift to Spiral, so he is able to receive a message from the spirit of Obi Wan Kenobi telling him to travel to the planet Dagobah. This is a marked change from how he received the crucial message that kicked off the first movie when he was on the move to Diamond, carried via technology by droids.

In response to Kenobi's psychic message, Luke goes to Dagobah, where he receives advanced training in the Force by ancient Jedi Master Yoda, who—like Obi-Wan—is at The Unity-Based Terrain (Infinity). Luke is faced with a big choice when his training is interrupted by a vision of his friends Han Solo and Leia in pain: whether to continue his Jedi training or to go save his friends. Being at Circle, he decides to follow his Heart and go save his friends, despite Yoda advising him against this.

It turns out that the vision of his friends had been a trap, and now Luke finds that he must face Darth Vader, who in his black mask is the very face of 'the system', a twisted distortion of the order that Luke so admired as a child at Square. Vader reveals himself to be Luke's father. He pulls on Luke's imperial conditioning as a child and tries to tempt him to the 'Dark Side' of the Force, offering him all the power of ruling by his side. In his critical moment of choice, Luke chooses to die rather than be corrupted and throws himself down into a bottomless reactor chasm. This profound act of integrity following his highest truth completes Luke's journey down the mountain and shifts him dramatically through the Event Horizon Of Perception from Circle to the Coherence-Based Terrain (Spiral).

Movie 3: Return Of The Jedi

At the start of the third movie, 'Return of the Jedi', set one year later, Luke is at Spiral. He is now a Jedi. Watching the way Luke holds himself, we can see that he is not the same mild mannered Square farm boy nor even the passionate Diamond rebel we used to know; he is now more centered, clearer about who he is, and much more Self-responsible. He is not quite yet a Jedi Master, but he is starting to be someone who leads by example, with humility, who is coming from acceptance rather than fighting to change the world. He is well on the Spiral journey of finding his own truth and holding to it even in the toughest of circumstances.

Yet once again Luke's Self is conspiring to bring him to his next and greatest evolutionary leap, organizing events to bring him to his biggest moment of choice in the entire trilogy...

In the cataclysmic scene at the end of this final movie, Luke faces both his father Darth Vader and the diabolical Emperor who is at the Will-Based Terrain (Pyramid), the Terrain of power-seeking and domination. As the Emperor eggs Luke on and threatens the lives of everyone he loves, Luke finally gives in to his anger and fights his father. He is winning the fight and even manages to sever his father's mechanical right hand.

But when the Emperor orders Luke to strike Darth Vader down and take his place, Luke glances at his own bionic hand and realizes he is on the verge of suffering his father's fate. He realizes he has been triggered out of his centre, regains his composure, deactivates his lightsaber and throws it away, proudly declaring his allegiance to the Jedi. He chooses not to fight, not to save his own life and not even to save the lives of his loved ones, choosing instead to trust in the Force, even in the face of death.

At that moment, Luke makes the monumental jump across the Event Horizon Of Perception to the Fractal-Based Terrain (Toroid). He ends the trilogy at Toroid, a true Jedi Master, living in a state of deepest trust.

Conclusion

So why is it that Luke Skywalker is able to grow and expand in his awareness so much that he shifts Terrain four times? Luke is an example of someone with a 'high Evolutionary Role', which means that he is here in this lifetime to grow and expand in order to raise the vibration of the entire Field.

Luke's enormous character arc—from Square to Toroid—is one of the most powerful and resonant in movie history, and it is one of the reasons that he is one of the most memorable characters of all time. Watching his journey through these three movies is a terrific way to deepen your understanding of the concepts we have been discussing in this chapter.

We recommend that you come back and read this case study again once you have read Part 3 of this book, 'Meet The Ten Terrains.' At that point, after reading the chapter about each Terrain, you will have a much deeper understanding of them than you do now and you will really see how Luke moves through them on his evolutionary journey.

OUR EVOLUTIONARY JOURNEY

AT ITS HEART, a person's evolution across the Continuum of Terrains is a progressive immersion into Infinite Consciousness. This is a gradual yet relentless journey, for the Universe is healing us all back to Unity just as smoothly as a cut on our hand heals itself.

PATTERNS

There are some patterns in how the Ten Terrains play out across the Continuum Of Terrains, as they move in a general arc from Matter to Void. Here is a short summary of some of those patterns:

1. The Terrains move from polarity to unity as they evolve along the Continuum.
2. The Terrains move from most limited in perception to most expanded in perception.
3. Just like a human body has two hands with five fingers in each and two feet with five toes in each, the human collective has two groupings of perceptions with five Terrains in each.
4. The first 5 Terrains are 'fear-reactive', meaning that one has a perception of separation from Infinite Consciousness that causes one to react to life from a place of mistrust and fear. The second five Terrains are 'love-responsive', meaning that one has a perception of interconnectedness with Infinite Consciousness that causes one to respond to life from a place of trust and Love.

5. The first five Terrains have a focus on 'survival', whereas the second five Terrains have a focus on 'thrival'.

6. The first five Terrains are 'outer-directed', meaning that one's motivations are in reaction to one's outer environment. The second five Terrains are 'inner-directed', meaning that one's motivations are in response to one's inner Being.

7. At the first five Terrains, learning is 'deductive', meaning people rely on external referencing to obtain information. At the second five Terrains, learning is 'inductive', meaning people have enough trust in their Self to obtain information inwardly.

8. There is a point on the Continuum where the Terrains move into multidimensionality. This happens at the Coherence-Based Terrain (Spiral). Therefore, the first six Terrains have a 3D awareness and the final four Terrains have a multidimensional awareness.

9. The first six Terrains are 'single-frame' Terrains, which means a person can only hold one single perception of reality at a time. Thinking that their perception is the 'correct one', they strive to make other people see the world as they do. The final four Terrains are 'multiple-frame' Terrains, which means a person can hold multiple perceptions, enabling them to truly see through another person's eyes. They are able to allow other people to be where they are at and see the world how they see it, without trying to change them.

10. The Terrains alternate between a more individual focus and a more collective focus, with the expression of these becoming more and more expanded.

11. The Terrains also alternate between masculine and feminine energy, with the expression of these becoming more and more expanded, ultimately integrating into Unity and then transcending even that.

12. Each Terrain also has a corresponding partner at the same position on the opposite side of the Continuum. These pairs of Terrains operate as bookends, exploring the same overarching theme in polar opposite and inverse ways: one partner explores it from an outer-directed perspective, and the other from an inner-directed perspective. Particle and No-Thing explore the theme of 'meaninglessness'; Radial and Infinity explore 'faith'; Pyramid and Toroid explore 'power'; Square and Spiral explore 'order'; and Diamond and Circle explore 'ethic'.

13. The Ten Terrains also play out the journey of Self-Governance in our world, moving from 'Chaos' to 'Submission' to 'Domination/Capitulation' to 'Consensus' to 'Revolution' to 'Evolution' to 'Involution' to 'Self-Rule' to 'Beinghood' to 'Presence'. This pattern also dances from an individual-focus to a collective one. It also falls into pairs of bookends, one at either end of the Continuum, with one half of each pair ceding the power of governance to something outside themselves and the other half governing themselves from within.

14. The ten visual symbols used to represent the Ten Terrains also express the above patterns. The physical attributes of the shapes of the symbols as they progress along the Continuum tell the story of human spiritual evolution, visually conveying the movement from randomness to meaning, from separateness to interconnectedness, from linear to cyclical, from manmade to natural, from three-dimensional to multidimensional, from matter to formlessness, and at a more symbolic level conveying the progression from outer to inner, from 'doing' to Being, from separation to Unity, and from fear to Love.

15. The Continuum of Terrains is exponential. As one moves along the Continuum, the perception of Consciousness expands exponentially, the rate of shift increases exponentially, and the Event Horizons Of Perception between the Terrains themselves get exponentially more subtle.

16. From the time-based perspective of the human ego-mind, the Continuum of Terrains appears to be linear from one end to the other, much like 'train stops' along a journey. However, from the perspective of the Infinite Self the Continuum is holographic, meaning that it is referencing all Terrains simultaneously in relation to itself and 'includes' within each Terrain—like Russian dolls—all other less expanded Terrains. From the Infinite perspective there is no journey at all, there is only ever this one 'Now' moment, and everything we are experiencing is a holographic projection created by the sum total of all our charge force.

We explain each of these patterns very thoroughly in *Mastering The Ten Terrains Of Consciousness*.

ALL TERRAINS ARE EQUAL

It is important to understand that we are NOT holding the Ten Terrains Of Consciousness as being ten 'levels'. Nor are they ten 'steps' on a hierarchical ladder. They are expanding rings of perception on the human evolutionary journey, each of equal value.

Just like it is no better to be 14 years old than to be 13, *no one Terrain is better than any other*. People at the more expanded Terrains are not any more 'mature' or 'intelligent' or 'wiser' or 'kinder' than those at the more constrained ones. Life doesn't magically get easier as a person moves through the Continuum. In fact the reverse is true: as a person expands to become All That Is, they are held to an increasingly greater degree of responsibility for their actions.

This idea will be most difficult to grasp for people at the Terrains of Particle, Radial, Pyramid, Square and Diamond, where the sense of self comes from outside oneself and one therefore compares oneself to the outside world in order to evaluate where one stands. Nevertheless, it is the truth. If you are at Diamond, those people around you at Spiral and Toroid are no better than you, no more advanced than you and no closer to the 'finish line' than you. From the perspective of Infinite Consciousness we all have the same spark of Divinity in us; it is only the ego that seeks to assign rank.

Always remember that each Terrain serves a particular evolutionary stage in a person's development. Each Terrain provides important lessons that a person needs to learn and experiences that a person has chosen to have. Each Terrain presents its own challenges and brings its own gifts. Each Terrain is like a fun playground with its own rides and games to explore and enjoy. Every Being has chosen their current Terrain Of Consciousness for their highest Spiritual development in this lifetime and as part of our Collective Agreement. There is no hierarchy here—there is no separation—ever.

IT IS NOT A RACE

Always remember, if you can, that evolution along the Continuum of Terrains is not a race and it is not a competition. No one is 'ahead' of you or 'behind' you. *Where you are on the Continuum is exactly where you are meant to be.*

This is not a board game where everyone's goal is to get to No-Thing before the time runs out. There is no goal or destination. There is no start time and no end time. Indeed there is no obligation to move around the board at all. There is no goal to even shift to the next Terrain. If there is any goal at all in this evolutionary journey, it is to BE fully where you are and who you are in each and every moment.

Indeed, from the perspective of Infinite Consciousness, you are an immortal Being with infinite lifetimes to play, experience and learn. When you are infinite and immortal, there is no other place to be but *here, now.*

As we have already said, it is futile to seek—through willpower or the power of mental intention—to rush your own evolution beyond the speed at which your Infinite Self is ready to move. You are at the Terrain you are meant to be at at this point in time, for the learning you are here to do now, the experiences you are here to have now, and the gifts you are here to give now.

Indeed, your *life purpose* in this lifetime may require you to be at a particular Terrain and it may require you to stay there. For example, if your life purpose is to create a revolutionary new telecommunications device that completely changes how people communicate, or to launch a social revolution that changes how people live, you will need to be at Diamond. If your life purpose is to codify laws or set up an orderly system of government, you will need to be at Square. If your life purpose is to master chi life force, teach vibrational energy or to anchor a new energy into the planet, you will need to be at Spiral. If your life purpose is to provide all of us contrast between 'good and evil' by doing acts of mass killing, you will need to be at Pyramid. If your life purpose is to bring forth a new body of teachings built upon Universal Principles that resonate as Truth throughout the ages, you will need to be at Toroid. These are simple examples, yet they illustrate how each Terrain has an important role to play in the unfolding of the human story, and that everyone is exactly where they are meant to be.

THE JOURNEY OF THE HUMAN SPIRIT

Ultimately, each of us is here on a spiritual journey as well as a physical one. Our spiritual journey is a journey of expansion through the Ten Terrains, moving from separation to Unity and beyond.

Some people will resist this whole idea of Terrains, because they don't want to be boxed in or 'typecast' (this kind of reaction can be particularly strong in those at the Reflection-Based Terrain, because for those at Diamond it is paramount that they feel that they are choosing their own destiny). However a person's spiritual development through the Terrains is no different than their physical development through chronological stages.

In our physical development, we pass through infancy, then childhood, then puberty, then young adulthood, then adulthood, then middle age, then old age, etc. Acknowledging these stages does not mean that we are being typecast or boxed in. They are simply natural stages of physical development. So too in our spiritual development do we pass through various stages: the Ten Terrains Of Consciousness. We move along the Continuum of Terrains as we grow and expand in our spiritual awareness, just like we move through the physical stages as our bodies grow and age.

From the linear perspective of the human mind, a helpful way to think of your spiritual evolution is like a train journey with ten stops. At each stop, you get out of the train, have a look around and spend some time in this fascinating new place—maybe a day, a month, a year or even a lifetime. You meet some new people, you have some powerful new experiences and you learn some much needed lessons. Then you get back on the train and keep traveling to the next stop, where you get out of the train again. This continues until you reach the end of that particular voyage. Then maybe another day you get on the same train line, but this time you start at a different stop and ride the train to a new destination.

The Ten Terrains Of Consciousness are the ten stops on humanity's evolutionary train ride. Along your journey, at each Terrain you stop at, you will explore something profound and powerful that your Infinite Self wishes you to learn, to experience, and to give. It may take you several years or even several lifetimes to 'get it', but once you have learned it, you will get back on the train and keep riding. In another lifetime, you may get back on this evolutionary train ride at a different stop and travel to a different end point, depending on what charge force you've taken on in the previous life and what your Infinite Self wants you to experience and learn this time round.

On this particular train journey—the Continuum of the Ten Terrains Of Consciousness—no one stop is any more valuable or worthwhile or important than any other. They are all simply part of the human journey. As with all such traveling, *it is the journey itself which is of value*, not the destination.

So what are the ten lessons that we are all learning on our evolutionary train ride? Let's look at the entire journey, from the very first stop at Particle all the way through to the final stop at No-Thing.

STOP 1:   SEPARATION
STOP 2:   FAITH
STOP 3:   FREE WILL
STOP 4:   SELFLESS DUTY
STOP 5:   UNIQUE EXPRESSION
STOP 6:   HEART CONNECTION
STOP 7:   INNER TRUTH
STOP 8:   UNIVERSAL TRUTH
STOP 9:   ONENESS
STOP 10: BEING

On this evolutionary train ride, if you were to be born at the first stop—The Matter-Based Terrain—and expand during your lifetime all the way through to the final stop—The Void-Based Terrain— you would learn ten incredibly powerful and profound lessons. You would learn first what it means to live in separation, then how to have faith in a spiritual force outside of yourself, then how to exercise your own free will, then how to act in selfless duty for the good of the majority, then how to express your unique self and make a unique contribution to the world, then how to connect to the Web of Life, then how to come to full inner coherence, then how to recognize Universal Principles and live from trust, then how to let go of everything that is holding you in separation so that you can come into full Unity with Infinite Consciousness, then how to experience the immortal simplicity of simply Being.

Everyone's train ride is unique—starting at a different stop and finishing at a different stop. Some people will continue their ride over the course of many lifetimes, typically picking up the journey in their next life where they left off at the end of the previous one. Others will be flung back to an earlier stop upon reincarnation and will have to make that part of the journey again. This is because, from the perspective of the Infinite Self, all points in time are one point and therefore this evolutionary journey is holographic, not linear.

Although everybody's particular train journey is unique, we are all riding along the same train line, the Continuum of Terrains. This is the profound spiritual journey that every single person on this planet is moving through, at their own speed and in their own time. In addition, as we will see in Part 4 of this book 'Collective Terrains', every culture and civilization in our world is also moving along the Continuum of Terrains as a collective spiritual journey.

LOOKING FROM THE OTHER DIRECTION

So far, we have been discussing the evolutionary journey through the Continuum of Terrains that we all experience once we have been born into our human body, the journey that moves in one direction from Particle to Radial to Pyramid to Square to Diamond to Circle to Spiral to Toroid to Infinity to No-Thing. We have been discussing the expansion of perception from separation to Unity that is humanity's spiritual evolutionary journey.

However, the Continuum of Terrains can also be looked at *from the other direction*. This is a very deep esoteric approach, which we explore much more fully in our other educational materials. However, for now, just as a taster, here is a simple summary.

The Journey From Infinite To Incarnate

This is a highly simplified description of vast bodies of esoteric science, so please read it as such. It is provided to give a very broad conceptual framework of 'reality'.

To begin, beyond your physical self living in this 3D body within the bounds of time and space, your Self is pure Consciousness. It has infinite awareness of all things. Like a drop of water in the Ocean, it knows that it is not just One with everything, it IS everything. It is Infinite Consciousness in a state of unconditional Love. It is fully at peace and surrendered, with no agenda or goals. It simply

IS. Essentially, your Self is deep in the Void beyond the illusionary bounds of space and time, at the outer realms of the Terrain Of Consciousness we are calling 'No-Thing'.

As No-Thing contracts into the first polarity that exists at Infinity creating *'everything and all possibility'*, imagination focuses on some 'things' and then your Infinite Consciousness as Self makes the choice to extend part of itself into the Fractalating Quantum Field, and at this dimension, into incarnation in a human body. At that point your journey of 'forgetting' begins. Your incarnated Self contracts through the various layers of vibrational density from the Void of No-Thing into the unity of Infinity on into the heavier density of Toroid and then into the even heavier and heavier densities of the more contracted Terrains. As your incarnated Self contracts from the more expanded realms of Consciousness into the increasing densities of this dimension of matter, your perception of reality becomes increasingly more limited.

An easy way to conceptualize this is to think of the analogy of a Hot Air Balloon that can float higher up in the air or sink lower down towards the ground. In this analogy, your Spirit is the vacuum of outer-space, beyond the Earth's atmosphere, infinitely expansive. When it is ready to incarnate part of itself into a human body, it sends that part down in the Hot Air Balloon. How far down the balloon descends—whether to the stratosphere, down into the atmosphere, down to the clouds, down to the treetops, or all the way to the ground—depends on where your Spirit wants to send that part of itself for its experiences, explorations and lessons in this lifetime.

The crucial point to remember is that your 'scope' of view from the balloon gets narrower and narrower as the balloon floats down towards the ground. Whereas, in its fully expanded state your Spirit had an infinite view of the entire Universe, as this incarnated part of your Spirit descends in the hot air balloon, it can first see the entirety of planet Earth floating as a ball, then as it descends down through the clouds all it can see is a vast stretch of curving land, then as it descends down to the treetops, all it can see is a smaller tract of flat land, then if it were to descend all the way to the ground, all it would be able to see is the few yards of turf around it to the trees at the edge of the field where you landed.

However, to continue this analogy of the hot air balloon, most incarnated Spirits do not descend all the way to the ground at birth. Each Spirit descends down to a different point, and begins its life there. Some hover at a higher altitude (a more expanded Terrain), with a wider, bigger perspective. Others hover at a lower altitude (a more contracted Terrain), with a narrower, more limited perspective.

So what causes our ballon to come down to that one specific height, that is, to incarnate at that particular vibrational density, in that specific Terrain Of Consciousness? Well this depends—just like the position of our metaphorical balloon depends on the amount of hot air inside it—on how much 'charge force' our 'energy bundle' comes in with. This creates the 'Geometry' that we experience in this lifetime. We incarnate into a situation with the exact factors reflecting the sum total of this charge force, which anchors us when we are a small child into our Terrain. Such factors include the environment's resonance at the time of our conception, gestation and birth (epigenetics)—this consists of things like the consciousness of our parents and extended family, the life circumstances we are born into, the culture we are born into and the physical environment around us—and even broader factors such as our parents' ancestral DNA memory and the sum total of our previous lives.

So each Spirit incarnates into life at a specific Terrain, that best suits the sum total of its accumulated charge force. Some people remain at that Terrain their entire lives—their balloon hovering at this one height with its one perspective. Others start to expand their Consciousness into new Terrains, their balloon floating back up towards their natural, fully-expanded, original state of No-Thing.

To continue our analogy, you could imagine that this balloon has a rope that is pulling it upwards, or even that it is fueled by helium rather than hot air, so it is always straining to rise back up. Remember when you were a child and you let go of a helium balloon and watched it float up up and away into the clouds? This balloon is like that. It wants to rise back up. Only our Spirit's desire to keep learning at that same Terrain holds it down there, creating the earthly conditioning that keeps it down… as powerfully as gravity.

Now that you have seen the full story of the Continuum of the Ten Terrains Of Consciousness, told from both directions, you can see that our natural state as one whole is always pulling us back to Unity.

3

MEET THE
TEN TERRAINS

WHAT YOU ARE
ABOUT TO READ

YOU ARE about to read a brief summary of each Terrain. These summaries have been designed to give you a general feel for each of the 10 Terrains. By the end of these brief summaries, you should have enough of a sense of each Terrain to be able to start observing the world around you with an eye to spotting what Terrain people, groups, ideas, systems and products, etc. are coming from. You may not always be able to map Terrains accurately, but you will have enough of a sense of the Terrains to start playing with them, to discuss them with your friends and to take part in the growing conversation about the Ten Terrains Of Consciousness that is spreading around the world.

Each Terrain summary will include the following information:

1. An indication of the approximate percentage of people likely to be at that Terrain in the Western World right now.
2. A brief description of the three foundation stones of each Terrain: its 'Event Horizon Of Perception', it's 'Story' and its 'Strategy'. The Event Horizon is the evolutionary threshold that is crossed when a person shifts into that Terrain from the previous Terrain, the quantum leap in perception that radically shifts their relationship with reality. The 'Story' is essentially their unique way of seeing the world. The 'Strategy' is the

specific approach used by people at that Terrain to navigate their world. In the case of some Terrains this is a 'Survival Strategy' and in others it is a 'Thrival Strategy'.

3. A brief description of the core perceptions, fears, orientations and beliefs that make up the operating system of that Terrain. It is these core drivers that are causing the behaviors that can be observed in the world by people at that Terrain.

4. A brief description of the Key Elements of that Terrain; that is, whether it has an individual or collective focus; whether it has masculine or feminine energy; whether it holds either a single or multiple 'frame' of reference; whether it is fear-reactive or love-responsive; and whether it is outer-directed or inner-directed.

5. An explanation for why the particular visual symbol that represents that Terrain was chosen and what it means.

6. Several examples of what a typical person's life might be like at that Terrain.

7. A description of what changes in a person's life as they start to move from that Terrain to the next Terrain.

8. Some examples of famous people who have shown up at that Terrain throughout history.

9. Some examples of books, movies and TV shows that illustrate that Terrain.

10. A summary of the purpose of each Terrain from a spiritual perspective: that is, the learnings, challenges and gifts that each Terrain brings, and the unique 'Journey' of that Terrain.

CAVEAT: TERRAIN vs. BEHAVIOR

When reading the following ten Terrain summaries, please bear in mind that in this book we are describing the kinds of behaviors that *typically* accompany a person's Terrain. Essentially we are describing people who are very clear examples of their Terrain. This will usually be the case when someone is 'Stationary' at their Terrain and has not yet started moving towards the next Terrain.

Of course, once a person has started moving towards the next Terrain, they may begin to be influenced by ideas, teachings and practices from that Terrain, and their behavior may change somewhat to reflect this. Nevertheless, their core perception will still remain at their original Terrain and someone familiar with the Ten Terrains Model will still be able to pinpoint their true Terrain.

In addition, there are circumstances where a person's behavior does not reflect their Terrain at all. When you observe such people, they may appear to be at a completely different Terrain than they are truly at. In these cases, it takes someone with deep training in the Ten Terrains Model to ascertain the person's true Terrain.

We will now discuss three situations in which a person's behavior can be unrepresentative of their Terrain: the cases of lagging behavior, expanded behavior and temporary behavior.

(1) LAGGING BEHAVIOR

Sometimes a person's 'external persona' that they present to the world is to some degree lagging behind their true inner Terrain Of Consciousness. This means they are not yet fully embodying their true Terrain in all their behaviors and are instead exhibiting some behaviors of a previous, more contracted Terrain. This is a very common phenomenon, occurring in approximately 50% of people, to some extent or other.

It is important to understand that *in most cases, this kind of lag in behavior only happens in certain specific areas*, for example in the area of money or relationships or health. In all other areas, the person will exhibit the beliefs and behaviors that one would expect to see from someone at their Terrain. Only certain parts of themselves are lagging behind and are behaving as if they were at a more contracted Terrain than they truly are at. For example a person at the Connection-Based Terrain (Circle) may find it difficult to form intimate sexual relationships due to being sexually assaulted as a child, even though they are at a Terrain that usually allows for deep intimacy.

The reason for this lag in the person's behavior is usually to do with their childhood wounding, their cultural conditioning or the impact of the collective Field's Prevailing Terrain upon them. Sometimes lagging behaviors can be caused by the person feeling they need to modify their behaviors in order to gain love and approval, or because they hold certain judgments about the more expanded behaviors that flow from their true Terrain. In all cases it has to do with an as yet unresolved 'charge' being held in their field—usually borne from a trauma that is holding the lagging behavior in place.

In addition, if someone has had a very sudden Terrain jump, or has moved through several Terrains very fast—for example, after having a Near-Death Experience—it can sometimes take some time for the old behavioral, emotional and mental conditioning and habits to transmute and fall away. Until then, the person's sense of self is still lagging behind; their cellular and DNA memory holding it where it is. This is why they can project an external persona out to the world that is more contracted than their truly expanded inner state.

This issue of lagging behavior can sometimes make it tricky to determine which Terrain a person truly is at. Yet usually, with time, as the person grows and evolves and learns their life lessons, their lagging behavior will fall away and their external persona will catch up with their true inner Terrain. At that point, their behaviors in all areas will be in alignment with their internal Terrain, their energy will be coherent and their true Terrain will become much more obvious.

It should be noted that these cases of lagging behavior can be more dramatic where the person's internal Terrain is very expanded. For example if a person at the Fractal-Based Terrain (Toroid) had a Square upbringing and is living in a Square culture, then any Square behaviors they still have as a result of their conditioning will stand out like a sore thumb in their otherwise Fractal-Based life. However, such lagging behavior tends to get more quickly resolved at the more expanded Terrains, as people there are taking greater degrees of Self-responsibility to catch themselves when they are out of alignment and to clear their conditioning.

(II) EXPANDED BEHAVIOR

There are also two cases where a person's behavior can make them appear to be at a more *expanded* Terrain than they are really at: (i) the case of someone at Square who is taking on more expanded traits in order to play a particular role, and (ii) the case of someone at Diamond who is self-identifying with a more expanded Terrain and presenting that image to the world. We will discuss both of these briefly in the Square and Diamond chapters. In both of these cases, the person at Square or Diamond may appear to be at a much more expanded Terrain than they are really at, and their behavior is not indicative of their true Terrain.

(III) TEMPORARY BEHAVIOR

In addition, people's behavior may stray temporarily from the kind of behavior you would expect to see from someone at their Terrain.

From time to time, a person make exhibit more contracted behavior than usual. This can happen for many reasons, including the following:

+ Triggering
+ Childhood wounding
+ Programming and conditioning
+ Inter-dimensional Interference
+ Past life reactions
+ Influence from the Prevailing Terrain they are living in
+ Influence from the people around them at the time
+ Moments of extreme fear

In addition, a person may temporarily exhibit more expanded behavior. This can also happen for many reasons, including the following:

- Expanded spiritual experiences like deep meditation or shamanic journeying
- Psychedelic drugs and plant medicines
- Life-Or-Death moments
- Ecstatic moments
- Being surrounded by a roomful of people at a more expanded Terrain
- Moments of profound connection like in sacred lovemaking
- Moments of extreme presence, like childbirth

In all of these cases, people can have experiences at Terrains other than their own and can exhibit behaviors, albeit temporarily, that can make them appear to be at a Terrain other than their own. However, just because a person can have experiences and behaviors that are more or less expanded than their Terrain does not mean that they are jumping around from one Terrain to another!

Again, we remind you: *Terrain is not behavior.*

A person does not change their fundamental relationship with reality from moment to moment. They may have experiences, awarenesses and understandings from other Terrains, but their core operating system remains the same. They may be triggered or temporarily inspired into behaviors different to their Terrain, but their core operating system remains the same.

When a person returns from their moment of contraction or their moment of expansion, they will still be at the same Terrain they were at before (unless the experience has caused them to have a Terrain Shift). They will analyze that experience through the filter of their Terrain, talk about it through the filter of their Terrain and remember it through the filter of their Terrain.

To think that a person's Terrain can change from day to day is to reveal a misunderstanding of what a Terrain Of Consciousness is. It simply means you have confused Terrains with behavior.

STAY ALERT

Therefore, the analysis of a person's Terrain Of Consciousness is more complex than first meets the eye. So stay alert, and stay tuned in, and don't always believe the face that other people present to you. Feel with your Heart into what is really driving them at their core, and observe how they respond when in very confronting or emotional situations, when their Heart is wounded or their financial security is rocked. In these kinds of testing times, do they come from Love or fear? How quickly do they return to their center once they get triggered? Do they play the victim card or are they Self-responsible? And always remember to observe them *without judgment*, for they are simply doing the best they can to survive and thrive, as is everyone.

In *Mastering The Ten Terrains Of Consciousness* we explain in great detail why some people exhibit behaviors that appear to be more contracted or more expanded than that Terrain would normally produce. We also explain people who may appear by their behavior to be at a particular Terrain, yet in truth are not. This is one of the reasons why you are encouraged to study the complete foundational material of the Ten Terrains Model in order to accurately map the true Terrains of people you encounter in the world, in cases where it is not reflected in their external behavior.

SIT WITH IT

While you read the following ten Terrain descriptions, you will probably try to work out which of them is YOUR Terrain. That is totally natural!

It's very tempting to rush into that decision, but we want to advise you to keep that as an *open question* until the end of this book and until you have completed your Terrain Analysis Questionnaire. It will be tempting to jump to conclusions about your Terrain earlier than that, as you are reading the examples given in the following descriptions. You may think *"Ooh that guy sounds just like me!"* or

"*I do that too!*" or "*Yes, I'm passionate about that!*" But as we have just seen, that may not necessarily indicate which Terrain is truly yours.

At some level, we all *know* our own Terrain Of Consciousness. We know deep down how we are fundamentally seeing the world and the kind of relationship we have with reality. But sometimes our sense of self and the way we like to see ourselves can get in the way of us being able to consciously recognize our own Terrain. It is the water we swim in and the air we breathe, and those things are not always so easy to see.

So as you are reading the following chapters, ask yourself, "*Which Terrain am I living at?*" and then sit back… and wait. The answer will come. Trust that. It may not come while you are reading these pages; it may come a few months later, once you start applying what you have learned here in your life. Or it may come to you in a dream, or in a discussion you have about the Terrains with a friend, or some other way.

When reading our descriptions of the 10 Terrains in the following chapters, don't just focus on which behaviors, opinions and values described there match your own. Feel into the *deeper core perceptions and fears* that come with each Terrain and sense if they apply to you or not. Sit with it. Sleep on it.

And if you require confirmation of your Terrain, make sure to complete your Terrain Analysis Questionnaire, available at www.tenterrains.com.

THE MATTER-BASED TERRAIN (PARTICLE)

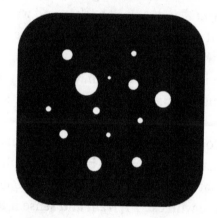

THE MATTER-BASED TERRAIN OF CONSCIOUSNESS (PARTICLE) is the first evolutionary stage on the Continuum Of Terrains. A person at this Terrain is experiencing 'The Journey Of Separation'. As of 2015, we estimate that approximately 2.5% of people in the Developed World are living at the Matter-Based Terrain.

The Event Horizon Into Particle

People at Particle fundamentally believe the great human illusion: the illusion of separation. They believe that they are completely alone in this life, separate from all other people, from nature, from their higher Self, and from Infinite Consciousness. There is a corresponding complete and total lack of trust in other people, in the natural world, in the spirit world and in the wider universe.

There is not really a true 'Event Horizon' here, in the sense that we use this term in this Model, meaning a jump in perception from a previous Terrain. The Matter-Based Terrain is the first Terrain on the Continuum, so a person has not shifted here from any other Terrain. However, the jolt a person at Particle gets upon incarnating into a human body at this most constrained of Terrains is like an Event Horizon. It is the biggest jump of all, from total Oneness with All That Is to utter separation.

The Story At Particle

People at Particle are the only people on the Continuum Of Terrains who have no Story to explain their world. They believe that there is no meaning to life and no explanation for what happens to them; instead, they see life as being entirely random and events as being unconnected. They feel completely powerless, believing that things happen 'to' them, as a victim of circumstance. They see themselves as being completely at the mercy of the world around them.

The Strategy At Particle

As a result of this lack of Story, people at Particle have nothing comforting to believe in and no hope. They have no way to predict or control their world or their future. They have no Survival Strategy of any kind—save living hand to mouth—for they do not believe it is possible to ever be truly safe, given how dangerous the world appears and how completely alone they perceive themselves to be. All they can do is react in the moment to whatever life throws at them, trying to stay alive, using blind instinct.

CORE FEATURES & DRIVERS OF PARTICLE

Survival

The attention of people at the Matter-Based Terrain is focused on base survival needs, such as finding food, staying warm and keeping safe from predators. Life is a moment-to-moment fight to stay alive.

People at Particle are not concerned with more complex needs like earning a living, making friends or improving their health, nor with more sophisticated drivers such as exploring art, culture or technology, etc. People at this Terrain are so preoccupied with simply satisfying their immediate visceral needs and with staying alive, that the subtler pursuits of the human condition simply have no meaning for them.

Physicality

The reason that this Terrain is called 'Matter-Based' is because people at this Terrain are focused on the densest, most physical of things: eating, sleeping, keeping warm, staying alive. They are not focused on subtler things such as emotions, feelings, thoughts, ideas, energies, spiritual forces, etc. Their focus is entirely on the 3D realm of physical matter, the most primal focus in the human experience.

The Now

People at Particle live in the present moment. This is by necessity, as they are so focused on their immediate survival that they do not have the luxury of thinking ahead or dwelling on the past. They are in a moment by moment battle to stay fed, warm and alive. They operate by instinct, in reaction to each moment, without strategy or planning, and without a past or future story.

Body-Centered

At Particle, the Terrain is of the body. There is not even a split yet between the body and the mind or between the body and the emotions. The only driver is the body. Here 'body language' takes precedence over spoken or verbal language. This is a body-centered, gut-based, instinct-driven, animalistic world. Even the urge to procreate extends purely from immediate physical needs rather than from any desire to form bonds, gain power or create a family. This is a primal Terrain.

Local Consciousness

At this Terrain, Consciousness is most definitely experienced as local. There is no awareness of, belief in or even concept of an infinite intelligence or a higher power of any kind. Life is completely divorced from Spirit and there is only an awareness of 3D matter. To the eyes of the person at Particle, the world appears to be fragmented, inanimate, non-sentient, and completely random.

Scarcity

Those at the Matter-Based Terrain have a fundamental belief that resources are scarce, that they must be fought for, and that life is a struggle. The Particle person believes that at every moment they are at war with Life to simply stay alive. Given that the world appears to be chaotic and coincidental, there is no trust that food will be there when they need it, or that resources or money will come. They have a fundamental belief that they will always have to scramble and fight to get their basic needs met.

Isolation

People at Particle live in isolation, mistrusting other people and life itself. They see themselves as being alone in an unfriendly universe, unsupported and left to survive by whatever means they can. The person at Particle does not trust other people, other tribes or other groups. They do not believe in any god or higher power, therefore they feel truly alone, even on a cosmic level. They have no one and no thing to turn to.

Victim Consciousness

The person at Particle feels that everything happens 'to' them. They see themselves as being completely at the mercy of the world around them. They feel that they have no control over their own life, over other people or over the world around them. Because they see themselves so completely as victims, they are indeed utterly powerless.

Randomness

At Particle, events are seen as unconnected and random. Things are seen as happening to you in isolation without any explanation or meaning. This means that the person at Particle feels constant uncertainty and fear about each coming moment, with no way to predict or prepare for what is coming. This compounds their feeling of being a victim, for in the Particle person's world, events happen to them with no order, no rhyme or reason, and no ability to predict or control the outcome.

It should be noted that this sense of meaninglessness is very different to the meaninglessness of the Void-Based Terrain (No-Thing) at the opposite end of the Continuum, which brings with it a feeling of complete peace. What is perceived as terrifying randomness at Particle is blissful formlessness at No-Thing.

Atomized

Like the dots in the symbol of Particle, people at the Matter-Based Terrain are atomized individuals, each operating separately from each other, even when standing in close proximity. There is no community (common unity) and no connectedness. At this Terrain, there are no organized group structures, like we find at the other nine Terrains. Here the only time people come together is to band together against a common threat, where this is necessary for their survival. However there is no group identity, no loyalty or allegiance to the group and no sense of belonging. It is an arrangement of pure necessity. As soon as the danger has passed, the group will disperse back to its separate atomized parts.

Disassociated

People at the Matter-Based Terrain are in an extreme state of disassociation. They are disassociated from other people, from life and from themselves. They are not connected to their Heart, to their will, to their emotions, to their unique thinking mind or to their Higher Knowing. They are only connected to their gut and their instincts. They are disconnected from the deeper aspects of human existence. This means that they are unable to connect with their dreams, their inner yearnings, their desires or their visions. They are merely able to react in the moment to what life throws at them, with very basic, knee jerk, instinctual, survival actions.

Resistance

People at Particle experience extreme resistance to growth, resistance to change, resistance to expansion and resistance to life itself. They see the world as a place they cannot influence, they see other people as being beyond their power to control, and they see themselves as being unchangeable. They do not seek growth or transformation; in fact, such thoughts do not even occur to them. Their internal resistance to growth keeps them firmly focused on the survival of the present moment rather than on their own personal evolution or the transformation of their world.

Inertia

The Matter-Based Terrain is the hardest Terrain to shift from, as the force of inertia is at its strongest here at this end of the Continuum, keeping a person in extreme fear, separation and doubt, unable to expand towards Unity. As a result of the inertia and resistance of Particle, people at this Terrain are the most fixed, the most rooted, and the least likely to expand along the Continuum.

Entropy

The inertia of Particle always tends to disorder and chaos. Because people at this Terrain do not have any strategy beyond surviving the present moment, they tend to put little or no effort into generating forward progress, thus entropy causes an inevitable decline and degeneration over time of whatever social fabric may have begun to take hold. Add to this the transient propensity of those at Particle, and nothing tends to having any lasting permanence. It seems that those at Particle are always having to 'start over' again and again.

Separation

On the spiritual evolutionary journey, people at Particle are here to experience the most traumatized, fragmented aspect of their Self. It is a mistake to call them the 'least evolved' on the Continuum of Terrains; rather, they are the most separated from their 'I AM' Self.

KEY ELEMENTS OF PARTICLE

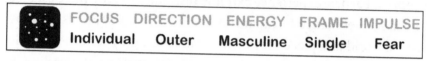

	FOCUS	DIRECTION	ENERGY	FRAME	IMPULSE
	Individual	Outer	Masculine	Single	Fear

The Matter-Based Terrain is an individual-focused Terrain because people at Particle are necessarily self-centered for pragmatic reasons of survival.

The Matter-Based Terrain is the most outer-directed of all the 10 Terrains because it relies strictly on external sense perception, with people at Particle always on guard and aware of their surroundings in every moment.

The Matter-Based Terrain has the most disempowered masculine energy of all the 10 Terrains, as people at Particle believe that nothing and no one has their back; therefore, there is no inner strength in their stand, and typically the slightest threat will cause them to turn and run for their lives.

The Matter-Based Terrain is a single-frame Terrain, which means that those at Particle can only see reality from their own perspective and therefore there is no way for them to be swayed from their fundamental belief in their own victimhood.

The Matter-Based Terrain is the most fear-reactive of all the 10 Terrains, for people at Particle have a perception of separation that causes them to have an overwhelming core fear of death, mother nature, other people, Infinite Consciousness and life itself, and they are not able to allay this fear in any way with either a Story or a Strategy.

SYMBOL OF PARTICLE

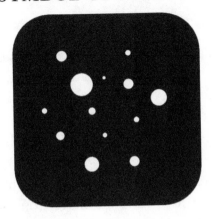

The symbol of the 'particle' best describes the Matter-Based Terrain because at this Terrain Of Consciousness, people feel completely disconnected from themselves, from each other and from the interconnectedness of All That Is. They experience the events happening to them as being completely random and without explanation. Atomized, separated and isolated, they feel that they are completely at the mercy of life.

The random disconnected spread of the dots in this symbol reflects these core ways that the Matter-Based person perceives their world. The largest dot in this symbol represents the Matter-Based person looking out at what they perceive as pure chaos all around them.

EXAMPLES OF PARTICLE

A historical example of people at Particle is the prehistoric caveman, who lived a visceral, instinct-driven life, focused moment to moment on survival.

A modern example of a person at Particle might be someone who has grown up in a war zone, in a famine or in a fight-for-survival situation on the streets, where there is no guarantee of food, shelter or safety at any moment, who has never expanded in their awareness past the immediate drive for survival.

PARTICLE MOVING TO RADIAL

From Separation To Faith

The examples of Particle we've just provided are most likely to describe someone who is *stationary* at Particle, that is someone who is living in the valley of Particle and is not yet moving up the mountain towards the Faith-Based Terrain (Radial). Such a person is deep in the pocket of the Matter-Based Terrain, learning its biggest lessons.

How long a person stays there will be different for each person. Nevertheless, as we have said, the move from Particle to Radial requires overcoming a great deal of inertia, therefore most people will remain stationary at this Terrain for a very long time, possibly for lifetimes.

Once a person has learned the most fundamental lessons of Particle, deeply lived the experiences of Particle and received the evolutionary gifts of Particle, they become someone who *fully embodies* this Terrain. They are now ready to start the long journey towards Radial. At this point, if it is on their life path to expand, their Infinite Self will start to orchestrate their journey up the mountain, and their life will start to noticeably change.

As the person at Particle starts to move up the mountain towards Radial, they will start to notice *patterns* in what is unfolding in their life and in their world. They may start to notice events repeating in the natural world at particular times, seemingly linked to particular factors. They will start to notice that there is cause and effect at play in their environment. The world will begin to seem a little less random and a little less terrifying.

They will also start to notice that their own actions have consequences. As they start to notice this, they will have the first hints of a dawning realization that they might one day be able to exert some control over what happens to them in their life. They still won't have a real Survival Strategy until they get to Radial, but at least the possibility of one will begin to emerge.

As the person at Particle moves up the mountain and down the other side towards Radial, they will increasingly begin to believe that survival might be possible. As a result of this, their attention will now be able to move to things beyond simply staying alive. They may find they have moments where they are able to focus on things such as relating to other people, taking in their surroundings, and enjoying the intake of food and drink. They may find that they now have the luxury to sometimes think about the past and the future, rather than always being on the alert in the present moment. They may start to have some emotional experiences beyond pure fear, such as excitement or passion.

Such a person who is on the move to Radial would seem to an outside observer to be a very different person than they were when they were stationary in the valley of Particle. However, until this person actually crosses the Event Horizon Of Perception into Radial and perceives the possibility that they can receive protection from a supernatural force, they are still lacking the kind of faith that leads to a sense of safety in the world. They are still being driven primarily by fear.

HISTORICAL FIGURES AT PARTICLE

We have been unable to find any famous historical figures at the Matter-Based Terrain. Most people at Particle are too busy trying to stay alive to gain any kind of acclaim or renown.

MOVIES, TV & BOOKS AT PARTICLE

There are not many modern works of fiction that include characters at Particle or depict aspects of life at this Terrain. However, two works of fiction that do so are the movie 'Quest For Fire' and the book 'The Inheritors' by William Golding.

BIGGER PICTURE OF PARTICLE

From the spiritual perspective of Infinite Consciousness as Self, the Matter-Based Terrain can be seen as 'The Journey Of Separation'. The lesson a person is learning while at this Terrain is to experience the pain and suffering that comes from separation. The gift that this Terrain brings is the ability to stay present in the Now. The challenge it brings is how to keep one's overwhelming fear at bay in order to stay alive.

THE FAITH-BASED TERRAIN (RADIAL)

THE FAITH-BASED TERRAIN OF CONSCIOUSNESS (RADIAL) is the next evolutionary stage on the Continuum Of Terrains. A person at this Terrain is experiencing 'The Journey Of Faith'. As of 2015, we estimate that approximately 6.5% of people in the Developed World are living at the Faith-Based Terrain.

The Event Horizon Into Radial

As a person crosses the Event Horizon Of Perception into the Faith-Based Terrain, the huge shift in perception is that they now believe that events are not random. The person at Radial now sees that events have patterns and meaning and are therefore understandable. This allows them to see meaning in life, and to believe in the possibility of being safe and of being able to influence the world around them.

The Story At Radial

People at Radial attribute this meaning and explanation for events to supernatural forces that are outside of themselves, such as a god, a deity, a spirit or a magical creature. They believe that this supernatural force has the power to shape their life and that they are completely at its mercy. This is the Radial Story.

People at Radial see the motivations of this supernatural force as being beyond man's ability to understand, and believe that it acts on its own whim. If they get sick, they assume that this force is displeased; if they get well, they assume this force is pleased. Some people at Radial believe that their chosen supernatural force has created our world and is omnipotent over all life. Others merely believe that their chosen supernatural force has power over them as an individual or over their particular family, clan or village.

Regardless of the scope of power being attributed to the supernatural force, the consistent theme here is that the person at Radial believes that this supernatural being or force is outside of them, completely separate from them; that it has the power of life or death over them; and that it acts capriciously on its own whim. They are therefore in a position of total submission to it.

The Strategy At Radial

As a result of this belief in the complete power that this supernatural force or deity has over their fate, people at Radial believe that at any moment their fortune can turn because this supernatural force may decide to 'punish' them or 'reward' them. Earning the favor of the deity is therefore paramount, whether by praying, carrying out rituals or doing other submissive acts.

Some people at Radial spend their life trying to develop a benevolent relationship with their deity either by dedicatedly serving it with devotion so as to win its favor, trying to make friends with it or trying to win its affection. Others do everything they can to avoid incurring its wrath. This approach of appeasing and pleasing a supernatural force is the Survival Strategy at Radial.

CORE FEATURES & DRIVERS OF RADIAL

Separation From Spirit

Like all the fear-reactive Terrains, the Faith-Based Terrain is fundamentally rooted in separation. Here, the focus of that separation is between man and Spirit, that is man and Infinite Consciousness as Self. At this Terrain, man's true spiritual nature (that which is fully owned at Infinity) is projected outwards externally onto anthropomorphized spirits and angels and gods who are seen as being apart from man. The disowned internal spiritual Self is projected fully onto the external divine being, with all the Self's vast powers being transferred there along with it.

Capricious Deities

Because man at Radial sees the gods as being separate from himself, he can never fully understand their motivations or patterns. Therefore he experiences his chosen deity as being capricious and unreliable. This keeps him groveling before his deity, trying to cater for their every perceived whim, follow their every perceived law and praying fervently for the gift of their favor. Life at this Terrain feels very uncertain and unstable, because when one believes one lives at the whim of capricious gods, one can never fully relax.

Appealing To A Higher Power

People at Radial cannot command their deities, who they see as all-powerful. Neither can they manipulate or trick their gods into helping them. All they can do is throw themselves upon the capricious mercy of their gods and appeal to them, pray to them, supplicate them, make offerings to them or beg them. However, the fact that those at Radial can take even this much action, gives them at least some sense of being able to control their environment. This is a big jump from the total powerlessness experienced at Particle.

Religion

Many of the major world religions, although initially founded from a very expanded Terrain such as Toroid or Infinity, were influenced at some point during their history by people at the Faith-Based Terrain. Throughout history, those who were drawn most strongly to formalized religion have tended to be at Radial, and their devotion has led to them rising to positions of leadership. Many religions, which began as quite simple teachings, over time became highly complicated, ritualized, formalized and rigidified under the leadership of these devout Radial rulers.

Fundamentalism

The difference between someone at Radial and your average religious person at the Order-Based Terrain (Square) is that the person at Radial believes that their very life and death depends on pleasing their god. They do not just go to church or to the mosque out of a sense of tradition or duty, but because they genuinely believe their god will smite them if they don't. People at Radial tend to live fundamentalist, disempowered lives, completely devoted to their god or chosen mystical force. Their deity becomes the center of their existence.

When one believes that one's God or gods have complete and total power over one's fortunes, one's health, one's life, one's death and even one's happiness after death, one will do everything one can to please one's deity. This means that all rules or decrees set down in the name of one's deity must be obeyed to the letter. Sacred words must be spoken correctly, offerings must be made with the exact right contents, rituals must be carried out in the exact right way at the right time, or risk offending one's gods.

Furthermore, all commands seen to be coming from one's deity must be obeyed. Indeed, people at Radial will commit seemingly heinous acts in blind obedience to what they believe to be the commands of their gods and will fight to the death in defense of their deity. Whilst in the past this took the form of holy wars, in the modern era it can be seen in the fanatical actions of the suicide bomber.

Spiritistic

People at the Faith-Based Terrain are animistic and spiritistic, tending to believe in supernatural acts such as magic and witchcraft or miracles, either carried out directly by a deity, or by a person imbued temporarily with divine powers. For example, while there are millions of Christians in the world who believe in the teachings of Jesus Christ, only those at Radial truly believe that he was born by a miraculous virgin birth and that he will one day come back to save them.

In some cultures, groups at Radial believe that elements in the natural world are possessed of magical spirits—such as certain animals, kinds of plants and bodies of water—and as a result they worship these elements. Some people at Radial believe that material objects are imbued with magical or divine powers, such as totem poles, voodoo dolls or crucifixes.

Superstition

People at Radial are highly superstitious. Things have meaning and significance for them that would not occur to those at a more expanded Terrain. For example, if it rains or a certain numbers of babies are born, then this means their god is pleased; if famine or plague arrives, then this means their god is displeased.

Those at Radial attribute superstitious meaning to their own actions too. For example, they may believe that if they spill salt, it will let the devil in; wearing a bracelet made by a witch doctor will protect them against evil spirits; if they confess their sins before they die, their 'immortal soul' will be saved, etc.

Clans And Sects

At the Faith-Based Terrain, people self-organize into groups so that they can better serve their chosen deity and thereby ensure their own survival. In ancient societies (and in recent primitive societies), this self-organizing took the form of tribes or clans of people who shared a common belief in the mystical force that ruled their lives, and who followed the rituals and rules that they believed would keep them protected by that force. In the modern Western world, this tribal expression of Radial often takes the form of fundamentalist religious sects. These are close-knit groups where people unite around their shared belief in an all-powerful God and follow a shared body of rules and rituals to ensure they retain the favor of that God.

People in Radial clans or sects share a collective disempowerment relative to their chosen mystical force, giving up their own person needs and even sometimes the needs of the group in order to please it. For many people at Radial, the worst thing that could happen to them would be to be banished from their clan or excommunicated from their religious sect. This is because they believe they would no longer have the backing of their deity if they were no longer part of the group that is officially protected by it.

Mistrust

Due to the fundamental perception of separation at Radial, this Terrain is ruled by mistrust. Those at Radial deeply distrust anyone who is not a member of their clan or sect and tend to see people who are not of their faith as 'infidels', and oftentimes as a threat. Frequently they feel superior to people who are not 'believers', seeing themselves as the chosen ones who will be protected by their god. Other times they pity those who are not 'of the faith', believing that they will suffer grave consequences for being non-believers, such as being doomed to go to hell in the afterlife.

Atomistic

The Faith-Based Terrain is atomistic; that is, the opposite of holistic. Everything is segmented and reduced to its separate parts. Therefore while this is a collective-focused Terrain, each small clan at Radial functions as its own discrete unit. In times of history where Radial was the prevailing Terrain, there were multiple clans spread across vast geographical areas, who were apt to war with each other in the name of their gods. The same kind of atomism operates even now among the fundamentalist religious groups in our modern world. Each one is an island unto itself. They do not cooperate with each other, nor are they open to each other's views or ideas. And if their spiritual views are challenged, they will fight each other.

To The Death

The Faith-Based Terrain is a single-frame Terrain, like all of the first six Terrains on the Continuum. Because people at Radial believe that their entire survival depends on pleasing their deity, the existence of that deity must never be questioned or doubted. Anyone who dares to say that *"your deity is not the one true deity"* must be silenced. It is simply too frightening for people at Radial to allow free debate on this point.

People in Radial clans are not interested in stealing another clan's territory, wealth or power (as we will see happening at Pyramid), yet if another clan was to challenge their god or their way of life, they would defend it to the death. Therefore, war is a common behavior among those at the Faith-Based Terrain, not because of any inherently violent nature, but because those at Radial cannot allow even the slightest kind of challenge to their hallowed view of their gods or risk feeling the terror of total annihilation.

Lore

Most Radial groups will tend to build up a body of 'lore' that explains the particular rules and preferences of their chosen mystical force, so that they will know exactly how to behave in order to retain that deity's protection and to avoid its wrath. Whatever the lore of that group, it must be followed to the letter, or risk death by exposing oneself to the chaos of the natural forces. In the modern world, we can see this consciousness in those fundamentalist Christians and fundamentalist Moslems who believe that the Bible and the Qur'an is the literal word of God, to be obeyed to the letter without exception.

In a Radial consciousness, breaches of the lore are punished brutally, without trial, defense or repeal for any excuse. Often the punishments are administered publicly, to frighten others so much that they don't make the same transgression. In ancient Radial cultures this took the form of public stoning, hanging and other brutal forms of punishment that regularly took place.

Divinely Ordained Leadership

Radial is a collective-focused Terrain, where the group is hierarchically organized around their belief in a particular mystical force. Groups at Radial often believe their human leaders are imbued with divine powers and will obey them as they obey their god. In some primitive Radial societies, the clan leader was seen to have the powers of magical spirits invested in him. In modern religions that were formalized from a Radial consciousness, the leader of the faith is followed because they are seen to be divinely ordained. Even today, people in the highest positions of authority in the major world religions are often at Radial, as they are the most devout and dedicated to their faith, with unquestioning devotion to their god.

Ritual

Ritual is core to life at the Faith-Based Terrain. In most Radial groups there tends to be a strict calendar of rituals, religious ceremonies, religious celebrations and festivals scheduled for particular times of year, which must be conformed to if one is to remain in favor with the clan or sect and continue being blessed and saved by one's deity. Many Radial rituals may have originally been created as one-off events or as recurring rhythms in harmony with natural cycles, but over the years they have become locked in and formalized.

Darker Rituals

This is also the Terrain where we find more nefarious and twisted rituals, such as those found in cults and secret societies. In the completely submissive environment of Radial, people will commit acts like ritual sacrifices, sexual rites and other traumatizing rituals if that is what they perceive is needed or required to please their god, those who claim to be representatives of their god or their cult leaders. Throughout history, much of the entrapment of the human soul has taken place through manipulative rituals where people have so completely given up their power to forces being perceived as divine that they have allowed heinous acts to be inflicted upon themselves and upon others.

Cults

People at Radial are peculiarly susceptible to being enrolled into cults. Coming from the 'magical child' perception that they need a supernatural force to believe in, such people are easily taken in by the charismatic leaders of cults who promise salvation in many forms. People at Radial can fall prey to promises of wealth, health, benefits in the afterlife, or other things in return for giving their lives over to the cult.

These cults function for adherents in much the same way as fundamentalist religious groups do, however, there is a distinct difference between religious groups and cults. Fundamentalist religions are generally led by devout believers at Radial who see themselves as being representatives of their god, whereas cults are generally headed by ego-driven leaders at Pyramid who have an agenda of manipulation or charismatic leaders at Diamond who seek followers.

Shaming

As we will see, fear is the tool used to control people at Pyramid and guilt is used to keep everyone homogenous at Square; however, here at Radial the tool of control is *shame*. People at Radial—given this Terrain's collective focus—seek above all else to be socially accepted by people who share their faith, and the antithesis of this is to be publicly humiliated and shamed. For example, when a Radial group gives 'the silent treatment' to one of its members, great humiliation will be experienced by that member.

Because of this, a strategy used by leaders at Radial to keep people in their clan well behaved is to shame them. Children are taught to follow the dictates of their god rather than give in to the 'shameful' natural urges they would otherwise feel, such as their sexual urges. People are shamed into ignoring the desires of their own ego and the yearnings of their own heart, and instead are encouraged to submit fully to the higher power and to whatever they believe that their deity is asking of them.

Disempowerment

While their belief in a supernatural force gives those at Radial much more comfort and sense of safety than people at Particle have, it is still a very disempowered, dependent place to be, rooted in a deep fear of life. People at Radial believe that some non-human, divine force is the only thing standing between themselves and obliteration by the forces of nature. They believe that no human person can protect them from death and destruction, and they believe that they cannot protect themselves.

KEY ELEMENTS OF RADIAL

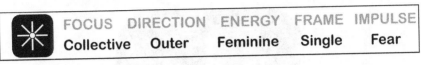

	FOCUS	DIRECTION	ENERGY	FRAME	IMPULSE
	Collective	Outer	Feminine	Single	Fear

The Faith-Based Terrain is a collective-focused Terrain, because at Radial people come together in their shared belief in the power of a particular supernatural force, believing that they can better please their deity as a group than as individuals.

The Faith-Based Terrain is an outer-directed Terrain, for people at Radial focus their entire behavior outward toward the appeasement of the mystical forces they believe are 'out there'.

The Faith-Based Terrain has the most disempowered feminine energy of all the 10 Terrains, for those at Radial submit completely and utterly to the will of their deity. Their own personal will and desires are completely set aside in the face of the perceived demands of supernatural forces.

The Faith-Based Terrain is a single-frame Terrain, for the belief that one's entire survival depends on pleasing a deity leads to a kind of fundamentalism whereby the existence of that deity must never be doubted, and anyone who dares question either the existence or the nature of one's god must be challenged, defeated and silenced.

The Faith-Based Terrain is an extremely fear-reactive Terrain, with the fear of nature and life being so strong that those at Radial believe that they will be obliterated unless they have the protection of an all powerful supernatural or mystical force.

SYMBOL OF RADIAL

The symbol of the 'radial' best describes the Faith-Based Terrain because it is at this Terrain that people first come together in community around a common belief that their collective safety will be assured by sacrifice and submission to mystical forces greater than themselves, represented by all the spokes meeting in the center of the symbol. The large central point in the middle of the symbol represents the Faith-Based person looking outwards at their world, rather than inwards at themselves, always seeking salvation from outside themselves. They place their lives in the hands of deities, gods and spirits 'out there', with a profound faith that offers them great comfort but is ultimately an illusion. This is represented by the outward-reaching spokes of the symbol.

EXAMPLES OF RADIAL

You might think that the Faith-Based Terrain only existed back in primitive times when spiritistic clans lived with a belief in magical beings, performing ritualistic and animistic acts. However, like all Terrains, the Faith-Based Terrain is not linked to a specific era, rather to a specific relationship with Consciousness.

Some typical examples of people at the Faith-Based Terrain in our modern world include:

- a religious fundamentalist who believes their God has full power over their life, death and afterlife;
- a member of a cult who believes that they will attain salvation or 'ascend' if they do everything that their cult leader tells them to;
- a suicide bomber who gives his life up for his God, on the promise of receiving rewards in the afterlife;
- a person who asks voodoo spirits for protection and blessings of good fortune;
- an adult developmentally stuck in the 'magical child' stage, who still believes in elves, fairies, goblins and wizards, etc.; and
- a mentally ill person who is living in their own delusional reality with its own magical rules, completely dependent on others to look after them.

The above examples are simplified stereotypes of people at the Faith-Based Terrain, designed to give you a feel for this Terrain. There will be many people at Radial who do not resemble the above examples at all; and you may meet people who fit the above descriptions yet who are not at Radial. Accurate analysis of someone's Terrain requires extensive training in the Ten Terrains Model and must never be assumed based solely on someone's behaviors.

RADIAL MOVING TO PYRAMID

From Faith To Free Will

The examples of Radial we've just provided are most likely to describe someone who is *stationary* at Radial, that is someone who is not yet moving up the mountain towards Pyramid. Such a person is deep in the pocket of the Faith-Based Terrain, learning its biggest lessons. How long a person stays there will be different for each person, depending on how long it takes them to fully absorb the lessons of Radial.

Once a person has learned the most fundamental lessons of Radial, has deeply lived the experiences of Radial and has offered the fullest expression of their gifts at Radial, they are *fully embodying* this Terrain. They are now ready to start the long journey towards the Will-Based Terrain (Pyramid). At this point, if it is on their life path to expand, their Infinite Self will start to orchestrate their journey up the mountain, and their life will start to noticeably change.

As a person at Radial starts to move up the mountain towards Pyramid, they will start to perceive the disempowerment inherent in their Survival Strategy. They will start to realize that they are a slave to the supernatural force that they depend upon to protect them. They will start to feel trapped by this, and a restlessness will start to grow within them. They will begin to question their total, fundamentalist obedience to that external force. Although they still believe that their life depends on pleasing their god, they will start to wish that it were otherwise.

The further the Radial person travels up the mountain and down the other side towards Pyramid, the more they will start to question their total subjugation to the will of their god. They will start to suspect that maybe their life does not depend fully on divine whim. They will start to sense that they have a choice in what happens to them, in how their life turns out. They will start to yearn to be free, to be able to make their own choices, to be master of their own destiny. They still won't have the courage to take action to step away from the protective arm of their deity, but the impetus towards that huge step is building within them.

Such a person who is on the move to Pyramid will look back at their time when they were stationary in the valley of Radial and feel that they have changed a great deal. They may even feel like a completely different person. People in their religious order or clan may start to look at them differently, as if able to smell potential heresy on them. However, until they actually cross the Event Horizon Of Perception into Pyramid this person at Radial on the move is still trapped in the disempowerment of their faith. This will be the case until the moment when they cross the Event Horizon into Pyramid and realize that it is *they* who control their destiny, not any supernatural being.

HISTORICAL FIGURES AT RADIAL

A few famous historical figures who were at the Faith-Based Terrain are Queen Elizabeth I, St Augustine and Martin Luther. To see a full list of famous historical figures who were at the Faith-Based Terrain, make sure to get your free eBook *The Terrains Of Famous People In History*, available at www.tenterrains.com. It includes names of hallowed religious leaders, monarchs, theologians and philosophers from throughout the ages, who were at Radial.

MOVIES, TV & BOOKS AT RADIAL

There are a few works of fiction that illustrate aspects of life at Radial and characters at Radial, such as the movies 'The Ten Commandments' and 'Left Behind', and the TV show 'Big Love' which has a subplot involving some characters at Radial. There are also many works of fiction coming from other Terrains that warn of the dangers of fundamentalism at Radial, such as the novel 'The Handmaid's Tale' by Margaret Atwood.

BIGGER PICTURE OF RADIAL

From the spiritual perspective of Infinite Consciousness as Self, the Faith-Based Terrain can be seen as 'The Journey Of Faith'. The lesson a person is learning while at this Terrain is to place hope and faith in supernatural forces outside themselves. The gift that this Terrain brings is being able to hold firm to one's beliefs and to one's faith. The challenge it brings is how to ignore temptation and follow the dictates of the supernatural force that one believes in.

If you are at this Terrain, we suggest that you read the *'Guidebook For The Radial Terrain'*. In this booklet we go into far more detail about the lessons you are here to learn on 'The Journey Of Faith'. We explain much more about the unique gifts and challenges of Radial. We also give you invaluable tips and strategies to help you navigate life at this Terrain.

THE WILL-BASED TERRAIN (PYRAMID)

THE WILL-BASED TERRAIN OF CONSCIOUSNESS (PYRAMID) is the next stage on the Continuum Of Terrains. A person at this Terrain is experiencing 'The Journey Of Free Will'. As of 2015, we estimate that approximately 10% of people in the Developed World are living at the Will-Based Terrain.

The Event Horizon Into Pyramid

The Will-Based Terrain is the Terrain of free will. As a person crosses the Event Horizon Of Perception into Pyramid, the huge shift in perception is that they no longer believe they are at the mercy of a higher power; instead, they believe that they alone have power over their own destiny. They realize that they can protect themselves—without the need for 'other' forces beyond them to do so.

At Pyramid, the relationship between man and Infinite Consciousness dramatically changes. Instead of appealing to gods or other supernatural forces to save him, man now declares that he will no longer live at the whim of the gods. He now perceives himself as able to be the master of his own destiny. He waves his fists at the gods and says *"I will do what I want!"*, like an angry child finally standing up to its parents.

The Story At Pyramid

Just like all those at the fear-reactive Terrains, people at Pyramid see the world, nature and life as being inherently dangerous. However, in the case of Pyramid, this general fear of the world is projected out onto other people and takes personified form. Here, it is not just nature and the forces of life that are to be feared, it is the people around you.

Those at Pyramid do not believe in the essential goodness of man, instead they believe that people are inherently selfish, cruel and heartless. They see the world as a jungle, where everyone is out for themselves, and where people are untrustworthy and will turn on you in a heartbeat.

The Story at Pyramid is that the world is a dog-eat-dog place where everyone is out to get you. This is very much a 'Wild West' mentality, where it is every man for himself and he who can draw his gun fastest wins.

The Strategy At Pyramid

As a result of this story, people at Pyramid believe that the only way to protect themselves is to acquire as much *power* as possible in order to be able to dominate others and exert their will over them. This is their Survival Strategy.

'Power' at Pyramid is not the kind of true Universal Power found at the Fractal-Based Terrain (Toroid); rather it is earthly power. Earthly power is the ability to dominate others and make them do what you want. It means the ability to exert your *will* over someone else's. It is measured by wealth, property and territory, and by how much you can manipulate and control the behavior of others.

Those at Pyramid work hard to acquire and hold onto such 'earthly' power and they will go to any lengths to achieve it, including manipulation, lies, scheming, trickery, fear-mongering, abuse, violence and war; believing that the end of keeping themselves safe and 'on top' justifies the means.

The ultimate goal of all people at Pyramid is to accumulate power. However, not everyone at Pyramid is successful at this. Those who are not powerful in their own right understand that they need to align themselves with someone who is powerful, in order to stay safe. That is why people at Pyramid often join gangs, submit to mafia-style protection and obey the whims of powerful charismatic leaders who command hierarchical power structures.

Essentially, the Survival Strategy at Pyramid is to become the Alpha Male / Queen Bee or to align oneself with the strongest Alpha Male / Queen Bee one can find. This is the way people at the Will-Based Terrain control the world around them in order to manage their internal fear.

Illusory Safety

What is important to note is that this is the first Terrain on the Continuum of Terrains where man believes he can personally control the world around him. This is an absolutely *enormous shift*. Instead of feeling that he is at the mercy of a capricious god or deity, man now feels that he can influence his own fate. This brings with it a higher feeling of safety than was experienced at Radial, and as a result people at Pyramid live in less fear and feel less disempowered than did those at the Faith-Based Terrain.

Nevertheless, the power that the Pyramid safety depends upon is ultimately illusory; it is not true Power at all, but merely 'force'. It needs all the kings horses and all the kings men simply to keep it going. It must be held onto tightly because it can be taken away at any moment. Therefore inside their fortified castles, those at

Pyramid can never feel truly secure, which is why they strive to gain ever more wealth, power and territory and never feel that they have enough.

CORE FEATURES & DRIVERS OF PYRAMID

Independence

People at the Will-Based Terrain refuse to be controlled or told what to do by anyone in a position of authority. They consider themselves to be masters of their own destiny. This is a kind of lawless 'frontier mentality' where people refuse to knuckle down because someone else tells them to and seek to get away with wild and rebellious acts.

Ego

The Will-Based Terrain is all about the pure unadulterated expression of the ego—that childlike part of a person that causes it to assert its own will at all costs. This is a 'me-focused' Terrain, driven to satisfy the ego's needs for power, as well as other indulgences such as bodily pleasure.

The Pyramid person looks out for themselves alone. They do not do things because of a higher power (as at Radial) or for a larger cause (as at Square), instead they do what they want to do and act in their own interest at all times.

Instant Gratification

At this ego-driven Terrain, what the ego wants, the ego gets, regardless of the consequences. It is not only the consequences to other people, to society and to the planet that people at Pyramid ignore, but also the consequences to their own long term good. Think of Veruca Salt in the movie 'Willy Wonka And The Chocolate Factory' demanding that her father buy her a golden goose, still singing *"Don't care how, I want it now!"* as she falls down the shoot for bad eggs.

Hedonism

Accompanying this need for instant gratification at Pyramid is a kind of hedonistic lust that puts the goal of pleasure above all else. People at Pyramid will go to great lengths in the pursuit of pleasure and the avoidance of pain. They will ignore later consequence to both themselves and others, in order to have even a moment of pure pleasure.

Addictive substances such as alcohol, drugs, cigarettes and sugar, and dopamine-raising behaviors such as video games, sex and gambling are often used by people at Pyramid to spike the pleasure centers in the brain. This enables them to avoid negative feelings, living instead in a hyper-stimulated state. Whereas those at more expanded Terrains are able to walk away from these behaviors when their health, work or family life begins to suffer, people at Pyramid do not do that. They see that their behavior has consequences, yet they have a *"Damn the torpedoes—full steam ahead!"* attitude.

Entitlement

People at Pyramid not only want what they want, but they feel entitled to get it. They feel that it has their name on it, whether it is a chocolate bar or an empire. In order to go after something they want, those at Pyramid do not feel that they need the blessing of a 'god' (Radial) or permission from those in authority (Square). They simply feel that if they want something, it is their right to have it.

If the person at Pyramid needs to step over other people, manipulate them, deceive them, charm them, bribe them, intimidate them, fight (or even kill) them in order to get what they want, then they will do so. And if somebody seeks to get in their way, they will not hesitate to mow them down. It is not that they do not care about the feelings of others, it is simply that their feeling of entitlement to the desired object trumps all other considerations.

Greed And Conquest

Those at the Will-Based Terrain inherently see life as a pyramid, with scarce resources and only room for a very few at the top, who rule the world from on high. This is therefore the Terrain of greed—the driving need to acquire more wealth—and of conquest—invading the territory of others to seize it for yourself.

Think of the game of Monopoly—the quintessential Pyramid board game—where the sole aim is to acquire more property and more wealth. The more money and territory that a person at Pyramid has, the safer they feel.

Empire

It is this Pyramid lust for conquest, control and ever growing power that is at the heart of Empire building. Empires throughout history— such as the Mongol Empire, the Roman Empire, the Spanish Empire and the British Empire—have all sprung from rulers at the Will-Based Terrain who had an insatiable urge to control greater and greater swathes of territory. The more territory that a leader controls, the more people they can dominate and the more resources and wealth they have at their fingertips; this then gives them a feeling of greater earthly power that helps them to feel safe in their fear-reactive reality and sated in their ego.

Of course, because the earthly power is not true Power at all, merely force, the feeling of safety is illusory. Therefore deep down, the Pyramid leader can never feel truly safe, no matter how much wealth and territory he controls and no matter how many peoples he subjugates. This fuels him to always want to conquer more land and more peoples, and to expand his empire even more. In this ego-driven Terrain, the needs of the ego are insatiable and are never satisfied. Not even total world domination would satisfy it.

Domination

This Terrain is called 'Will-Based' because, at its core, this Terrain is about the imposition of one person's will over another's—and thereby over nature and all life. This Terrain is about one person making another do what they want them to do. It is this domination of will that makes the person at Pyramid feel powerful and therefore safe from the terrifying forces of nature and from the dog-eat-dog world that they perceive around them.

This is a *'power-over'* Terrain, rather than a *'power-with'* Terrain such as at Toroid. What is important to remember is that when one person at Pyramid dominates another person at Pyramid, both sides are actually comfortable with this at a deep subconscious level—even if they protest outwardly—for it accords with their perception of a dog-eat-dog universe where the 'alpha male' dominates.

Control

This perception of life being a pyramid combined with the belief in the scarcity of resources means that those at the top must necessarily control those at the bottom. Inherent in this Terrain is the belief that if the masses are not controlled, they will rise up like ants and knock those at the top of the pyramid off their perches and take their precious resources.

This is why those in power at the Will-Based Terrain do everything they can do to protect their privileged positions, while hiding behind layers of security. Domination of the masses—whether using Pyramid tools like terror, brutality and conquest, using Square tools like mind-control and propaganda or using Diamond tools like celebrity, influence and technology—is key to the strategies of the wealthy at Pyramid. It is how those at Pyramid who have accumulated their precious power survive.

Ends Justifies The Means

The mantra 'the ends justifies the means' is the catch-call of Pyramid. Moral and human considerations do not matter here, for the closer one gets to the top of the pyramid, the less one is connected to those at the bottom, and the easier it becomes to manipulate them with moral impunity.

A key feature of people at the Will-Based Terrain is that they are unattached to their methods of gaining power. They will do whatever is needed and whatever works. When it stops working, they will do something else. They are not excited by original thinking or new ideas, they are excited by what works to get them more power.

While those at Pyramid will do whatever is needed to achieve their goals of power, there are some standard tools commonly used. These include fear mongering—both by violence and the threat of violence and by the manufacturing of catastrophe and chaos; manipulation—including bribery, trickery, deception and blackmail; and abuse—including physical abuse, sexual abuse, mental abuse and emotional abuse. These tried and tested Pyramid tools create fear, trauma and dependency in the victim and allow them to be more easily manipulated and controlled.

Individualism

People at the Will-Based Terrain are individualist by nature. They only unite as a group when they have a perceived common enemy to fight or a common predator they need protection from or want to gain advantage over. All throughout history as well as in our modern times we see factions, nations, even whole regions of the planet at Pyramid align together to protect their common interests, only to disband once they are again secure or have achieved their goals of dominance; and then later to be seen regrouping with others, often against those who were previously their allies.

Extended Ego

The idea of individualism is a little more complex at Pyramid than it is later at Diamond, for people at the Will-Based Terrain consider their children and descendants to be extensions of themselves. The ego is so strong at this Terrain that the person's egoic sense of self extends beyond their own life through their progeny. Therefore, they accumulate power not only for themselves, but for their entire bloodline and its future generations. This is the Terrain of the 'dynasty'.

The Family

Blood bonds are strongest at Pyramid. At this Terrain the 'family' is everything. This applies to both a birth family and an *adopted family*—such as a gang, army unit or sporting team—that becomes one's entire identity.

At this Terrain, oaths taken and promises made in the name of the family or adopted family are taken very seriously, and grudges are jointly held by everyone in the gang and maintained sometimes for generations. Each adopted family has its own unique rituals, which are carried out with pride by all members. They often also have their own way of dressing, secret codes and words, and sometimes even their own dialect, which enables all the members of the group to identify with it and feel that it is their family.

This Pyramid approach to 'family' can be seen most clearly in the Mafia, where family members stick together to work for the dominance of the entire clan. It is considered crucial at Pyramid to protect one's family, gang or cabal at all costs. In the dog-eat-dog world that people at Pyramid believes themselves to be in, only members of one's own 'family' can be trusted. Everyone else is seen as an enemy, there to be climbed over, profited from, manipulated, vanquished, enslaved, submitted or otherwise controlled, in order to gain more power for one's gang.

Alpha Leaders

As we have said, those at Pyramid who are unable to themselves acquire power will align themselves with an Alpha Male or Queen Bee who does have power, usually by joining their gang or cabal. These leaders are generally charismatic, heroic, larger-than-life figures, who rule by fear and wield their power ruthlessly. They tend to become corrupted by their power and can end up as megalomaniacs.

Those beneath them always know where they stand in the pecking order and how to appease and obey those above in order to survive.

Leadership By Fear

At Square, people will work for you because they are loyal by nature, and because they believe in order and the greater good. At Diamond people will work for you if they believe passionately in your vision, if they think they will learn something or if they think it will ultimately further their career path. At Circle, people will work for you if they feel that you share their values and they feel a Heart connection to you and to your cause. However, at Pyramid the only motivator is power—either the lust for it or the fear of it. Therefore, no person at Pyramid will work for you unless they feel they can somehow gain power over others from that position, or unless they are so fearful of you that they feel they have no choice. Thus leaders at Pyramid use fear to keep those who work for them in line, and every rung in a Pyramid hierarchy rules those below it through fear.

Hero Worship

Whilst these tyrannical leaders at Pyramid are feared, they are also often worshipped, for people at the Will-Based Terrain celebrate acts of heroism and conquest by individuals, and admire people who have power and glory.

The Pyramid 'hero' not only does glorious feats, but he does not show weakness, sensitivity or emotion. He must be tough and push himself to his limits. He is aggressive and demands respect. He throws himself in the face of the dragon, hurls himself in front of the oncoming army or football tacklers, and dives off the stage at his own rock concert. He lives life large and shows no fear. And he is greatly admired for it by others at Pyramid.

Us Versus Them

The core fear at the Will-Based Terrain is the fear of other people, which is rooted in a deep sense of separation and causes a driving belief of 'us' vs 'them'. At Pyramid, you are either *"with us or against us"*. There is no middle way with the ego.

This belief is the basis of racism, sexism and all other social divisions where one group decides that another is 'less than' and turns on it. At its most extreme, this aspect of Pyramid expresses itself in a belief that one's own blood or race is superior to that of others and even in an urge to exterminate those who are 'other'.

Battle Of The Sexes

The 'us vs them' mentality of Pyramid combined with the me-focused sense of entitlement at Pyramid means that the relationship between men and women at this Terrain becomes a 'battle of the sexes'. At Pyramid men see women as 'objects' to be used sexually for their own physical needs, and women see men as pawns to be manipulated by sex for their own financial needs. As a result, there is a continual power play between the sexes at this Terrain, which has been greatly glamorized by Hollywood and by the pornography industry.

Exploitation

Another facet of the 'us vs them' mentality of Pyramid is that the ethos of Pyramid is harsh and exploitative, with people divided into 'haves' and 'have nots'. In times where the Prevailing Terrain of a population is at Pyramid, you will see slavery as a common feature of the society. As we will see in Part 4, slavery is a key Pyramid collective behavior. This is because those at the Will-Based Terrain consider that people are lazy and untrustworthy by nature and that they will only work for you if they are coerced, bribed or forced.

Victim Mentality

In the dog-eat-dog world of Pyramid, people genuinely believe that others are out to get them and that in some profound way the whole world is against them. This deep fear of other people causes those at

Pyramid to have a strong 'victim consciousness'. They frequently feel wronged by other people or feel 'hard done by'.

Those at Pyramid rarely take responsibility for the situations they create in their lives and instead place all the fault squarely on other people. A common cry at Pyramid is *"how could they do this to me?"* This feeds the Pyramid person's need to have enemies and to fight heroically against perceived injustices.

Emotional

At the Will-Based Terrain, the emotional body begins to drive the ego. This means that people at Pyramid can sometimes be very emotional, temperamental and demanding and can often act quite wildly and impetuously.

Indeed, because of the victim-mentality mentioned above, people at this Terrain often carry simmering anger and resentment towards people who they perceive to have wronged them. They may even carry a catalogue within them of all the people who have ever hurt them, betrayed them or wounded them. This anger and resentment inevitably boils to the surface at some point, often leading to aggressive, violent behavior.

Aggression

Life at Pyramid can be very combative, as a core driver here is the expression of aggression. Those at Pyramid will often fight simply for the thrill of 'blood lust' or to get their emotions out, rather than for any greater cause as do those at Square.

In the modern world, you will often find people at Pyramid signing up for careers in the military or in the police force, to give them a way to express both their yearning for heroism and their pent up aggression. You will often see those at Pyramid on the other side of the law too; these are the untamable rebels, larrikins and hooligans who refuse to fit into the ordered system of Square.

Violence

Because of the mix of ego and emotion that is operating at the Will-Based Terrain, the separation between man and man that is found here can be a violent and antagonistic separation. The Pyramid ego fights hard against any threat it perceives to its territory. And when the passion and emotion of Pyramid meet with the sense of entitlement, the lust for power and the sense of 'us vs them', that is where we see some of the most violent and senseless conflicts on the planet. This is the bloody world of gang wars all the way up to global territorial warfare that has been such a large feature of the human story over the last few thousands years.

Sports Fanaticism

A prevalent example of Pyramid in the modern world is that of sports fanatics. We are not talking here about people who merely like to watch sport, we are talking about those people who follow their team fanatically, think and talk obsessively about their team, and whose happiness depends on how their team fares from week to week.

Being able to fanatically follow a sporting team satisfies many of the core Pyramid drivers. Firstly, it allows those at Pyramid to extend their ego and their identity out to an adopted family who is able to have heroic victories on their behalf. Sporting fanatics at Pyramid identify with their team of choice so much that their emotional response to a win or defeat is exactly the same as if their clan had won or lost a battle in days of old. Sporting fanaticism also gives those at Pyramid a safe opportunity to vent all their pent up emotions and to express their separation mentality without having to actually physically fight anybody, by passionately cheering for their team and vehemently jeering the opposition. The opponent on the sporting field becomes the personification of all things 'other', a representation of all things that are to be feared, fought and defeated, if one is to reign supreme in this dog-eat-dog world.

KEY ELEMENTS OF PYRAMID

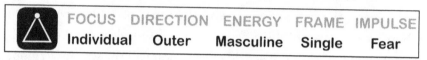

	FOCUS	DIRECTION	ENERGY	FRAME	IMPULSE
	Individual	Outer	Masculine	Single	Fear

The Will-Based Terrain is an individual-focused Terrain, for here we see the emergence of a distinct 'self' separate from the tribe, who wants to obtain power for its own gain.

The Will-Based Terrain is a strongly outer-directed Terrain, for as the Pyramid person now perceives that they can conquer and control their environment through their own will, they direct their attention outward to build an empire they believe will assure the immortality of themselves and their lineage.

The Will-Based Terrain is a fairly immature expression of masculine energy, with the emphasis being on conquest, domination and force.

The Will-Based Terrain is a single-frame Terrain as, being fundamentally fearful of other people and their motives, those at Pyramid are fiercely protective of their individual perspective and will tend to fight anyone who disagrees with them.

The Will-Based Terrain is a fear-reactive Terrain, for people at Pyramid have a perception of separation that causes them to have an overwhelming fear of other people and see the world as a threatening jungle filled with predators, such that they consider it acceptable to dominate and manipulate others in order to accumulate power, so as to keep themselves feeling safe.

SYMBOL OF PYRAMID

The symbol of the 'pyramid' best describes the Will-Based Terrain because this is the Terrain of domination and control. The large point at the top represents the Will-Based person looking down on his world seeking to exert his will upon it and to dominate and control everyone in it so that they submit to him. The pyramid shape also represents the fact that this Terrain is hierarchical and based in scarcity-consciousness, with those at the top seeking to hoard power and wealth for themselves. There is only room at the top for a very few, and the countless ants at the base of the pyramid must be kept from wresting power from those at the top by means of fear and force.

EXAMPLES OF PYRAMID

Historical examples of people at the Will-Based Terrain include megalomaniacal Monarchs and Emperors who sought to expand their empire by invading other countries, and feudal lords who believed their slaves to be their 'property'. Modern equivalents include the powerful families of the Oligarchy, who many would say are running our world behind the official Square governments, the so-called 'Powers That Be'.

However, it is important to remember that not all people at Pyramid are megalomaniacs seeking world domination. Most people at Pyramid are ordinary good-natured folk going about simple daily lives, not seeking to hurt or control anyone. Yet they have a relationship with reality that is based in scarcity and 'us vs them' thinking that comes from their Terrain.

To show you the wide range of the Will-Based Terrain, here are some typical examples, ranging from the common man all the way to billionaire elites.

- a member of a street gang who is devoted to his 'hood' and fights gang wars to defend it;
- a chronic smoker who refuses to give up the pleasure of cigarettes even though she is on her deathbed;
- a sports fanatic who lives and breathes for his team and vents all his pent up aggression while cheering for them each week;
- a beautiful young actress who uses her body to manipulate men and climb to the top;
- a larrikin who spends his days and night drinking in the pub and has no interest in holding down a regular job or settling down;
- a member of a biker gang, who rides where he wants when he wants and lives a free life outside the law;
- a couple whose use S&M power games in their sex life;
- a simple punter who nurses his grudges against his neighbors, resents government control and wants to stick it to 'the man'.
- a tattoo artist who wears leather and chains and engraves death symbols on his body;
- a matriarch of a large wealthy family who married the biggest 'catch' in town and believes her family is superior to all others in the neighborhood;
- a member of the Ku Klux Klan who hates all negroes and wants America to be 'pure';

- a rock star living in the fast lane, addicted to women and cocaine;
- a charismatic mafia leader who rules his territory by fear and threat;
- a political leader who invades the surrounding countries and ultimately seeks world domination; and
- a billionaire in an 'elite' family who manipulates world events from the secrecy of his bunkered estate.

Please note that the above examples are simplified stereotypes of people at the Will-Based Terrain, designed to give you a feel for this Terrain. There will be many people at Pyramid who do not resemble the above examples at all; and you may meet people who fit the above descriptions yet who are not at Pyramid. Accurate analysis of someone's Terrain requires extensive training in the Ten Terrains Model and must never be assumed based solely on what someone does for a living or their external behaviors.

CONTEXT

From some of the above examples and descriptions, it may seem that people at Pyramid are the 'bad guys' in our world. They are certainly portrayed to be so in many works of fiction, and have indeed played that role in the history books. However, in the eyes of Infinite Consciousness there are no bad guys. Everyone is an equally important thread in the human tapestry, playing an equally valuable role in the unfolding play that is life.

Remember that the stage of Free Will is an important one that needs to be passed through in the journey of human evolution, after the isolation of Particle and the disempowerment of Radial. In addition, people at Pyramid play a very important role in the collective Field of humanity by providing contrast and choice for people at the more expanded Terrains.

Furthermore, it is important to understand that the earthly 'power' that people at Pyramid seek so strenuously is in fact not true Power at all. It is merely 'force'. It is only at Toroid, at the very opposite end of the Continuum, that one becomes truly 'Powerful'. Therefore, even with all the wealth and territory they can possibly accumulate, those at Pyramid can never truly take a dominant position for long in our world as they will always be overcome by people who are truly Sovereign in their Being—and eventually by life itself.

PYRAMID MOVING TO SQUARE

From Free Will To Selfless Duty

The examples we've just provided are most likely to describe someone who is *stationary* at Pyramid. Once a person is fully embodying all the lessons, gifts and experiences of Pyramid, their Infinite Self will start them on the long journey up the mountain to the Order-Based Terrain (Square).

As a person at Pyramid starts to move up the mountain towards Square, their wildness will begin to curb a little. They will be driven less by the overwhelming desires of their ego and will start to be able to exercise a little restraint in their behavior.

They will start to become interested in people beyond just themselves and their own blood line. They will still be driven foremost by their own ego needs, but if other people get caught in the crossfire, they will now feel some guilt and remorse.

They will begin to pay attention to the consequences of their actions; not enough to overcome their strongest ego desires, but enough to sway their less urgent whims and to take a more restrained course of action in some cases.

They will start to wish that they were a part of something bigger than themselves, even while they are still driven by the need to accumulate personal power. This need to be a part of something and to be of service will grow stronger and stronger inside them, as they proceed up the mountain and down the other side towards Square.

As this person at Pyramid continues to travel down the other side of the mountain towards Square, they will most likely start to suffer experiences that humble them, that cause them to start to knuckle down, and to pull in their ego. They may start to find that their grand plans for heroism, wealth, domination and power begin increasingly to be foiled, as life prepares them for the even greater humbling that will happen in the moment of their jump to Square.

Such a person who is on the move to Square will look back at their time when they were stationary in the valley of Pyramid and feel that they have changed a great deal. They may even feel like a completely different person. They may indeed look upon their old self in the valley at Pyramid with some judgment or shame. Indeed, if reading this book, they might even mistakenly feel that they have already shifted into Square. However, until they actually cross the Event Horizon Of Perception into Square this person at Pyramid on the move is still fundamentally driven by their ego and their own interests, for their sense of safety in the world still comes from amassing power. This will be the case until the moment when they cross the Event Horizon into Square and their need for safety now gets assuaged by being part of something greater than themselves.

HISTORICAL FIGURES AT PYRAMID

A few famous historical figures who were at the Will-Based Terrain are Genghis Khan, Al Capone and Adolph Hitler. To see a full list of famous historical figures who were at the Will-Based Terrain, make sure to get your free eBook *The Terrains Of Famous People In History*. It includes names of infamous monarchs, emperors, political leaders, military leaders, mobsters, gangsters, outlaws, drug lords, movie moguls, rock stars, gladiators and sporting heroes, from around the world, all of whom were at Pyramid.

MOVIES, TV & BOOKS AT PYRAMID

There is a vast body of fiction in our modern Western culture that celebrate aspects of life at Pyramid and characters at Pyramid, perhaps more so than any other Terrain. These include movies such as 'Rambo', 'The Godfather' and most Westerns; TV shows such as 'Revenge', 'Empire', and 'Game Of Thrones'; and books such as '50 Shades of Grey' by E.L. James and 'The Vampire Chronicles' series by Anne Rice.[4] There are also many works of fiction that depict the journey from Pyramid to Square, such as the movie 'Top Gun'.

Many works of fiction coming from other Terrains are about the dangers posed by the Pyramid hunger for power, such as novels 'The Lord Of The Flies' by William Golding and 'Animal Farm' by George Orwell. The 'bad guys' in many Square works of fiction tend to be characters at Pyramid; such as Voldemort in the 'Harry Potter' Series, Sauron in 'The Lord Of The Rings' and the larger-than-life bad guys in most comic books.

In addition, there are many famous non-fiction works written from the Will-Based Terrain of Consciousness, such as the very playbook of Pyramid: Machiavelli's 'The Prince'.

To learn about other popular books, movies and TV shows that illustrate Pyramid, watch our entertaining free videos on the 'Ten Terrains' YouTube Channel.

Other aspects of popular culture that express the Will-Based Terrain include:

- Video games and board games where the goal is to capture territory, acquire wealth or defeat enemies, such as 'Monopoly' and 'Stratego';
- Competitive team sports where the goal is to gain the other team's territory by scoring goals there, such as Football and Hockey;
- Competitive individual sports where the goal is to use physical strength to defeat the opponent, such as Boxing and Wrestling; and
- Reality TV shows involving gladiatorial competition, such as 'Survivor'.

BIGGER PICTURE OF PYRAMID

From the spiritual perspective of Infinite Consciousness as Self, the Will-Based Terrain can be seen as 'The Journey Of Free Will'. The lesson a person is learning while at this Terrain is how to use their power of choice for their own good. The gift this Terrain brings is empowered action. The challenge it brings is how to gain power when other people are resisting you. This becomes particularly challenging when the Pyramid person is living within an ordered Square society that is regulating them.

If you are at this Terrain, we suggest that you read the 'Guidebook For The Pyramid Terrain'. In this booklet we go into far more detail about the lessons you are here to learn on 'The Journey Of Free Will'. We explain much more about the unique gifts and challenges of Pyramid. We also give you invaluable tips and strategies to help you navigate life at this Terrain.

THE ORDER-BASED TERRAIN (SQUARE)

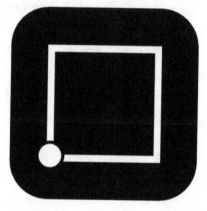

THE ORDER-BASED TERRAIN OF CONSCIOUSNESS (SQUARE) is the next evolutionary stage on the Continuum Of Terrains. A person at this Terrain is experiencing 'The Journey Of Selfless Duty'. As of 2015, we estimate that approximately 25% of people in the Developed World are living at the Order-Based Terrain.

The Event Horizon Into Square

As a person crosses the Event Horizon Of Perception into the Order-Based Terrain, the huge shift in perception is that they realize that there is something bigger than themselves that is more important than their own personal egoic will and desires: that is, the common good of the majority. At this Terrain, being a cog in a greater machine gives one a sense of place, of service, and of meaning. One's own ego desires are set aside out of a sense of duty, chivalry and public service.

The Story At Square

The Order-Based Terrain is still a fear-reactive Terrain, at a deep subconscious level untrusting of life and nature, but here the primary fear is of the wild, unpredictable, unrestrained unlawfulness that exists at Pyramid, and therefore the driving need is for *order*.

People at Square have a driving need for order in all areas of their life: in their family relationships, in their interactions with others, in their work, play, finances, health, economics, politics and every other aspect of society. The only thing that can provide this degree of order for those at Square is an external 'system', a centralized machine that manages all of its citizens and runs every aspect of their lives smoothly and fairly.

Therefore, the Story at Square is that a 'system' of social regulation is needed to provide order and that such a system is the only thing that can protect you.

The Strategy At Square

People at the Order-Based Terrain believe that their safety depends not on the accumulation of power, but on their ability to fit into 'the system'. This is their Survival Strategy.

The person at Square agrees to a 'social contract' in which they give up the right to do whatever they please in order to receive the protection of the system. They agree to follow society's laws, which are understood to be in place for the orderly functioning of the system as a whole.

The more a person at Square fits into the system by following the law, obeying authority figures, sticking to tradition, keeping up with whatever trends become mainstream, adhering to social norms and going along with the majority, the safer they feel.

CORE FEATURES & DRIVERS OF SQUARE

Mainstream

A simple way to understand the Order-Based Terrain is to think of the word 'mainstream', as it is generally used in the vernacular. A person at Square is a mainstream person. They are not pushing the envelope socially, politically, artistically, technologically or culturally. They are happy with the status quo and have found a place for themselves in the existing system.

Traditionals And Moderns

Using the language of sociologist Paul Ray, Ph.D.[5], who first came up with the terms 'Moderns', 'Traditionals' and 'Cultural Creatives', some people at Square would be considered 'Traditionals' and others would be considered 'Moderns'. This depends largely on the culture they are living in.

For example, in the conservative bible belt of the southern United States, you will find many people at Square who are Traditionals, who go to church every Sunday and live a parochial, old-fashioned life carrying on the traditions of their forefathers. In the big cities, you will find people at Square who are Moderns, living in suburbs with high-tech gadgets and fast-paced corporate jobs, wearing the latest fashions and reading celebrity magazines.

These two groups have very different behaviors and may even hold very different beliefs and vote for different political parties. Yet they are all at the same Terrain, regardless of this difference in their lifestyles and opinions. In the context of where they are living, they are the 'mainstream'.

Where Do I Fit?

From earliest life, one of the central questions a person at Square faces is: *"What part will I play in the system? Where do I fit?"* The nuances of this question will change as a person grows, but the core question remains the same.

For example, a child at Square might wonder if he should be an astronaut, an actor or a doctor when he grows up. A young adult at Square might think about whether he should study law or commerce or science. A professional at Square might agonize about whether they should work in the private sector or the public. A dancer at Square might ask themselves which company they should perform with. An athlete at Square might wonder which team they should join. An intellectual at Square might ask themselves if they should become an academic, a consultant or an analyst. A comedian at Square might wonder which sector they should lampoon: celebrities, the media or politicians. An activist at Square might wonder which political party he should join: the conservatives or the liberals.

At all points in their life, the person at Square is trying to figure out where they belong in the mainstream system. They are trying to find their place. Only when they have found their place do they feel stable and secure.

As difficult and individual as these decisions of *"where do I fit?"* are, they are still easier and more generic than the decisions of identity faced by people at Diamond, for at Square at least one is limited by choosing from options *within* the system. At Diamond a person is trying to create their own, entirely new options.

Roles

Once a person at Square has found where they fit in the system, this gives them their sense of self. This is because at the Order-Based Terrain, one's entire identity comes from the *role* that one plays in the system. At this Terrain, a person is a 'mother' or a 'lawyer' first, and an individual second. People at Square slot easily into institutionalized, corporate, family and societal roles. Indeed, without an assigned role in the system, the Square person feels lost.

Multiple Roles

People at Square do not always play only one role in the system. There is often some internal 'compartmentalization' of the person at Square into various discrete roles. For example, they may see themselves as a 'banker' at work, then a 'father' at home, then the 'president of the tennis club' on the weekends. The identity of the person at Square derives from this collection of roles, rather than from a unique sense of 'self' like we find at Diamond.

Changing Roles

Once a person at Square has defined themselves by their role or roles, they are reluctant to change these. They tend to put off retiring and can take it very badly when they are fired from a particular job or when their term in office is over. Similarly, they can struggle when a long term marriage ends or their children grow up. In both kinds of cases, their entire identity has come from the role they were playing at work or at home, and now that it has disappeared they no longer know who they are or what their purpose is.

The Institution

As the Story at Square is that safety comes from the order provided by 'the system', those at Square tend to believe wholeheartedly in official institutions such as the State, the Government, the Bureaucracy, the Justice System, the University, the Medical Establishment, the Political Party and the Corporation. If they are Square 'Traditionals' they are likely to also believe wholeheartedly in the Church and/ or the Monarchy. This embracing of the system extends to cultural institutions such as the institution of Marriage, to industry institutions such as the institution of Medicine, and to sporting and cultural institutions such as those of Cricket, Opera, Ballet, etc., all of which have heavily codified practices and regulations that have been practiced for many generations.

The Greater Good

As a Collective Terrain, a key feature of people at Square is that they do not work for self-interest, like those at Pyramid, but for the good of their family, their community or their country. They are focused on 'service-to-other'. These are people who do their best to help their neighbors, be good citizens, and to contribute to the fabric of the society they are in.

The downside of this commitment to the greater good is that people at Square generally only take into account the greater good of the *majority*. People in minority groups do not tend to be catered to, nor do those who do not conform to the cookie-cutter Square behavior or who live outside the system; such as people who live below the poverty line, are unemployed or homeless.

Authority

People at the Order-Based Terrain obey authority without question. They follow the rules laid down by whoever they consider to be an 'authority figure', be that their father, their government, their law makers, their King or their God. Within the family structure, those at Square will unquestioningly follow the rules set down by the head of the household. Within civil society, those at Square will strive at all times to be good citizens and follow the law to the best of their abilities. Those at Square who are religious will do their best to follow the dictates of their God as laid down in religious texts.

For those of you at a different Terrain, it is important to understand that people at Square will only do something if it has been given approval by someone in a position of authority. So if you try to introduce a new idea to someone at Square, they will be unable to hear you unless you can back that idea by some sort of official sanction such as a university degree, scientific study, government approval or coverage by the mainstream media.

People at Square do not obey authority out of fear or mindlessness, but because they believe, deep in their bones, that for there to be *order* someone has to be in charge; and for that person to lead properly, their commands must be obeyed. For those at Square, obedience is merely the price of order.

Following Rules

People at the Order-Based Terrain generally like to have clear rules to follow—it gives them a sense of safety and security. In addition, people within the Square system are encouraged—even conditioned—to feel guilty when they disobey the law, when they break social conventions, or when they stray from the flock in any way. They are taught to feel guilt if they give in to their own natural urges, whether those be sexual urges, creative urges or simply the urges and yearnings of their own true Heart. Even having an original thought can be enough to engender guilt for some people at Square.

Conformity

Not only do people at Square blindly follow rules and obey authority, they also unequivocally adhere to traditions and accepted practices. Observance of national patriotic holidays is one example. In addition, people at Square are very aware of what is expected of them and make sure that they act in ways that are considered 'normal'. They do not experiment, push the envelope or seek to stand out, instead they do what those around them are doing. This conformity is not due to a lack of imagination or a lack of original thought, but because people at Square believe their entire safety depends on conforming to the system and doing what has always been done.

Consensus Reality

People at Square live by a code of 'consensus reality' whereby what the majority decrees to be true becomes the truth. They base their actions on the opinions of the majority, seeking safety in numbers. The opinions of the *minority* are generally dismissed or ignored, as are their own deeper personal feelings.

Often, when something new enters the culture, it may take time for a majority opinion on it to emerge. In the interim, those at Square will tend to wait and watch, remaining skeptical of any changes until they can see that those deemed the 'authorities' in their society have approved of it and that the majority of their peers or neighbors have adopted it.

The majority view in any Square culture will generally conform with the views and opinions held by people in positions of authority. This is why it has always been fairly easy for those 'elites' at Pyramid to control and manipulate the opinions and actions of the masses at Square. They simply have to make sure that the universities, political and religious leaders and mass media outlets are putting forth the views that they wish the population to hold, and these views and opinions thereby become the norm with which everyone is expected to conform.

Cutting Down Tall Poppies

In many Square communities, people who seek to develop their own unique identity independent from their role in the Square system will be criticized or ridiculed. If a person starts to live their life differently than the norms of the culture, they may be heavily pressured to conform, and if they refuse, they may even be ostracized. In some Square cultures, if a person seeks to rise up above the status of the majority around them they will be cut down to size quickly and told they are getting 'too big for their boots'.

Ignoring One's Own Truth

In order to play their role in the system and carry out their strategy of conforming to the social contract, people at the Order-Based Terrain are necessarily disconnected from the authentic guidance of their own Heart. They will tend to sacrifice their own Heart's desires and to ignore their own truth in order to carry out what they see as their duty, to obey authority and to do as they are expected to do. This enables many profound acts of selflessness to be carried out by people at Square. However, this same switching off of one's true feelings has also enabled people at Square to carry out truly heinous actions throughout human history, under the instructions of their superior officer, their political leaders or in the name of their God.

Routine

The deep drive for order means that, at Square, life tends to be organized around routine, and people tend to behave in predictable ways. For example, those at the Order-Based Terrain tend to eat the same foods for breakfast they have always eaten, watch the same TV shows, drive the same car, go to the same job and follow the same sports team. They are generally slow to adopt new trends or fashions.

At Square, people will often even stick with something that is not serving them at all, simply because it is familiar to them. For people at this Terrain, *what is known is always safer than what is unknown.* For example, they are likely to stay in an unhappy marriage or an unsatisfying job for countless years because the thought of being single or jobless again, with all its inherent uncertainties, is terrifying for them.

Stability And Certainty

At Square, the future is planned for and all risks are managed. For example, people at Square prefer to have long term jobs, with a steady career path. They are much more likely to save for and buy a house than to rent for years. They will happily commit to a mortgage, as that actually provides them with a sense of continuity and a feeling that they are building towards a certain future. They are likely to live in the same home for many years, and if they do have to move, it will generally not be too far away. They like the certainty of knowing that when they wake up a year from now, they will be in the same place.

Work Ethic

People at Square tend to have a strong work ethic. They believe that success comes from hard work and persistence. They believe that if you work hard and save your money, you will be able to attain financial security. Even though they see life as a struggle, they know that they can turn things around by putting their head down and working, with commitment and dedication. Stories like 'The Little Engine That Could' perfectly capture the ethos of this Terrain.

Financial Security

People at Square have a driving need for financial security. They tend to hoard and save—money, assets, material possessions, even natural resources. They are very reluctant to make what they perceive to be 'risky' investments, preferring to let their wealth appreciate slowly over time in more traditional investments like property or slowly growing 'blue chip' stocks.

To create long term financial security, people at Square place great store in superannuation and retirement funds. They tend to have everything insured that they can afford to insure—their home, their car, their health, their life. They are likely to have their will and succession organized long before their death.

Border Security

The Square need for security extends to protecting one's borders, both those of one's home and of one's nation. At Square, family security takes the form of fences, alarm systems and strict rules for the children about times of coming and going. Collective security consists of tight border regulations and large military defense budgets. This is the Terrain where the population unites as a whole in its fear of a collective enemy that needs to be guarded against.

Predictability

At the Order-Based Terrain, people not only seek routine and continuity in their own behaviors, but they need the world around them to be predictable too. This tends to be possible within the boundaries of their local Square community, for any other Square people around them will also all behave in predictable ways and be following the same social rules as they themselves are. However, in the wider world beyond this, such predictability is not possible, particularly in our current Diamond Prevailing Terrain, where innovation is everywhere and the speed of change is ever increasing.

When societal change comes gradually, those at Square will always be the slowest to adapt. When societal change comes suddenly, those at Square will be the hardest hit, for they will not be able to spot the emerging trends and change course accordingly. When societal change comes dramatically, such as in times of financial or social collapse, when the very system they rely upon seems to be falling apart, then those at Square will be the ones who commit suicide in droves, as was seen during the Great Depression in the 20th century.

Homeostasis

The important thing to remember is that the person at Square is always trying to maintain a familiar homeostasis. They do not like change, not because of the specifics of the change itself, but because of the uncertainty it brings with it. They will always resist upgrading, modernization and innovation until the change has been around long enough to have gathered mass consensus and become mainstream. They will cling to their beliefs, traditions and allegiances. The only way they can safely let go of an old belief is if someone they respect in a position of authority replaces it with a new 'officially sanctioned' truth.

Disinterest In Personal Growth

Until someone starts to move up the mountain to Diamond, their life at Square will tend to perpetuate without too much intentional personal growth. You are unlikely to find many Square people at personal development seminars or reading self help books, unless they are already on the move to Diamond. The kinds of 'truth seeking' and 'soul searching' that are so prevalent at Diamond do not exist yet at Square, for people at this Terrain are not trying to choose between multiple options or to figure out what is uniquely right for them, rather they are doing what is expected of them and what they have always done.

Absolutism

The beliefs held by those at the Order-Based Terrain tend to be simple and absolutist, with things divided into unvarying 'right' and 'wrong'. For example, 'capitalists are good, communists are bad', etc. Right and wrong at Square are not determined by one's inner knowing, but by outer authority. This 'consensus reality' approach to morality takes the stress out of life, without any energy needing to be wasted on agonizing decisions coming from one's own inner truth or morality.

Propaganda

With this black and white mentality, people at Square are very loyal to what they consider to be the 'truth' (usually that which is officially sanctioned by the media and the government) and they will go to great lengths to defend it. This makes people at Square particularly susceptible to propaganda. People who are at the Order-Based Terrain are unable to believe that the organs of the mass media would ever lie to them, for that would undermine their entire faith in the system. So they willingly close their eyes even when there are inconsistencies in the official story and stick their head under the carpet when people at other Terrains try to point out the truth. This enables them to be very easily controlled and manipulated.

Discipline

Discipline is strict at Square, yet it always seeks to be ruthlessly fair and is always made pursuant to laws and rules, rather than by emotion or whim. This is not only the case in the legal system, but also within families, in churches, community groups and in corporate environments too.

While those at Square may grumble when the discipline is harsh, they will always obey it without question. Given the black-and-white morality of the Order-Based Terrain, the Square child knows when he has been 'naughty' and he feels guilty for breaking the rules. He expects himself to be punished when he has done wrong and will submit willingly to the punishment. Indeed, it is this very punishment that allows the person at Square to feel safe, for if he is being punished, then all other wrongdoers will also be punished, and therefore life in the Square world will remain regulated and safe for him.

Self-Monitoring

Not only do those at Square allow the watching eye of authority to monitor their behavior, and not only do they accept its discipline, but they themselves *are* that eye. They are constantly monitoring themselves for breaches of the rules and conventions of their society, and they are just as closely keeping an eye on their neighbors. This means that the enforcement and control of Square law and order does not depend solely on the use of assigned 'monitors' such as policemen, but flows naturally through the system as part of its core DNA.

Loyalty

At the Order-Based Terrain, people are held together firmly by loyalties and allegiances such as those based on family and kin. Those at Square tend to be very family-oriented people with traditional values. Often if you examine the motivations of a Square person's behavior, you will see that they are acting to try to do what they think is best for their family. Those at Square will be reluctant to break up the family unit. We see very few divorces where both spouses are at Square, although the numbers are increasing now that divorce is becoming more accepted as 'mainstream' in many countries.

Patriotism

This loyalty to kin extends to loyalty to one's nation. In contrast to the Radial allegiance to one's clan or religious sect and the Pyramid loyalty to one's gang or blood-line, people at Square tend to be held together by loyalties and allegiances based on their 'Nation State'. Square is the Terrain of patriotism, national pride and flag waving.

When a population is at Square, a national crisis such as a major war, revolution, famine or financial collapse will pull all of its people together to forge an even stronger national identity. The scale of global conflict we saw in the early 20th Century, where whole nations of young men went to war to defend what they perceived to be 'right over wrong' could not have happened under any other Prevailing Terrain than Square.

Acceptance Of The Political System

If a country is operating with a Square system of government, such as a two-party democracy, a constitutional republic or communism[6], then people at Square tend to accept the political system that they are living in, so long as that system is 'perceived' to be fair. If it crosses the line from a fair Square system into totalitarianism or fascism, or if it tips into Pyramid tyranny, then the Square population will become uncomfortable.

You may think that people who are considered 'left wing' cannot be Square, yet this is untrue. Any person who happily votes in standard national elections, without questioning the system, is likely to be at Square, regardless of which party they are voting for. This is in stark contrast to those at Diamond, who are generally trying to change the system, overthrow it, undermine it, upgrade it, revolutionize it or expose it.

Role-Based Hierarchy

The Square society is stratified, with everybody in it knowing their place. However, this stratification is very different to the hierarchy found at Pyramid, where we see caste systems based on birth and blood lines, operating by fear. At Square, the stratification of members into classes is based on efficiency and order. Those in the working class have certain roles they are expected to fulfill, as do those in the middle class and those in the upper class. Everyone has their place and everyone accepts it. It is only at Diamond that we see people wanting to climb up beyond their class and break out of the roles that have been assigned to them.

Statesmen

At Pyramid, leaders rule those below them through tyranny and fear. At Square, we have a system where a person is *appointed* to a position of leader (whether by election or some other means). They are there not because of their birth, wealth or power, but because they are considered by the group to be the right person to fill that role. The person at Square may not be particularly wealthy or powerful in his own right, instead his ability to make decisions over others comes from the *role* he is now playing and the power invested in that role. He only has this power for the duration of the term of the role. This is the difference between a lifetime King who is there by birthright (Pyramid) and a term-limited Prime Minister or President who is there by election (Square).

Outer Immortality

Being outwardly focused, as part of their deep need for certainty and stability into the future, people at Square tend to want the structures and systems in their world to endure. For example, they tend to want their family unit to endure through children and grandchildren. Buildings and products at Square are designed to stand the test of time, not to be replaced by the latest new thing as happens at Diamond. People at Square are likely to want to be buried with stone tombstones that will last.

As 'order from without', Square systems are built with strong foundations that will endure in the collective memory—such as long running systems of education, banking and government. Furthermore, at Square, duty to the system is rewarded by immortality through the system. For example, a leader or public servant at Square is rewarded for their service by having a monument built to honor them or a building dedicated to them with a plaque on the wall with their name on it.

ROLE–BASED PERSONA

It is important to note that some people at the Order-Based Terrain can appear to be at a Terrain different to their true internal Terrain. This can happen when they are taking on certain behavior in order to fulfill a role in a particular institution. This happens in the case of approximately 14% of people at Square.

For example, a person at Square who is in the military may have to take on certain Pyramid behaviors in order to play their role as a soldier. In another example, we know a man at Square who was for many years a facilitator in an organization where the Prevailing Terrain was Circle, and he adopted many Circle behaviors in order to play that role.

In these cases, the foreign behavior is taken on not because the person is somehow shifting to the other Terrain, but *because the person is at Square.* Their entire sense of safety comes from being part of 'the system' and their identity is based entirely on the role they are playing in that system. Therefore, in the rare case where the role they are playing requires them to engage in behaviors that are not natural to their Terrain, they have no choice but to adopt those behaviors and to adopt them completely.

Nevertheless, this is still just a role that they are playing. Their internal Terrain remains at Square. When they come home at night from playing their role or when they retire from their position, they will revert to more typical Square behavior. The behavior they were adopting is like a suit of clothing or 'uniform' they were putting on.

This is very different from the identification with a more expanded Terrain that we will see in the next chapter at Diamond. At Diamond, a person can perform behaviors from a more expanded (and in some rare cases more contracted) Terrain as part of an identity they have constructed, an identity that is continually reinforced until it becomes an impenetrable mask. The Role-Based Persona we find at Square is merely a temporary identity deriving from the necessity of the role the person is playing. It is not *how they see themselves*, they are not attached to it and they have no need to sustain it once their role has ended. It is simply a role they are playing, like an actor in a play.

KEY ELEMENTS OF SQUARE

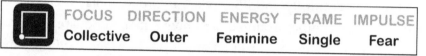

	FOCUS	DIRECTION	ENERGY	FRAME	IMPULSE
	Collective	Outer	Feminine	Single	Fear

The Order-Based Terrain is a collective-focused Terrain, for those at Square give up their own individual ego desires and needs in order to serve the common good of the majority.

The Order-Based Terrain is an outer-directed Terrain, for the focus is on conforming to 'the system', rather than on following one's own inner truth.

The Order-Based Terrain is a single-frame Terrain, for reality is that deemed by the consensus of the majority and the only truth is the 'official' truth, sanctioned by those considered by the collective to be 'in authority'.

The Order-Based Terrain is a feminine Terrain in that those at Square willingly surrender and submit to 'the system' in order to receive its protection.

The Order-Based Terrain is a fear-reactive Terrain, for people at Square have a perception of separation that causes them to have a deep fear of what they perceive to be chaos—both the chaos of mother nature and the chaos that results from human ego run rampant—and therefore to manage this fear, they seek to order and regulate every aspect of life.

SYMBOL OF SQUARE

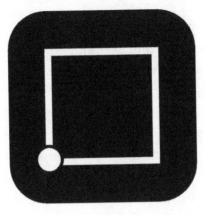

The symbol of the 'square' best describes the Order-Based Terrain because, with its stable four-sided shape, the square is a symbol of order and stability, which are key features of this Terrain. The square's right angles and it's perfect uprightness makes it very rigid, like the mindset at this Terrain. The square is also the shape used for most conventional houses in our era, and as such represents tradition and conservative thinking.

The large point in the bottom corner of the square represents the Order-Based person looking up at the enormous house-like edifice of the system they live in and feeling protected and safe inside of it. This point is placed at the bottom left cornerstone to indicate that the Square person is wanting to hold back the movement of progress and stay anchored in the known safety of the system.

EXAMPLES OF SQUARE

The behavioral expressions of Square can differ depending on whether a person is a 'Traditional' or a 'Modern'. On the next page are some typical examples of people who are Square Traditionals.

- a farmer who runs the family farm started by his great-grandfather;
- a wife who will not divorce her husband even though their marriage has been unhappy for many years;
- a father who believes his children should obey him without debate;
- a family who go to church every Sunday;
- a school headmaster who seeks to instill good traditional values and discipline into his students;
- a missionary who travels to Africa to bring God to the natives and 'civilize' them.

Here are some typical examples of people who are Square Moderns:

- a teenage girl who reads all the fashion magazines and makes sure her clothes are always in fashion;
- a young man who goes to all the biggest rock concerts and sporting events;
- a white collar worker who stays in the same corporate job for years;
- a woman who pours over the celebrity magazines, avidly following the lives and loves of her favorite celebrities;
- a couple who have saved to buy their first house and happily commit to a 30 year mortgage, knowing this investment will provide them with security;
- a doctor who performs the medicine she was trained to perform at medical school, without question;
- an accountant, lawyer, or bureaucrat working within the system;
- a news anchor or the host of a popular network TV show;
- a middle-aged man who happily eats the same foods year after year, drives the same kind of car, goes to the same holiday destination, votes for the same political party and believes the same ideas that he learned in high school; and

- a scientist who collects data to expand on existing scientific theories.

It should be noted that 'the system' also has sanctioned roles allotted within it for criticism and satire. The people in these roles, despite their apparent position as stone-throwers, are still at Square, such as in the following examples:

- a cynical political analyst who writes popular articles in major newspapers critiquing the government; and
- a popular comedian who spends his life making fun of all aspects of the mainstream world, without ever actually stepping outside of it himself.

Once again, we remind you that the above examples are simplified stereotypes of people at the Order-Based Terrain, designed to give you a feel for this Terrain. There will be many people at Square who do not resemble the above examples at all; and you may meet people who fit the above descriptions yet who are not at Square. Accurate analysis of someone's Terrain requires extensive training in the Ten Terrains Model and must never be assumed based solely on what someone does for a living or their external behaviors.

SQUARE MOVING TO DIAMOND

From Selfless Duty To Unique Expression

The examples we've just provided are most likely to describe someone who is *stationary* at Square. Once a person is fully embodying all the lessons, gifts and experiences of Square, their Infinite Self will start them on the long journey up the mountain to the Reflection-Based Terrain (Diamond).

As the person starts to move towards Diamond, while still needing order, security and tradition in order to feel safe, they may also start to feel a stir towards innovation and entrepreneurialism. They will not yet be ready to fully strike out on their own, but they will start to find that idea exciting.

The Square person on the move to Diamond may start to question the traditional life they have been living—even such core things as their job, their marriage, and their lifestyle. They will not yet have the ability to truly throw themselves into a new kind of life fully and fearlessly, however they will be starting to crave such change and beginning tentatively to build towards it.

As the person at Square hikes higher and higher up the mountain and then even more so as they start to speed down the other side towards Diamond, they will find the impetus towards change and innovation growing inside them.

They will start to increasingly question the things that authority figures are telling them, to question the role they have been playing in the system and to question the way they have always done things. They will start to take more and more risks in their life. They will start to make larger and larger changes in how they are living and to step further away from the herd.

Such a person will look back at their time when they were stationary at Square and feel that they have changed a great deal. They may even feel like a completely different person. Indeed, if reading this book, they might even mistakenly feel that they have already shifted into Diamond. However, until they actually cross the Event Horizon Of Perception into Diamond, this person at Square on the move still needs order so they can feel safe, and they will not fully throw out the rope that connects them to tradition and keeps them in the mainstream.

Nevertheless, the boat they are on is floating further and further from the safe familiar shore and the time is approaching when they will be ready to cut themselves free and sail away. As we will see in the next chapter, once they cross the Event Horizon into Diamond they will cast aside the last remnants of their fear of being 'different', will let go forever of defining themselves by the role they played in the system and will begin to design a unique life so as to express their own unique essence.

HISTORICAL FIGURES AT SQUARE

A few famous historical figures who were at the Order-Based Terrain are Abraham Lincoln, Margaret Thatcher, Grace Kelly, and J.R.R Tolkien. To see a full list of famous historical figures who were at the Order-Based Terrain, make sure to get your free eBook *The Terrains Of Famous People In History*. It includes names of celebrated political statesmen, revolutionary leaders, industrialists, novelists, poets, musicians, movie stars, economists, philosophers, historians and even astronauts, from throughout the ages, all of whom were at Square.

MOVIES, TV & BOOKS AT SQUARE

There is a very large body of works of fiction that celebrate aspects of life at Square and characters at Square. These include movies such as 'Chariots Of Fire', 'The Sound Of Music', 'Forrest Gump', 'It's A Wonderful Life', and even the 'James Bond' franchise; TV shows such as 'Downton Abbey', 'Perry Mason' and 'Happy Days'; novels such as 'Pride and Prejudice' by Jane Austen, 'Anne of Green Gables' by L.M. Montgomery and most classic fantasy works such as 'The Lord Of The rings' by J.R.R. Tolkien; children's books such as 'The Chronicles of Narnia' by C.S Lewis and the many books of Enid Blyton; and ancient texts such as 'The Aeneid' and 'Aesop's Fables'.

Many works of fiction created by people at Diamond depict the negative aspects of Square, such as the dangers to individual freedom posed by the Square system gone too far. This can be seen, for example, in the novel '1984' by George Orwell and the blockbuster movie 'The Matrix'.

There are also many works of fiction that depict the journey from Square to Diamond, such as the movie 'Dead Poets Society'.

To discover other popular books, movies and TV shows at Square, watch our entertaining free videos on the 'Ten Terrains' YouTube Channel.

BIGGER PICTURE OF SQUARE

From the spiritual perspective of Infinite Consciousness as Self, the Order-Based Terrain can be seen as 'The Journey Of Selfless Duty'. The lesson a person is learning while at this Terrain is how to set aside their own individual will and desires in order to fit into 'the system'. The gifts this Terrain brings are stability, loyalty and steadfastness. The challenge it brings is how to maintain the status quo while the world is constantly changing around them.

If you are at this Terrain, we suggest that you read the *'Guidebook For The Square Terrain'*. In this booklet we go into far more detail about the lessons you are here to learn on 'The Journey Of Selfless Duty'. We explain much more about the unique gifts and challenges of Square. We also give you invaluable tips and strategies to help you navigate life at this Terrain.

THE REFLECTION-BASED TERRAIN (DIAMOND)

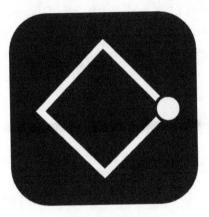

THE REFLECTION-BASED TERRAIN OF CONSCIOUSNESS (Diamond) is the next evolutionary stage on the Continuum Of Terrains. A person at this Terrain is experiencing 'The Journey Of Unique Expression'. As of 2015, we estimate that approximately 32% of people in the Developed World are living at the Reflection-Based Terrain. As we will discuss in Part 4, Diamond is currently the Prevailing Terrain in the Western World.

The Event Horizon Into Diamond

As a person crosses the Event Horizon Of Perception into the Reflection-Based Terrain, the huge shift in perception is their realization that they can choose their own *unique identity*, rather than being assigned an identity by 'the system'.

People at Diamond see themselves as unique individuals with a unique contribution to make. They choose to walk their own path and march to the beat of their own drum. They question 'the system' and refuse to conform to it. They seek to influence the mainstream culture to change, by technological innovations, political innovations or social, lifestyle or artistic innovations.

The Story At Diamond

Like all people at the five fear-reactive Terrains, those at Diamond have a deep subconscious fear of all aspects of Mother Nature, especially her cycle of life and death. The Diamond Story is that *the ingenuity of the human intellect* will keep them safe. This Diamond Story creates beliefs such as *"the next scientific discovery will solve all our problems"* or *"this latest cultural phenomenon will change the world"*.

The Strategy At Diamond

As a result of the Diamond Story, the core Survival Strategy of those at the Reflection-Based Terrain is to *influence their world using their thinking mind.* This is very different to the kind of influence sought by those at Pyramid, which comes through force and brawn, seeking to impose one's will upon someone else, in order to get one's way. In contrast, the influence sought by those at Diamond comes from reason, creativity, argument, persuasion and intellect, in order to gain approval, agreement and admiration.

People at Diamond use their mental powers to influence their world every way they can, using ingenuity, creativity, intention and force of mind to create the kind of life that their self-image wants. We will see this play out in many ways in the following section, nevertheless in all forms, when stripped down to its core, Diamond behavior always comes back to using your thinking mind to influence your life and the world around you.

CORE FEATURES & DRIVERS OF DIAMOND

Moderns & Cultural Creatives

Because of its central preoccupation with identity, the Reflection-Based Terrain is the most complex Terrain on the Continuum, and it expresses itself in a wide variety of behaviors. However, in the broadest terms, people at Diamond fall into two basic groups: the Diamond 'Moderns' and the Diamond 'Cultural Creatives'. Once again, these terms come from the work of sociologist Paul Ray, Ph.D.[7]

Approximately 65% of people at Diamond would self-identity as Moderns and 35% would self-identify as Cultural Creatives. The Diamond Moderns tend to be avid consumers, into technology, fashion, the latest gadgets, celebrity and fame. The Diamond Cultural Creatives tend to be 'seekers', passionate about new social systems, environmental causes, personal development, consciousness and the Zeitgeist. As different as these two groups are in their values and behaviors, their underlying Terrain Of Consciousness is still the same.

The vast majority of people who are interested in self-help and personal development are Diamond Cultural Creatives, as are most people in the 'new age' world. Indeed, many of you reading this book will be Diamond Cultural Creatives. While you probably see yourself as being *extremely different* from the Diamond Moderns because you live such a different lifestyle to theirs and hold such different values and beliefs than they do, when you look deeper you will start to see that you do indeed have a great deal of common ground with them. This can be a powerful jumping off point for deep self-inquiry.

Uniqueness

As we have said, the Event Horizon of Diamond is the realization that you have a unique identity, rather than one assigned by 'the system'. People at Diamond will spend much of their time trying to figure out what is their unique calling, passion, life purpose or talent. Their entire sense of self depends on them being able to determine what exactly is unique and special about *them* and what makes them different from people in the institutional, mainstream world.

There are whole industries in the Diamond world there to help people work out what is their unique gift and what is the contribution they are here to make—from personal coaches to personality profiling such as Myers Briggs all the way through to psychic processes that help dial in one's unique life purpose.

Unique Expression

People at Diamond spend a great deal of energy on clarifying and expressing their unique way of seeing the world. One sees this most clearly in the artistic milieu, where designers and artists will strive, often for years, to convey their own unique artistic 'point of view'. A Diamond artist or designer strives to ensure that their work could never be confused with the work of another. This is absolutely key to expression at the Reflection-Based Terrain.

Indeed, creativity at Diamond is driven by the urge to find and display one's own unique take on something, be it art or life. This is a beautiful and pure expression of the human Spirit, and it has led to some of the greatest works of art on this planet. We honor it as one of the great gifts of the Reflection-Based Terrain.

Standing Out

Another way that those at Diamond seek to assert their uniqueness is by standing out from the crowd. Unlike people at Square, who like to look and act like their neighbors, those at Diamond generally want to be different. They seek to do things in a way that shows who they are. They seek to excel and be extraordinary. This can often be hard if they live in a Square culture that seeks conformity and cuts down tall poppies.

Freedom

As a result of this deep yearning for unique self expression, a core driver at the Reflection-Based Terrain is the desire for freedom. Those at Diamond yearn to be free to act in ways that suit their own mental self-image, and refuse to fit into a role decided by someone else. They rebel against authority when it tries to control them. They abhor hierarchy, believing opportunities should be available to all.

People at Diamond resist the homogeneity of Square, preferring to self-organize into multiple *sub-cultures*, each with their own identity. They care about diversity, defend the rights of minorities and applaud multiculturalism and pluralism. They champion a free market and a level playing field that allows for healthy competition.

Influence

Not only does the person at the Reflection-Based Terrain refuse to follow the consensus of Square, but they also realize that they themselves have the power to *influence* that consensus. Indeed, this is why the symbol for the Reflection-Based Terrain is the shape of a diamond, as this is what a square looks like when it is 'pushed over' (influenced).

People at Diamond seek to influence their world in many ways. They seek to influence the outcome of their own life, by using mental techniques such as manifesting, goal-setting and affirmations (although many of these techniques are also used by people at Square those days, now that they have become more mainstream). They seek to influence other people, by using mental techniques such as persuasion, debate, marketing and win:win strategies to get others to agree with their convictions, buy their products, admire and follow them. They seek to influence the environment around them, by using their minds to take things apart, alter them and upgrade them. They seek to influence nature itself, by seeking to upgrade and improve upon the processes of life and death, and in the case of the Diamond Moderns attempting to render nature obsolete through technology.

Progress

One of the highest priority for those at the Reflection-Based Terrain is *progress*. People at Diamond are all about transforming things, improving things, growing things and moving things forwards. They are passionate about innovation, whether it is their own innovation or that of others. They admire ingenuity and original thinking. They applaud radical thinking. One of the catchphrases of Diamond is 'think outside the box'.

As a result of this high priority placed on progress, people at the Reflection-Based Terrain have initiated most of the major innovations of the past few centuries that have pushed humanity first into the industrial revolution, then into the technological era and information age we are in today. Not only have pioneers at Diamond spearheaded technological innovations, but also social innovations such as new political and economic systems, artistic and cultural innovations that have changed the worlds of music, literature, film, fashion and art, and lifestyle innovations that have changed such things as the way people do business, eat, exercise and relate to each other.

In their own lives, people at Diamond are committed to progress, always questioning the status quo, rebelling against traditions and seeking new ways to do things. Where those at Square will talk of how things 'should' be, those at Diamond will talk of how things 'could' be. They generally strive to be the most original, cutting-edge, or unique person they can be. They do not just accept their lot in life, they strive to change and improve it, to move up the ladder. They seek growth and expansion, whether it is growth in wealth, growth in success, growth in knowledge or growth in spiritual understanding. Indeed, most of the people who actively seek spiritual 'ascension' or 'enlightenment' are at this Terrain.

Innovation

As a result of their core Story that the ingenuity of the human thinking mind will keep them safe, those at Diamond have a passion for innovation and originality. They have a constant thirst for the *new*: for some this means new products or gadgets, for others new systems and for others new ideas.

There are two main groups of people at Diamond: the '*Innovators*'—the creative, original-thinking pioneers who are are always seeking new ways to do things—and '*the Adopters*'—the followers who are always seeking cutting-edge new innovations and trends to adopt.

The Diamond Innovators and Diamond Adopters exist in a symbiotic relationship. The Innovators invent new technologies, pioneer new social and political systems, create the latest art forms and fashions, and introduce new spiritual, health, financial and personal development approaches. The Adopters provide proof of concept and create a constant market for all these new innovations. No matter how great a discovery or invention by a Diamond Innovator, a new trend can only emerge when one or more Diamond Adopters—looking for the 'next big thing'—start to admire the discovery or invention, use it, and tell others about it.

There tend to be more Adopters in the Diamond world than Innovators, which works nicely, otherwise the market would be crowded with too many innovations and too few buyers. In the Diamond world, there is only room for a few leaders, but there is room for many followers.

The Four Arenas Of Diamond Innovation

The Diamond passion for progress, originality and innovation can take four very different forms, depending on the Diamond person's particular bent, personality and areas of interest. Some people at Diamond are innovators in the arena of science and technology (we call these the 'Diamond Technological Innovators'); others are innovators in the arena of art and culture (we call these the 'Diamond Cultural Innovators'); others are innovators in the arena of political, economic and social systems (we call these the 'Diamond Social Systems Innovators'); and others are Innovators and Adopters in the arena of lifestyle and personal innovation (we call these the 'Diamond

Lifestyle Innovators'). And of course, the Diamond Adopters also fall into these four groups, following the latest cutting-edge trends in one of these four areas.

There are some people who are Innovators or Adopters in more than one arena. A famous example of this, someone who truly personifies the Diamond Innovator, was the 'renaissance man' himself, Leonardo Da Vinci, who was a cutting-edge original thinker in many areas—art, culture, and science. He was both a Cultural Innovator and a Technological Innovator. This is rare. Usually a person at Diamond will specialize in one of the four arenas.

Innovation Is An End In Itself

It is important to understand that *not all innovation takes place at Diamond*. There is also a great deal of innovation at the other Terrains, however it is coming from a different place.

At Diamond, the drive to innovate is coming from a deep-seated need to use the power of the mind to influence the world in order to feel safe from the forces of life itself. At this Terrain, the mind is seen as supreme, even over nature. This is the Terrain where mankind feels it can harness, dominate and upgrade the forces of nature. It is this thinking that has led to the development of all kinds of technologies, ranging from the simple plough all the way to cloning, GMO foods, nanotechnology and robots. It is this thinking that has created our complex, highly developed, modern world.

Innovation has a very different driver at the other Terrains. At Square, people innovate in order to improve the smooth running of 'the system'. At Circle, people innovate to simplify life and to harmonize with nature, seeking to create the minimum possible human impact. At Spiral, people innovate to deepen their own connection with themselves. At Toroid, people innovate to bring to life a universal principle that has shown itself to them. This is very different to Diamond, where people innovate to overthrow the system, to modernize life, to harness and upgrade nature, and to change the world.

At the other Terrains, innovation is an effect or byproduct of another driver. At Diamond innovation is the goal, in and of itself. Something has weight in the Diamond world simply because it is new and original. The Diamond drive to innovate is so deep that it continually calls a person at this Terrain to question, overhaul, redesign and upgrade things. People at Diamond will innovate even when innovation is not needed, just for the sake of change.

Social Proof

At the Reflection-Based Terrain, truth is not arrived at by believing the dictates of authority figures as it is at Square, nor is truth arrived at through inner knowing as happens at the more expanded Terrains. At Diamond, truth is arrived at by confirmation from external reflection. People's choices are dictated by Social Proof. That is, something will be deemed to be of value if it has been adopted or popularized by the market.

As a result, if a Diamond Innovator can get a critical mass of Diamond Adopters to buy their product, adopt their idea, watch their movie or 'like' their Facebook page, then many other people at Diamond will too. And eventually even those at Square will come along, once enough time has passed for the innovation to be deemed 'mainstream'.

Vision

Vision is one of the great gifts of the Reflection-Based Terrain. It is at Diamond that people are first able to have a unique vision for their own lives, for other people and for the world, beyond that designed for them by 'the system' and conditioned into them by society.

There is a great deal of emphasis in the Diamond world on mental visioning techniques such as setting intentions, making declarations, saying affirmations, creating vision boards and writing mission statements. All of these are ways that a person at Diamond forms and declares their unique vision to the world so that they can bring it into being. Once they have formed their vision and declared it to the world, the Diamond person brings all their skills, talents and knowledge together to bring about that vision.

It is the Diamond ability to have a vision, hold onto it and work towards it, that drives a great deal of the innovation that we talked about above. For in order to be able to create something new, one first has to be able to envision it. In order to be able to follow through with all the work needed to bring the envisioned thing into being, one has to be passionate about it. And if people at Diamond are passionate about anything, it is their visions!

Success And Recognition

As a result of the unique sense of identity that develops at Diamond, a core driver at this Terrain is to succeed at one's individual endeavors and to be recognized and respected for one's unique achievements. The Diamond person's urge for recognition of their success can take many forms, such as seeking social recognition of their achievements and seeking material wealth and property as symbols of success. It can include seeking a large following and appearance on high-profile public platforms such as blogs or talk shows. In the case of the Diamond Moderns, it can include conspicuous consumption and the flaunting of possessions to show one's success.

Making One's Mark

The Diamond urge for recognition also expresses itself in the noble urge to make one's mark on the world, to make an impact, to change the world. People at Diamond strive to find the unique thing that will be their special contribution. For example, in their marketing they will seek out an audience who has a specific problem that only they can solve or they will seek out a problem that only they can fix. Driving this is the urge to make a difference, for their life to count, to be extraordinary. People at Diamond ultimately seek to be remembered for their achievements and to leave a legacy.

Walking Your Talk

We spoke above about how Diamond is a Terrain of vision. What must be understood is that this is not an abstract concept. As a result of the success driver we have just mentioned, it is very important to people at Diamond to actually bring their visions into being in a concrete manner. It is not enough for them merely to have original ideas. In order to be admired, respected, applauded and otherwise validated by others for their unique contribution, as they seek to be, they need to bring their vision into reality and create something in the world that can be seen by others and that can make a difference in reality not just in imagination.

The Head

Diamond is a very mental Terrain. In line with the Survival Strategy of the Reflection-Based Terrain, decision-making here is made by 'the head'. By the head, we are referring to the thinking mind, the brain, the intellect. People at Diamond use their head to try to control every step of their life themselves, rather than giving some of that control over to the wisdom of Infinite Consciousness, as happens at the more expanded Terrains.

People at Diamond use their thinking mind to decide who they are and what they want. They use their brain to decide where they want to go in life. They use their intellect to decide how they want the world around them to be. They do not allow other people to make these decisions for them, they do not leave these decisions to 'the system', nor do they leave them to the greater knowing of Infinite Consciousness as Self. They 'make their own mind up'.

As we have seen, people at Diamond use mental techniques a great deal. They use mental tools such as visioning and imagination to dream up a better future; innovation and creativity to construct their vision; persuasion and argument to enroll other people in their vision; and goal-setting and 'manifesting' to bring that vision into being.

Many of the greatest inventions, artworks and innovations in history have come from brilliant innovators at Diamond who sought to use their intellect to influence their world. However, regardless of how mentally brilliant the Diamond person is, they are ultimately *limited* in their intelligence to the intellectual capacities of the human brain, and are unable as yet to take full advantage of the quantum intelligence of Infinite Consciousness.[8]

Monkey Mind

Being a Terrain of the mind, at Diamond there can be a great deal of mental busyness. People at Diamond are using their minds to control and influence every aspect of their lives. This includes thinking about the past, planning for the future, analyzing, interpreting, visioning, setting intentions, worrying, scheduling, etc. All of this mental busyness drops away when a person shifts into Circle and life becomes a much simpler, more feeling-based existence.

This is why meditation is such a popular practice for Cultural Creatives at Diamond. A high percentage of people who regularly meditate are at Diamond. This is because at this Terrain of mental busyness, stilling the mind and separating oneself from the thoughts of the mind is essential. Otherwise, the Diamond person can start to become ruled by their thoughts and their fears, becoming too closely identified with them. It can be an exhausting way to live.

Frustration

A lot of the suffering experienced by people at the Reflection-Based Terrain comes from the fact that they try to make things happen that their *head* has decided should happen, in essence seeking to impose their own will on the Universe. This is amplified by the fact that people at Diamond are generally very attached to and identified with their mental visions, intentions and goals.

While the clarity of vision and intention found at Diamond can lead to great success, wealth and historical impact, it can also lead to a great deal of frustration. This is because each time a person seeks to 'manifest' an outcome from their head that is not on their higher life path, they inevitably meet resistance from the Universe. They face inexplicably roadblocks, obstacles and defeats, and often their vision does not come about at all. This can create great frustration and disappointment for the person at Diamond and further reinforces the very mistrust in life that caused their reliance on their thinking mind in the first place. In our 'Guidebook For The Diamond Terrain' we give many tips and strategies to help people at this Terrain reduce this frustration.

Expansion

A part of the Diamond mentality is the desire to be constantly growing things bigger. It is not enough simply to create something new or move something forward, it must also be continually expanded. For example, at Diamond if a person's business goes statewide, they will want it to go national. If they start a cultural revolution in one country, they will want it to go global. If a person gets a large number of fans for their blog, they will want to start a youtube channel, to get even more fans. If they lose weight, they will then seek new ways to become even more attractive, such as getting a makeover or building muscle. If they buy one electronic gadget, they will want more of them. If they get one spiritual insight, they will want more of them. The urge for growth and expansion at Diamond is insatiable.

Wealth Creation

Because Diamond is all about entrepreneurialism, original thinking and risk-taking, investment of money at Diamond is very different than at Square. It is more on the edge; leading to greater reward if it succeeds but greater disaster if it fails. People at Diamond have a faith in their own abilities that those at Square don't yet have. They believe in their own ability to create a unique life for themselves and they are willing to gamble on that. Therefore they will take the risks that are necessary to create great wealth out of nothing. Indeed, Wall Street and the stock market itself are Diamond innovations.

Financial Independence

One of the hallmarks of the shift into Diamond is that the focus moves from financial security to financial independence. The Square person wants money because to them it represents security and peace of mind. The Diamond person wants money because to them it represents choice and freedom. Ideas like self-employment, entrepreneurialism and the 'Four Hour Work Week'[9], all come from a Reflection-Based Terrain that seeks to free itself from the grindstone of work at Square, for they no longer feel any duty to contribute to 'the system'.

Competition

At Diamond, competition is prized over collaboration. This is an individualist Terrain, with emphasis not on collective wellbeing, but on individuals rising to the top by the ingenuity of their minds. In this Terrain, competition is considered healthy, for it is seen to stimulate innovation and growth, improve productivity and lead to more profit.

However, this does not mean that people at Diamond do not ever collaborate with each other. At Diamond, an entrepreneur or visionary can always find people to collaborate with him on his vision, his project or his mission, but that will be because these people also share his passion for that same vision, project or mission. At Diamond, the cry is always *"I want to find someone who believes in my work!"* This is different from the kind of collaboration found at Circle, where two people who are working on completely different projects can come together and support each other, finding the common ground like in a venn diagram, or where a group of people can work together in community for a common cause.

Conviction

As a result of the core driver for unique self expression at this Terrain, people at Diamond generally pride themselves on having their own unique opinions and beliefs about things. As a result, they can become quite attached to their opinions and perspectives. Their convictions often become a part of their identity. When that happens, as a part of their desire to bolster that identity, they will try to convince others to agree with their opinions, using reason, argument and persuasion.

When a Diamond person has a goal, they will often choose to follow a particular approach in order to achieve that goal, and will commit themselves to it wholeheartedly. For example, if their goal is weight loss, they may choose to follow the Paleo Diet or become a Raw Foodist. In many cases the approach becomes the person's *personal path* to their goal, and they will follow that path unless and until they find a new approach that suits their self image even more.

Because the approach becomes a part of the Diamond person's identity, they generally believe that their chosen path is the only way, and are often unable to question it. They can become very zealous about it, passionately trying to persuade others to their cause.

Ideology

This is the Terrain where we see competing schools of thought, philosophies and ideologies. Indeed, many new ideologies arise directly from the creativity of Diamond Innovators. A new idea by a Diamond Innovator gets transformed from an isolated opinion of that individual into an 'ideology' or 'philosophy' or 'school of thought' when it gets popularized by Diamond Adopters. At that point, people at Diamond will adopt this new idea as their chosen ideology if it fits with their self image and they agree with it. They will then attempt to convince others to adopt their chosen ideology, and can often become quite passionate about it, attached to it and even zealous about it.

There are usually big debates going on in the Diamond world between the proponents of opposing ideologies, taking place on the street, in the media and all over the internet. As a result, the Diamond world is very much a 'marketplace of ideas'. People at this Terrain compete for mindshare, and whoever has the largest number of people agreeing with him wins. Being a mental Terrain, the kinds of strategies used to convince others include mental strategies ranging from intellectual debate through to advertising, lobbying, marketing and PR.

Zeitgeist

People at the Reflection-Based Terrain love to be caught up in the large waves of cultural, social or political innovation that sweep civilization from time to time, particularly in the early phases where a movement is just gathering speed. In addition, at Diamond the urge to be 'current' and 'modern' often outweighs the need to be authentic, so people at this Terrain will tend to jump on the bandwagon and adopt as their own whatever groundbreaking causes are being promoted by visionary thinkers who they admire. This urge to be part of something cutting-edge that is changing the world takes over from the Square urge to be part of a system working for the common good.

Rationalism

An interesting feature of the Reflection-Based Terrain is that of all the 10 Terrains, Diamond has by far the largest percentage of people with a 'spiritually-closed orientation'; that is, people who are only able to conceive as truth that which they can perceive with their outer five senses and observe with their physical instruments (the gauges, dials and meters of science). These people believe in a materialistic universe, where consciousness is a local phenomenon that arises from the brain. Indeed, approximately 82% of people at Diamond have a 'spiritually-closed orientation', compared to approximately

35% at Pyramid, 24% at Square, 9% at Circle, 2% at Spiral and 0% at Radial, Toroid and Infinity.

The remaining 18% of people at Diamond, who are mostly Diamond Cultural Creatives, have a 'spiritually-open orientation'; that is, these people are open to the possibility that this is a spiritual universe that is intelligent, in which invisible forces beyond the scope of our outer senses and instruments operate alongside visible ones, where Consciousness is a non-local phenomenon. The fact that they have such a different spiritual orientation can cause these Cultural Creatives at Diamond to feel very different from the vast majority of people at their Terrain and out of sync with our Diamond Western world. If you are reading this book, are living in the Western World and are at Diamond, then it is likely that you fall into this camp and therefore you may feel like you don't quite fit into our modern world, even though you are living in a culture that is at the same Terrain as you are.

Personal Development

It is at Diamond that a person is most likely to be drawn to self-help books and to personal development approaches such as Neuro Linguistic Programming (NLP), Landmark, wealth creation and self-empowerment training. This is because it is at this Terrain that a person starts to see their *human potential*, beyond simply being a cog in the machine. The same pull towards growth and progress that fuels someone at Diamond to invent a new technology or start a new artistic trend also pulls them to improve themselves, to grow in their self awareness, to expand in their self image, to clear their old beliefs and to reinvent themselves.

The kinds of personal growth processes used at Diamond tend to be talk-based, mentally-focused therapies, aimed at rewiring beliefs, changing behavioral habits and shifting unconscious patterns. This is because Diamond is a mental Terrain, and therefore personal development at this Terrain tends to be focused on the mind.

There are a great many personal development teachers and trainers at the Reflection-Based Terrain. Indeed, the 'Human Potential Movement' that started in the 1960s around the world is a Diamond phenomenon. Most of the personal growth and self help gurus of our time are very successful Lifestyle Innovators at Diamond. These pioneers are sharing their own learnings with others in order to make a unique contribution to the world and in order to have their identity as an innovator in this area reflected back to them en masse.

While the journey of personal inquiry starts at Diamond, it continues on into the next four Terrains, becoming a deeper and more inward-looking journey at each one, as we will see.

IDENTITY

The reason why Diamond is called the 'Reflection-Based' Terrain is that the central preoccupation for people at this Terrain is *identity*. The Diamond person's need to construct a unique identity, sustain that unique identity and have their unique identity reflected back to them by other people is at the root of every other core feature of this Terrain. Therefore, we are devoting an entire section of this chapter to this single core feature.

Mental Self-Image

As we have seen, the Event Horizon of The Reflection-Based Terrain (Diamond) is a person's dawning awareness that they can construct their own unique identity, rather than merely live with one assigned to them by the systems of the collective at The Order-Based Terrain (Square). The identity that the Diamond person constructs is one that reflects their own internal mental 'self-image'. This means their sense of self, how they see themselves.

Those at Diamond can often spend much of their life trying to figure out how they see themselves and which identity best reflects that. They are consumed by trying to work out things like "*What is unique about me?*", "*What do I stand for?*" and "*What is my purpose?*"

Who Am I?

In the first stage of choosing an identity to build, the person's mind is seeking to figure out '*Who am I?*' This stage tends to happen when someone first shifts to Diamond from Square; or in the case of someone who is born at Diamond, this stage tends to happen during teenage and early adult years.

Being an outer-focused Terrain, people at Diamond will look *outside themselves* to those around them in order to answer these questions, rather than looking inwards. The process of choosing an identity usually starts by them looking around the world and deciding first who they '*are not*'.

Often they will start with the mainstream Square world, the one that has been trying to fit them into cookie cutter roles. They will find themselves thinking things like "*No, I'm not going to be a corporate monkey, I'm going to be an entrepreneur*" or "*No, I'm not going to be a stay-at-home Mom, I'm going to be a Women's Empowerment Expert*". They might find themselves refusing to participate in the Square institutions that once offered them a secure place, like the Church, the Government or the Corporation, or artistic institutions like the Ballet or the Opera, etc.

They will often tend to look to the mainstream media for a reference point in choosing their identity, usually going down one of two paths. They will either choose to build their identity by being at the very leading edge of what is in fashion in the Square world, becoming cutting-edge trend-setters who push the envelope, or they will rebel against it entirely and turn to one of the many alternative Diamond sub-cultures to help them design their identity.

As we saw earlier in the section on Innovators and Adopters, the Diamond World is essentially divided into four main quadrants— Technological Innovators, Cultural Innovators, Social Systems Innovators and Lifestyle Innovators. The Diamond person seeking to find their own identity distinct from both the Square roles and the mainstream media may look to any and all of these four quadrants for pointers and suggestions of an alternative identity to adopt.

For example, they may look to the music and fashion worlds of the Cultural Innovators, and identify themselves as something edgy like a 'goth' or an 'emo', etc. They may look to the scientific world of the Technological Innovators and identify themselves as a 'science geek' or a 'techie'. They may look to the environmental and social activism of the Social Systems Innovators and identify themselves as a 'human rights activist' or a 'hippie'. They may look to the Lifestyle Innovators and identify themselves as an 'entrepreneur' or an 'alternative health pioneer' or a 'new ager'.

As the Diamond person looks around the world at all the many identities already in play, they ask themselves, *'Is that who I want to be?'* After appraising all the thousands of Identities being paraded around the Diamond world, they will eventually see one that fits them perfectly or cobble together a unique compilation of several, or they will create an entirely new one all of their own, and they will decide *"that is who I am!"*

Building A Personal Brand

Once a person at Diamond has settled on a unique identity that reflects their self image, they will express their chosen identity to the world in every way possible, including: the kind of work they do; the things they talk about and the way they speak; the products they buy; the lifestyle choices they make; their artistic 'point of view'; their fashion style; their 'presence' on social media; their convictions and ideology; and much more. Essentially what they are doing is building a personal 'brand'.

Reflected Identity

Once a person at Diamond has settled on their identity, they display it to the world, hoping that the world will reflect this chosen identity back to them, confirming that *"yes, this is who you are"*. Reflected identity is essentially a feed-back loop a person has with their outer world; in other words: *do others see me as I believe I am?*[10]

The outside world reflects back the Diamond person's displayed external identity in many ways, such as by social recognition, applause, validation, fame, marketshare and mindshare. One common form of mass reflection of identity is the modeling and copying of one's identity by people who are one's 'fans'. A Diamond person's identity will be most bolstered if other people not only recognize that they are who they say they are, but in fact want to take on the same identity too.

Indeed, at Diamond, the larger the number of people who know you exist, who validate who you are, and who think you are great, the more solid your constructed identity becomes and the more you come to believe that you are who you think you are. This drives the Diamond urge to get oneself 'out there', to be known, to be seen, and to be famous. Of course, the more recognition you get, the more you come to depend on this mass reflection and crave it, and the more desperately you try to cling to it when it starts to fade or the tide of approval starts to turn.

Mutual Reinforcement

Another way of having one's identity externally reflected is by peer group acknowledgement, which comes from those with the same or similar chosen identity as one's own. If your peers accept you as a fellow 'gamer' or a fellow 'new ager' or a fellow 'trekkie', then this confirms that you are who you say you are. People at Diamond will often tend to seek out others with a similar identity to theirs and form sub-cultures where there is mutual reinforcement of identity.

The Desire For More

Reflected identity underlies the Diamond need to constantly acquire 'more'—whether that is more wealth, fans, customers, or impact on the world. This is because the bigger and more visible a Diamond person becomes in their footprint on the world, the more confident they feel about the solidity of the identity they have created.

Image

Being an outer-directed Terrain, at Diamond one's success, fame and mindshare is always relative to the success, fame and mindshare of others. As a result of this, people at Diamond and especially the Diamond media, are always assessing the appearance and actions of people, to find cracks in their public persona. In reaction to this, a great deal of energy at Diamond goes into 'image management' and 'spin doctoring', not only by celebrities, politicians, and major brands, but also by everyday folk who strive to ensure that their public image matches their chosen identity at all times.

Swapping Identities

The person at Diamond is always in charge of creating their own identity and will create themselves however they wish to be. Sometimes a person at Diamond may choose to change their identity, if their sense of self changes so much that they feel their old identity doesn't suit them anymore. For example, a person at Diamond might choose to change from being a consumerist Modern techno-geek to being a tofu-eating socially-conscious Cultural Creative. In such a case, the person's values and behaviors may change, their ideologies and beliefs may change, and indeed their entire lifestyle may change. However, this is NOT a Terrain Shift, it is merely the construction of a new identity.

Fragility

It is important to understand that, under the peacock-like Diamond show of identity, in fact lies a very fragile sense of self. For the Diamond identity does not come from a true knowing of oneself, but from a mental image one has of oneself. If it is not constantly propped up and bolstered by reflection back from other people, it can easily be shattered. Therefore, it is important to have compassion for people at Diamond. Underneath their external persona, there can often lie a great deal of confusion, self-doubt and even anxiety.

PROJECTED IDENTITY

The fact that Diamond is such a *mental* Terrain causes a unique issue that is not faced by people at the other nine Terrains. People at Diamond can sometimes be quite advanced in their mental understanding of spiritual principles and practices, which can lead them to *appear* to be at a Terrain beyond their own. For example, a person at Diamond may have studied energy work, be familiar with vibrational principles and have taken courses learning how to connect with their Higher Self. Such a person, while still being at Diamond, will have many *understandings* that a person at Spiral would have. We call such a person 'Spiral-Aware at Diamond.' Whilst still being at Diamond, they have a conceptual understanding of Spiral principles far beyond most other people at their Terrain.

In some cases, the person at Diamond has so much understanding and experience with the principles and practices of a more expanded Terrain that they are living 'as if' they were at that Terrain. They speak in the language of that Terrain and engage in the behaviors of people at that Terrain. To the outside world, they may appear to be at that more expanded Terrain, even though they are not.

What complicates this situation is that, for many people at Diamond who are 'Circle-Aware', 'Spiral-Aware', 'Toroid-Aware' or 'Infinity-Aware', their expanded spiritual knowledge has become a part of their very *identity*. This means they see themselves as more expanded than they really are, and they tend to be very attached to that belief. Their sense of self has been constructed around what they have come to know and understand intellectually, rather than around what they have experienced and are embodying within themselves.

In essence, these people are 'split' between their mental image of themselves and their true Terrain Of Consciousness. This kind of split can happen for a number of reasons, all of which we discuss at great length in *Mastering The Ten Terrains Of Consciousness*. Such a split can create problems for these people in cases where their true relationship with reality conflicts with the spiritual principles that they intellectually understand.

This split between the self image of the mind and the true Terrain of the Self is a fairly common phenomenon. Approximately 15% of people at Diamond identify with a Terrain beyond their own. In the case of Diamond Cultural Creatives, this percentage increases to approximately *40%*. Therefore, it is likely that a *large number* of the people reading this book will fall into this category, which is why we are discussing it at some length in this section.

Diamond Is Still Diamond

All of these people at Diamond who see themselves as more expanded than they truly are will generally reveal their true internal Reflection-Based Terrain when facing situations of real stress and challenge; for in those moments they will come from reaction rather than response, as is natural for someone at Diamond. In addition, they will still tend to focus outwards on the outside world and on other people, rather than looking inwards. This is because, underneath their intellectual understanding of expanded principles, their relationship to Infinite Consciousness is still fear-reactive and outer-focused.

In addition, those people at Diamond who identify with a more expanded Terrain will tend to see the spiritual ideas and principles of that Terrain through a Diamond filter. For example, a person who is 'Spiral-Aware at Diamond' might believe that they can create synchronicities through the power of intention. Someone who is 'Toroid-Aware at Diamond' might believe that they can achieve enlightenment through meditation or gnostic practices. The classic Diamond need to influence one's world with one's mind extends here to influencing one's own spiritual journey through intention, visualization, choice and will. This is very different to how those who are really at Spiral and Toroid see their spiritual evolution.

Identity Not Deception

It is important to understand that when a Diamond person is identified with a more expanded Terrain, this is not an attempt to deceive others, it is how the Diamond person genuinely sees themselves. They are not wearing a mask or deliberately trying to fool anyone. Just like everyone else at Diamond, they are doing their best to convince not only themselves, but the rest of the world, of their mentally-constructed identity.

This means that they will go out into the world talking and acting as if they are at a more expanded Terrain than they are at and will do the best to reinforce this identity at every opportunity. Such people are often very learned in the kinds of ideas that belong to the more expanded Terrain with which they are identifying, and they will often be very committed to practices that go along with that Terrain too, therefore their lifestyle helps to reinforce the image they are presenting to the world.

There Is Nothing Wrong Here

It is important to remember that there is nothing wrong with people who are identifying with a Terrain beyond their own. If a person is at Diamond, *it is part of their life work to explore identity.* They are here to delve deeply into this question of *"who am I?"*. Seeing themselves as being other than where they really are and projecting forward to a Terrain beyond their own is sometimes a necessary part of this learning.

It is not anyone's place to judge or change these people. It is simply for us to be aware of what is going on in the Diamond world, and always to look deeper, beneath someone's values and behaviors, to their true relationship with reality and Consciousness, in order to ascertain what Terrain a person is at and not be confused by their outer persona. This helps us to truly connect with people and accept them for who they authentically are, rather than for how they see themselves.

Indeed being mentally projected to a Terrain beyond your own can be seen as a very positive thing, for it means that you are focused on expansion, rather than contraction. If you are going to be goal oriented, as is the case at Diamond, then there are definitely worse goals to have than that of being 'awake' or 'enlightened'!

In addition, there are advantages to having an identity that is based on a more expanded Terrain. People at Diamond who are 'Circle-Aware', 'Spiral-Aware', 'Toroid-Aware' or 'Infinity-Aware' will often have many of the mental understandings of people at those Terrains, therefore they can be a great resource of knowledge for those around them. In addition, in many cases, by creating a split in the Diamond person between what their mind knows and what their Being is yet truly embodying, their Infinite Self may well be preparing them for a time in the future when they will truly be at the Terrain with which they are now identifying. Their Self may be giving them training now in many of the ideas and concepts and practices that go with that Terrain, so that when they arrive there one day they will already know the lay of the land and it will be easier for them to adjust to being there.

If the person does one day shift into that expanded Terrain, no more will they be living with a mere understanding of its expanded concepts, they will now be fully embodying those concepts in an authentic, heart-centered way. They will most likely look back at their days at Diamond with a smile, realizing that what they thought they knew then was merely a hint of the truth, like the dimness of reflected moonlight compared to the full direct radiance of sunlight.

The Outer Trajectory

The reason it is easy for people at Diamond to project forward to Terrains beyond their own is that Diamond is a mental Terrain, and the mind is capable of great feats of intellect and understanding. The Diamond person who is 'Circle-Aware', 'Spiral-Aware', 'Toroid-Aware' or 'Infinity-Aware' is projecting their identity forwards from their mind. It is a mental construction, not a fully embodied experience. The giveaway of all people in this category is that, no matter how enlightened they are mentally, they are not yet living from their Heart, as they have not yet made the jump to Circle.

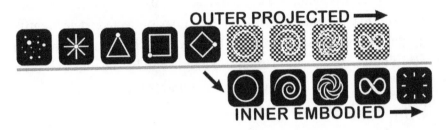

As you can see in the above illustration, the biggest shift on the entire Continuum of Terrains is the jump from Diamond to Circle. At the first 5 Terrains, a person is on an *outer* trajectory; that is, they are expanding in their external relationship with the world. At the second 5 Terrains, a person is on an *inner* trajectory; that is, they are expanding in their internal relationship with their Self. The big shift from outer to inner happens at the jump from Diamond to Circle.

The Diamond Projected person is still on that outer trajectory, even though their mental understanding has expanded. They can project forwards to Circle, Spiral, Toroid and even Infinity, yet that projection is merely mental, which is why we have represented it with dotted lines in the above image. Once a person shifts to Circle, they now move into a whole new phase—the *inner* path. Here the expansion from Circle to Spiral to Toroid to Infinity is real and embodied, as the person progressively expands in their relationship with their Self.

The Jump From Diamond To Circle

As the above graphic illustrates, the longest journey and biggest jump a person will make in their spiritual evolution is from the head to the Heart, as it means moving from reacting to a world 'out there' to beginning the process of taking responsibility for our world we are creating 'in here'. This is what is meant by the age old adage that enlightenment is an 'inside job'.

If a person at Diamond who is identifying with a more expanded Terrain one day truly shifts to Circle, they will retain all the intellectual learning they have accrued at Diamond, yet the transformation within them will be so dramatic as to make them virtually unrecognizable. This will be particularly so if the person has projected their identify very far out, such as to Toroid or Infinity. The shift that will happen within them should they expand to Circle will be the massive jump from head to heart, from outer to inner and from fear to Love.

Is This You?

A person who is identified with a Terrain beyond their own will most likely not recognize this to be the case, not even when it is pointed out to them, as they are usually very attached to their constructed identity. *So if you are such a person, you may not actually be aware of it.* The best way to find out for sure is to complete your Terrain Analysis Questionnaire, which is very detailed and is designed to pinpoint your Terrain exactly.

Nevertheless, as you yourself read the remaining Terrains in this book, if you find yourself resonating with any of them, it is useful to ask yourself, *"Am I really at Circle / Spiral / Toroid / Infinity, or is this simply how I like to see myself?" "Am I really living my life fully embodied at this Terrain or do I simply understand these concepts mentally and like to talk about them?"*

If you start to feel a suspicion that you yourself are at Diamond identifying with a more expanded Terrain, do not worry about it. This split between your self image and your Terrain is simply another opportunity for self-knowing and growth. If the results of your 'Terrain Analysis' questionnaire show that you are at Diamond identifying with another Terrain, you will be able to read the *Guidebook* we have written specifically for people in this situation. This *Guidebook* explains how to make the most of the incredible knowledge and wisdom you have already gained from the more expanded Terrain with which you have been identifying, so that you can integrate that knowledge into the Terrain you are at now. It contains lots of advice and strategies how to manage life at one Terrain while being identified with another, and how to reconcile the two, so you can continue your spiritual journey with ease and grace.

KEY ELEMENTS OF DIAMOND

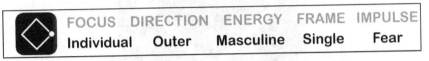

	FOCUS	DIRECTION	ENERGY	FRAME	IMPULSE
	Individual	Outer	Masculine	Single	Fear

The Reflection-Based Terrain is an individual-focused Terrain, for people at Diamond have moved away from aligning themselves with the majority consensus of Square and are now focused on individual expression, individual success, personal achievement, and personal advantage.

The Reflection-Based Terrain is an outer-directed Terrain, for people at Diamond are always looking to the world around them to reflect back their identity.

The Reflection-Based Terrain is a masculine Terrain, for people at Diamond seek to influence their world through the use of vision, intention and direction to create the life they want.

Despite being a Terrain of multiple ideas, opinions and ideologies, the Reflection-Based Terrain is a single-frame Terrain. People at Diamond are only able to see things from their progress-centric, individualistic perspective, and cannot truly be at peace with the order-driven motivations of those at Square or the connection-driven motivations of those at Circle.

The Reflection-Based Terrain is a fear-reactive Terrain, for people at Diamond have a perception of separation that causes them to have an underlying unconscious fear of their environment, of the forces of nature and of life itself, which causes them to seek to influence their life and the world around them with their thinking mind.

SYMBOL OF DIAMOND

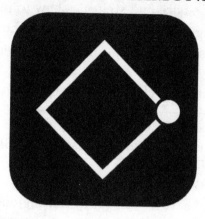

The symbol of the 'diamond' best describes the Reflection-Based Terrain because this Terrain is all about shining brightly in one's uniqueness, and this is what diamonds are known for, and indeed revered for. A diamond has multiple facets, like this Terrain, which is the most complex of all the 10 Terrains. Also, if one holds up a diamond, one can see oneself reflected in it from many angles, and this represents the fact that people at this Terrain are always seeking reflection from everyone around them. The large dot on the right point of the shape represents the fact that people at the Reflection-Based Terrain are always pushing the envelope against the rigidity of the square Order-Based Terrain and seeking to change it by innovation and rebellion. The point being on the right of the shape also represents the Diamond person looking forwards towards the future, for Diamond is the Terrain of progress.

EXAMPLES OF DIAMOND

The Reflection-Based Terrain expresses itself in a much wider variety of ways than do the other nine Terrains. This is because it is a Terrain of mentally constructed identity, and the number of different identities that can be created by the thinking mind is vast. When one also factors in 'spiritually-open' and 'spiritually-closed' orientations, differing values such as those of the 'Moderns' and the 'Cultural

Creatives', whether a person is an Innovator or an Adopter, and whether the person is identified with a Terrain beyond their own, the kind of behaviors that can show up in the Diamond world are almost endless. Nevertheless, we will provide you with a few examples, so you can get a sense of the scope of this Terrain.

Moderns

Here are some typical examples of people who are Diamond Moderns:

- an urban trendsetter passionate about fashion and design;
- a young indie singer who dreams of being a superstar;
- a visionary entrepreneur who wants to build a global brand;
- a scientist creating the next great technological innovation;
- a cutting edge graphic designer who really pushes the envelope in his designs;
- a person starting their own small business who dreams of financial independence;
- a woman who gets plastic surgery to create her own unique sexy look;
- a teenage goth who wears all black, listens to goth music and rebels against his parents;
- a tech geek who is anxiously awaiting the release of the latest iPhone;
- an edgy artist with their own unique look and distinct artistic point of view.

Cultural Creatives

Here are some examples of people who are Diamond Cultural Creatives:

- a radical social-justice activist;
- a yoga teacher who creates her own style of yoga and packages it to the world as a global brand;
- a movie star who thinks outside the box to raise money for humanitarian causes;

- a diet and nutrition pioneer who creates a cutting-edge alternative approach to health;
- a motivational guru with a legion of fans;
- a man who used an alternative therapy to cure himself of cancer and now is trying to bring that therapy out to the world, believing it is the only true cure;
- a young man who buys all the most innovative green products and goes on all the climate change rallies; and
- a couple who meditate every day, pride themselves on their ability to watch their thoughts and who see meditation as the path to enlightenment.

Diamond Projected

Here are some examples of people at Diamond who have deep understandings of principles from Terrains beyond their own, so much so that they become identified with and may appear to others to be at that more expanded Terrain:

'CIRCLE-AWARE' AT DIAMOND:

- an expert in permaculture who teaches courses in biodynamic farming, yet who does not actually viscerally feel a connection to the Web Of Life;
- an expert in raw food and juice fasting who runs a vegan retreat centre, yet who uses tools such as 'goal-setting' and 'manifesting' to make things happen;
- a tantra teacher who has polyamorous relationships with his students and is a treated like a rock star at the conscious festivals.

'SPIRAL-AWARE' AT DIAMOND:

- a 'create your own reality' expert whose goal is to build a highly commercial following around the world;
- an expert on chanting who has taken on a sacred Hindu name to reinforce her identity as an awakened person;

- someone deeply schooled in sound healing and vibrational medicine, who uses it to heal other people but never really looks inwards at themselves; and
- someone who teaches integration of the shadow self, yet who, when having relationship conflicts, blames the other person.

'TOROID-AWARE' AT DIAMOND:

- a learned teacher of gnosticism who thinks that their gnostic school is the only path to enlightenment;
- a teacher of profound universal principles whose understanding of these is purely intellectual rather than being embodied and lived in action;
- a self-proclaimed mystic who wants to 'ascend' or become 'enlightened'.

'INFINITY-AWARE' AT DIAMOND:

- a spiritual guru who seems to heal people by his sheer presence, yet it is merely the power of his charisma that causes total belief in him and leads to placebo healing.
- someone who has glimpsed Oneness during Ayahuasca journeys and now believes themselves to be enlightened, who is so identified with their plant medicine that they believe it is the only path to spiritual growth.

As you can see, the expressions of the Reflection-Based Terrain vary widely. Indeed, if all of these people met each other at a party, they would be stunned to find out that they are all at the same Terrain. What these people have in common, however, is their fundamental relationship with reality. Though their behaviors and values differ, they all share the same Terrain Of Consciousness.

Once again, we remind you that the above examples are simplified stereotypes of people at the Reflection-Based Terrain, designed to give you a feel for this Terrain. There will be many people at Diamond who do not resemble the above examples at all; and you may meet people who fit the above descriptions yet who are not at Diamond. Accurate analysis of someone's Terrain requires extensive training in the Ten Terrains Model and must never be assumed based solely on what someone does for a living or their external behaviors.

DIAMOND MOVING TO CIRCLE

From Unique Expression To Heart Connection

The examples of Diamond we've just provided are most likely to describe someone who is *stationary* at Diamond. Once a person is fully embodying all the lessons, gifts and experiences of Diamond, their Infinite Self will start them on the long journey up the mountain to the Connection-Based Terrain (Circle).

As they start to move towards Circle, the Diamond person will start to feel the stirring of their deeper Heart that lies beneath their mental sense of self. They may start to find themselves wanting to live a more authentic life. They may start to feel a little constrained by the identity they have constructed, as if it doesn't quite fit them anymore, or they may start to experience some challenges to their identity from the outside world.

The Diamond person on the move to Circle may start to find themselves wanting to connect more with their feminine side. They may start to feel a pull towards being more receptive to life, to surrendering to the flow rather than trying to manifest and plan everything.

They may begin to question their longing for success and accomplishment. They might start to feel a pull to leave the rat race and live a quieter life. They may start to feel an urge to spend more time in nature, to connect more profoundly with trees and animals. They may start to feel a call to 'be' rather than 'do'.

They might begin to feel a calling to getting more deeply in touch with their body, perhaps by exploring ecstatic dance or somatic movement processes, sacred sexuality practices, natural healing, raw foods or natural beauty.

They might begin to feel the stirrings of a yearning for community and a deeper connectedness with people. They may start to become interested more in collaboration and co-creation rather than entrepreneurialism and visioning.

They may start to feel the pull to be more authentic and vulnerable about their emotions, to allow people to see their weaknesses and their flaws, rather than showing such a carefully constructed image to the outside world. They may start exploring being more present while listening to others rather than being wrapped up in their own thoughts and responses. They may start practicing speaking from their Heart rather than from the head.

As the person at Diamond moves up the mountain and down the other side towards Circle, the pull to authenticity, to the Heart, to nature, to community, to sacred sexuality, to being in touch with the body, to deep connection, to vulnerability, to flow and to the Feminine start to become stronger and stronger. The person will still be mostly governed by the need to influence their life and the world around them from their thinking mind, nevertheless they will be feeling a deeper and deeper yearning to be free of that and to be truly living from their Heart in every moment.

Such a person who is on the move to Circle will look back at their time when they were stationary in the valley of Diamond and feel that they have changed a great deal. They may even feel like a completely different person. Indeed, if reading this book, they might even mistakenly feel that they have already shifted into Circle. However, until they actually cross the Event Horizon into Circle this person at Diamond on the move is still driven by an unconscious need to have their own unique identity and for it to be reflected back by the world; and their deepest sense of safety still comes from influencing the world with their thinking mind. This will be the case until the moment when they cross the Event Horizon into Circle and all of that falls away for good.

HISTORICAL FIGURES AT DIAMOND

A few famous historical figures who were at the Reflection-Based Terrain are Charles Darwin (Technological Innovator), Martin Luther King Jr. (Social Systems Innovator), Pablo Picasso (Cultural Innovator), and Sigmund Freud (Lifestyle Innovator).

To see a full list of famous historical figures who were at the Reflection-Based Terrain, make sure to get your ebook *The Terrains Of Famous People In History,* available at www.tenterrains.com. It includes names of greatly admired Technological Innovators such as nobel-prize-winning scientists, inventors, mathematicians, engineers and entrepreneurs; famous Social Systems Innovators such as human rights activists, social reformers, abolitionists, suffragettes, political writers, satirists, social commentators and political philosophers; celebrated Cultural Innovators such as composers, painters, sculptors, architects, novelists, poets, movie stars, rock stars, fashion designers and movie directors; and influential Lifestyle Innovators such as diet and nutrition pioneers, exercise and fitness gurus, parenting and relationship experts, founders of alternative medicine modalities, success coaches, personal growth gurus, psychiatrists, psychologists, and spiritual gurus, all of whom were at Diamond.

MOVIES, TV & BOOKS AT DIAMOND

There are many works of fiction that celebrate aspects of life at Diamond and characters at Diamond. These include classic movies such as 'Citizen Kane' and 'Sunset Boulevard'; modern movies such as 'Being John Malkovich', 'Swingers', 'Lucy' and 'The Breakfast Club'; TV shows such as 'Sex and the City', 'Entourage', 'House' and 'Glee'; and novels such as 'The Great Gatsby' by F. Scott Fitzgerald, Sir Arthur Conan Doyle's novels about Sherlock Holmes and many classic works of science fiction.

There are also many works of fiction about the dangers posed by the Diamond obsession with progress and innovation, such as the novel 'The Lorax' by Dr. Seuss (written from a Circle point of view) and the classic novel 'Frankenstein' by Mary Shelley (written from a Square point of view).

A good example of a Diamond character who is mentally projected to a Terrain beyond their own is the hero Neo in the movie 'The Matrix.'

To discover other popular books, movies and TV shows at Diamond, watch our entertaining free videos on the 'Ten Terrains' YouTube Channel.

Other aspects of popular culture that express the Reflection-Based Terrain include:

- Board games, card games and video games where the goal is to use strategy and ingenuity to win points or defeat an opponent, such as 'Bridge';
- Competitive sports where the goal is to perform a particular skill better than one's opponents, such as figure skating; or to use ingenuity and strategy to defeat one's opponent, such as golf; and
- Reality TV shows that take the form of a talent show, a test of mental skills, or a popularity contest, such as 'American Idol' or 'Big Brother'.

BIGGER PICTURE OF DIAMOND

From the spiritual perspective of Infinite Consciousness as Self, the Reflection-Based Terrain can be seen as 'The Journey Of Unique Expression'. The lesson a person is learning while at this Terrain is to march to the beat of their own drum. The gifts this Terrain brings are intellect, vision, and originality. The challenge it brings is how to find one's own unique identity and stand out from the crowd.

If you are at this Terrain, we suggest that you read the '*Guidebook For The Diamond Terrain*', available at www.tenterrains.com. In this booklet we go into far more detail about the lessons you are here to learn on 'The Journey Of Unique Expression'. We explain much more about the unique gifts and challenges of Diamond. We also give you invaluable tips and strategies to help you navigate life at this Terrain.

THE CONNECTION-BASED TERRAIN (CIRCLE)

THE CONNECTION-BASED TERRAIN OF CONSCIOUSNESS (Circle) is the next evolutionary stage on the Continuum Of Terrains. A person at this Terrain is experiencing 'The Journey Of Heart Connection'. As of 2015, we estimate that approximately 18% of people in the Developed World are living at the Connection-Based Terrain.

The Event Horizon Into Circle

As a person crosses the Event Horizon Of Perception into the Connection-Based Terrain, the biggest shift that happens is that their Heart opens enough for them to be able to *feel* a visceral connection with the Web Of Life. They feel personally connected to the Earth, to plants, to animals, to other people, to their ancestors, and to future generations.

The Story At Circle

As a result of this huge shift, it is at Circle that the illusion of separation first starts to be questioned. People at Circle not only understand interconnectedness as a concept, but they actually FEEL it as a truth. For example, if a tree gets cut down near a person at Circle, the person will feel it. Therefore, the Story at Circle is that all things in our 3D world are interconnected, from the smallest microorganism to the largest galaxy.

The Strategy At Circle

Since people at Circle and the Terrains beyond this feel fully and deeply connected to the Web Of Life, they no longer subconsciously fear nature and the forces of life and death; rather, they now inherently trust these. Therefore, they do not need a 'Survival Strategy'; instead, they now have a 'Thrival Strategy'.

At all the Terrains from Circle onwards there is a Thrival Strategy rather than a Survival Strategy, yet each Thrival Strategy is different. So what is the Thrival Strategy at Circle? It can be summed up in one simple word: *cooperation*.

People at Circle seek to cooperate with the Web Of Life in every way they can. They cooperate with nature by living a simple life according to her cycles, being in synergetic harmony with her ecosystems and honoring her laws. They cooperate with other animal species by attempting to preserve their habitats and being honoring of them in their food choices. They cooperate with past generations by respecting wisdom traditions. They cooperate with future generations by considering the long term consequences of their actions on the planet. And they cooperate with other people, by coming together in community and working together for the welfare of the whole.

Different people at Circle will focus on the above kinds of cooperation to different degrees; some will be more drawn to the community aspect, some to connection with animals, etc. Yet they are all ultimately committed to cooperation with the Web of Life, in whatever way their Heart calls them.

CORE FEATURES & DRIVERS OF CIRCLE

Heart-Guided

One of the biggest shifts that happens as a person moves from the Reflection-Based Terrain to the Connection-Based Terrain is that they stop thinking from the head and start feeling from the Heart. This does not mean that they are sensing the literal beating organ that pumps blood through their body any more than someone at Diamond, but that they are tuning in to their 'Energetic Heart Field'. The Energetic Heart Field is the part of us that feels our connection or disconnection from Infinite Consciousness as Unity, the part of us that feels our separation from unconditional Love, and the part of us that suffers the pain of this division. This is commonly referred to as 'feeling one's Heart'.[11]

Of course people at the Terrains before Circle have access to their Heart, and can tune into it if they choose. However, the more urgent drivers coming from their Terrain—such as the Pyramid need for power, the Square need to conform and the Diamond need to influence the world with one's mind—create filters that often distort or drown out the impulse of their Heart. It is at Circle, where these filters have fallen away, that a person is first able to truly and continuously listen to their Heart.

People at Circle spend a great deal of time learning how to tune into their Heart so that they can make decisions by following its unique impulse. Indeed, at Circle, the Heart becomes the *navigator* and the head merely becomes the wheel used to steer the person to the destination chosen by the Heart.

This navigation from the Heart sets the person at Circle on the beginnings of a trust walk that will continue to expand throughout the remaining Terrains. For when a person is operating from the Heart, they simply feel into each moment and make decisions based on how their Heart feels, without knowing or worrying about where that decision will take them. It is like walking down an unlit path, guided only by an internal compass.

Feelings

Circle is the Terrain of feelings. Here the mental focus of Diamond is replaced by emotional awareness, empathy and non-linear subjective thinking. At Circle, people are less interested in the outcome of a project than in the *process* used to bring it about. They focus on how something feels, rather than on the idea that underlies it.

People at Circle tend to feel very free to express their feelings to each other, to be vulnerable with each other and to share what emotions are 'up' for them in the moment—indeed this is encouraged in social situations in Circle communities. When working together, there is much sharing of feelings and speaking of one's truth at this Terrain, so that everyone knows how everyone else is feeling and therefore everyone is on the same page.

This is the Terrain where people hold space for each other. Often at this Terrain people sit in circles together—whether that be in a men's group or a women's group, in a community group or in a work group—and simply listen to each other, in a supportive, non-judgmental way. People at Circle intuitively understand how important it is for everyone to be 'heard' and 'felt' and truly met, so they strive to experience this themselves and also to provide it for others.

Transparency

The Circle way of relating is built on dialogue, cooperation and building relationships. Therefore trust, openness and transparency are key to the Circle way of doing things. Because the Diamond need to display an identity that others admire has melted away at Circle, people at this Terrain are more able to be honest and open about their vulnerabilities, their weaknesses and their mistakes. This is often a culture of confessions and the sharing of truth. People at Circle intuitively understand that sharing their vulnerabilities makes connections with others even deeper.

The Welfare Of The Whole

People at Circle tend to take into account the welfare of 'the whole' when making decisions, whether that is the whole local community, the whole human species or the whole planet. They do not take a 'somebody else's problem' approach, but instead know that their actions will affect the well-being of everyone else in the interconnected web. Therefore they take a great deal of responsibility to make decisions that are in the highest good of all life on Earth.

Stewards Of The Earth

Due to the fact that they can feel the Web Of Life, those at the Connection-Based Terrain tend to be passionate about caring for the Earth. They see themselves as stewards of the land rather than owners of it, and they generally seek to leave as small a footprint on it as possible. They do not see any part of nature as capital to be hoarded, wealth to be traded, or as a resource to be plundered for profit.

People at Circle tend to see the Earth as a giant living organism (sometimes known as 'Gaia'). They understand intuitively that the Earth is a living biosphere; an integrated, balanced, intelligent, self-organizing system with its own natural rules, natural patterns, natural mathematics and natural laws. They realize that if humans mess with the natural running of this system, they can throw it out of balance; therefore people at Circle choose to live in accordance with the natural cycles and laws of nature as much as possible.

Defending The Voiceless

People at the Connection-Based Terrain tend to be passionate defenders of the rights of the 'voiceless' members of the Web Of Life: young children, animals, future generations, indigenous tribes and mother Earth herself. Those at Circle are not defending these voiceless groups out of any intellectual ideal of freedom, diversity or a level playing field, as happens at Diamond. They are doing so because their connection to the Web Of Life means that they viscerally and empathetically feel the pain that these groups are experiencing.

Activism

It is at Circle that people will fight most passionately for the values that are close to their heart. People at Circle can be very angry and fired-up about things that are happening in the world that breach what they perceive to be 'natural law', such as harm to animals and to the Earth. It is at this Terrain that we find the more extreme types of activism such as lengthy sit-ins, hunger strikes, extended marching in the streets, chaining oneself to a tree, etc.

While there are also many activists at Diamond, their acts of protest are driven by their mental belief in the cause they are protesting about and their identification with that cause. In contrast, at Circle a person protests because they can *feel* the wrongness of the thing they are protesting about. It literally hurts their Heart that these things are happening. They will work tirelessly and fearlessly to 'change the world' so that these perceived wrongs are eradicated.

Activists at Circle can be very effective at fighting for the causes that they are passionate about because they are so interconnected to each other as a community that they self-organize rapidly as a group.

Community

The Connection-Based Terrain is fundamentally about community. Many people at the Connection-Based Terrain either live in close-knit communities or participate regularly in community activities. Even those who are introverted by nature or prefer to have 1:1 connections rather than group interactions still tend to form close heart-connections with people of similar values.

People at Circle tend to prefer to shop locally and support community-grown food. For health treatments, they generally prefer to go to known practitioners in their own community. They prefer to buy products that are recommended by people who share their values rather than seeking out the latest innovations.

In their careers, people at Circle tend to work not for personal gain or fame, but for personal connection, human contact, and to contribute to their community. Often they work in areas that provide things for their community, such as growing and selling food, health and wellbeing services, caring for the local land, education and care of children in the community, etc.

Shared Values

People at Circle seek to fit into their community, not out of fear of being different or out of a need for acceptance, but rather as a way to express their shared value and their kinship. At Circle, the more people one knows in one's community, and the more people with whom one has deep Heart-connections, the better and safer one feels.

The positive side of this is a real sense of community and a supportive, accepting environment. The downside is that Circle communities can be quite exclusive and cliquey, and often come across as suspicious and unwelcoming to people of other Terrains, as well as to people at the Connection-Based Terrain who they don't yet know.

Tribe

The Circle idea of community is summed up in the modern idea of the cultural 'tribe'. People at Circle like to connect with other people from their tribe, that is others who share their values, their open-heartedness and their connection to nature. People at Circle identify with their tribe as an expression of their own true Heart-chosen values, which is why they often tend to dress in their own very visible alternative fashion, live their own very recognizable alternative lifestyle and frequent certain kinds of alternative activities and festivals that are familiar to everyone in the tribe.

The Sum Of The Whole Is Greater Than Its Parts

People at the Connection-Based Terrain intuitively know that working together in synergy brings about greater results than striving towards something by oneself. Rather than focusing on individual success and celebrating healthy competition, as happens at Diamond, people at Circle treasure the feeling of connectedness that one gets from collaboration, from working together for a common end.

Lateral Organization

At Circle, organizations and projects are structured laterally rather than hierarchically. Decisions are not made by those on high, whether they be rulers, elected leaders or boards of directors. Decisions are made by the community or group as a whole, using dialogue and consensus. In Circle decision-making processes, everyone is given a chance to speak and be heard, and decisions are made by consensus. Where there is a disagreement of opinion, the minority viewpoint will not be overruled, rather the conversations will continue until a solution can be found that meets everybody's needs. While this process can be slow, here the efficiency and rapid progress of Diamond are sacrificed for connection, fairness and the feeling of belonging. Circle is a Terrain that is focused toward the long term.

Due to the lateral nature of Circle communities, leaders at Circle operate more as *facilitators* than as rulers, law makers or experts.

They are there to hold space for the wisdom of the group to emerge. They facilitate discussion and input from all, mediate in cases of conflict, and make sure there are structures in place to allow everyone to contribute their piece and shine.

Collaborative Learning

In contrast to Square and Diamond, Circle is not a Terrain where 'experts' teach from on high. Learning at Circle takes place collaboratively. When a person is in the position of teacher at Circle, they know that they have just as much to learn from their pupil as they have to teach them. It is not a situation of hierarchy, rather a mutually beneficial exchange.

Teaching structures at the Connection-Based Terrain are often communal. In traditional Circle cultures, children were often taught by the collective wisdom of the tribe. The traditional African proverb, *"it takes a village to raise a child"*, is a Circle idea that has been widely quoted in recent times when examining the partnerships required during the maturation of our youth. A modern example of this Circle approach is community home schooling, where different parents teach different subjects depending on their areas of expertise.

Nature-Based Spirituality

One of the most spectacular things about the jump from Diamond to Circle is the dramatic turn around in a person's spiritual orientation to the world. At Circle, 91% of people have a 'spiritually-open' orientation, compared to only 18% of people at Diamond. This means that the vast majority of people at Circle are able to conceive of an animating spiritual life force underlying their 3D world. They are able to see some kind of Divine life force at play in aspects of nature, and to see all living Beings—both human and animal—as interrelated aspects of one living organism.

At Circle, much of the spirituality that takes place is connected with nature. It can include various earth-based and body-based practices such as connecting to mother Earth and to nature spirits, celebrating feminine goddess energy, honoring sacred natural cycles, exploring plant-medicines, working with sacred sexuality and enjoying ecstatic forms of dance. People at Circle may be drawn to Ashrams as part of their spirituality, although this is more for the Heart-centered community life found there than for the mind-stilling benefits of meditation, which appeal more to people at Diamond.

Body Ease

Due to their sense of connectedness with nature, people at Circle tend to be comfortable with their bodies and with bodily functions such as birth, death, menstruation and breast-feeding; without the fear, shame and guilt that plagues people at the more contracted Terrains. People at Circle tend to eat more natural foods, honor the animals and the plants that they are consuming and be drawn to health practices that cleanse the body, such as eating raw living foods, doing cleanses and detoxes, and fasting.

For people at this Terrain, their relationship with their body is generally one of ease and acceptance. As a consequence of this, people at Circle tend to display their appearance more naturally than do people in the mainstream Square world of makeup and fashion or the identity-creating Diamond world of plastic surgery and unique looks. Most people at Circle tend to wear simple natural clothing, with little or no makeup and many also abstain from unnatural practices like shaving and leg waxing.

Sacred Sexuality

Sexuality at Circle tends to be more about expressing natural physicality and integrating the body with the Heart, rather the shaming found at Radial, the power games found at Pyramid, the conformity and guilt found at Square, or the yearning to be seen as sexually desirable that is found at Diamond. It is at Circle that we generally see people exploring the deep heart-connection of tantra and the interconnectedness of sacred sexuality practices.

The Feminine

Those at the Connection-Based Terrain do not fear life, instead they cherish it. Circle is devoted to the feminine principle. It is because of this that at Circle we see a worshipping of the sacredness of Gaia— the feminine energy of mother Earth. This is why at Circle we see a return to feminine forms of leadership, that are more collaborative and consensus based. It is why we see a return to living in harmony with nature, rather than in domination of it. It is why we see an honoring of people's feelings and emotions. It is why there is a pull towards more sacred sexuality. These are all fundamentally feminine principles.

From Doing To Being

The shift from the Reflection-Based Terrain to the Connection-Based Terrain is, in essence, a shift from 'doing' to 'Being'. At Diamond, as we have seen, there is a great deal of emphasis on making things happen, creating one's reality, achieving success and making an impact. This urge to 'do' things in the external world falls away when a person shifts to Circle.

Of course, people at Circle are still active in the world. They still work, create and build things. Yet they are coming more from a place of 'Being', from an inner connectedness to themselves. They do things as an expression of their inner Heart, not in order to make an impact on the world around them. They tend to spend time sitting in stillness, often in nature, feeling into themselves, sensing their feelings, listening to their body. Their doing comes from this quieter place of Being.

Interestingly, many women who struggle with their health while at the goal-oriented, 'make it happen' Terrain of Diamond can experience a deep healing when they shift to Circle and find themselves drawn to this more Heart-centered, flowing, feminine way of Being rather than the masculine approach of 'doing'.

A Simple Life

The Connection-Based Terrain is a dramatic departure from the Reflection-Based Terrain, largely because it moves from the complexity of the head to the simplicity of the Heart. Those at Circle yearn for a simpler, less technological life, more in tune with the cycles and rhythms of nature. They prefer to be out in nature or connecting with people rather than being wired to computers, televisions, cinemas and video games. They are less interested in the latest gadgets and luxuries than those at Diamond, preferring to live with basic, practical amenities and little more. Instead of using modern chemicals to clean their houses and processed foods to feed their bodies, they choose to use simple natural ingredients that people have successfully used for thousands of years.

At Circle, because people focus more on Being than doing, the busy-ness of life at Diamond falls away. Those at Circle generally avoid stressful, high powered careers, preferring instead to work hours that give them lots of free time to spend with their family, their community and with nature—and to explore their connection with their inner Self which they are now glimpsing for the first time. They tend to choose jobs that fill their Heart with joy, where they can be in service to their community or to the land, rather than jobs aimed at gaining status or wealth which would stress them out. Much more time is spent in communal activities, service-based activities like volunteering and charity work, and healthy relaxing self-care; and less time is spent on the mental stimulations that people at Diamond use to distract themselves from the possibility of just *Being*.

Emotional Work

The interest in personal growth that started at Diamond continues into Circle, but shifts in focus. Instead of the kinds of mental therapies that we saw at Diamond, which focus on shifting beliefs, changing behavioral patterns and rewiring unconscious habits, people at Circle tend to focus on the body and the emotions. Indeed these two focuses are really one, for at Circle emotions are seen as being simply the natural movement of energy in the body. Many Circle modalities are designed to facilitate the expression and movement of this energy.

The personal growth work becomes deeper at Circle, and also more raw. Repressed emotions are allowed to be expressed. Emotional wounds and memories are brought up to be healed. One's 'inner child' is heard and supported. There is much sharing with others, and communal healings are common. There is also a beginning of the self nurturing, stillness and deep inner listening that will deepen further at Spiral.

People at Circle are generally drawn to experiential modalities, rather than talk-based or mentally-focused therapies. They prefer to focus on the *process* of what is happening in the session, rather than the content. So for example, here we see modalities that involve breath-work, dance, emotional expression, interactive processes, touch, movement, art-therapy, etc.

Love

The Connection-Based Terrain is the first of the love-responsive Terrains on the Continuum. Of all the drivers that are present at Circle, Love is the strongest. Concepts such as brotherly Love and unconditional Love are very important to people at this Heart-driven Terrain. People at Circle focus on Love as an explicit contrast to the fear-reactive, head-driven nature of Diamond. Love is something that they talk about, act from, live for, cultivate within themselves, and seek to spread. You could almost say that people at Circle are in love with Love.

Indeed, the ideals of 'free love' that flowed through Western culture in the 1960s came from people at this Terrain. The classic Beatles song from that era, 'All You Need Is Love', could well be the catchphrase of Circle. If you visit a Circle community even now you will hear those same high ideals of Love espoused and see them being lived in action. When it comes to Circle, Love—not profit—is the bottom line.

KEY ELEMENTS OF CIRCLE

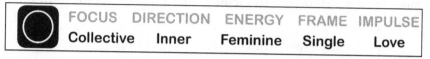

	FOCUS	DIRECTION	ENERGY	FRAME	IMPULSE
	Collective	Inner	Feminine	Single	Love

The Connection-Based Terrain is a collective-focused Terrain, where people choose their groups and communities based on shared Heart-values and passions rather than on tradition, religion or cultural heritage.

The Connection-Based Terrain is the first of the inner-directed Terrains, for, in contrast to the conditioned thinking mind that has guided decisions at Diamond, people at Circle are ruled by their own authentic Heart.

The Connection-Based Terrain is a much more expanded expression of the feminine than at Radial or Square, for at Circle one can feel one's connection to life and to the natural forces; therefore rather than fearing them, one celebrates them.

The Connection-Based Terrain is the last of the single-frame Terrains. This is why people at Circle simply cannot understand why everyone else doesn't share their values and why other people don't want to protect the Earth and live in community like they do. Because they care about issues so deeply from their Heart, those at Circle will often fight more passionately for their perspective than those at Square or Diamond.

The Connection-Based Terrain is the first of the love-responsive Terrains, because a person at Circle can now feel the Web Of Life. Instead of 'reacting' to life by seeking protection from it or trying to dominate it, they begin to 'respond' to life, by trusting it and cooperating with it.

SYMBOL OF CIRCLE

The symbol of the 'circle' best describes the Connection-Based Terrain because this Terrain is all about coming together in community, with everyone having an equal voice, as happens when people sit in communion in a circle. The 'outer-focused egoic self' represented by the large dot in the symbols of the five prior Terrains has now dissolved inwardly into the circle of equals. People at this Terrain value connection above all things, and in a circle, there are no individual points or edges; everything comes together in connected union.

The shape of the circle is also apt because this Terrain is the first one where a person can connect deeply to the 'Web Of Life' and is thus very drawn to the simplicity of nature. Compared to angular manmade structures, the circle is the shape of all homes in nature, from the egg to the nest to the burrow to the womb; indeed it is the shape we all live in for the first nine months of our life. It represents coming home to nature and to the Heart, which is the gift of the Connection-Based Terrain.

EXAMPLES OF CIRCLE

Historically, many of the pagan cultures were at the Connection-Based Terrain. Indeed until recent times, many people in indigenous cultures were living at Circle, in a very harmonious relationship with the Earth, before their cultures were decimated by 'Western' (Radial, Pyramid and Square) invasion and assimilation. Some, like the Australian Aboriginal peoples, had lived that way for tens of thousands of years, without depleting the Earth in any way or leaving any marks on her.

Typical examples of people at Circle in our modern world include:

- a person who lives a simple life close to nature, in tune with the seasons, animals & plants;
- someone who works tirelessly in the local soup kitchen feeding the homeless without seeking recognition;
- a naturopathic healer using herbal medicines to facilitate self-healing;
- someone who organizes community resistance to the harming of the local land by mining, deforestation, etc;
- a raw foodist who does regular cleanses and juice fasting while living a simple life in nature;
- a volunteer who works abroad in a third world country helping villagers build water infrastructure;
- a family who live close to the land, growing their own food and celebrating the natural cycles;
- a doula who assists at natural home births;
- a person who cares for animals injured in bush-fires;
- a man who facilitates a men's group as a space for empathy and sharing amongst men;
- a woman who teaches other women how to get deeply in touch with their bodies and the sacred feminine;
- someone who uses body movement processes like five rhythms and ecstatic dance as their spiritual practice;
- a teenager who plants trees in their spare time to repopulate forests.

Once again, we remind you that the above examples are simplified stereotypes of people at the Connection-Based Terrain, designed to give you a feel for this Terrain. There will be many people at Circle who do not resemble the above examples at all; and you may meet people who fit the above descriptions yet who are not at Circle. Accurate analysis of someone's Terrain requires extensive training in the Ten Terrains Model and must never be assumed based solely on what someone does for a living or their external behaviors.

CIRCLE MOVING TO SPIRAL

From Heart Connection To Inner Truth

The examples we've just provided are most likely to describe someone who is *stationary* at Circle. Once a person is fully embodying all the lessons, gifts and experiences of Circle, their Infinite Self will start them on the long journey up the mountain to the Coherence-Based Terrain (Spiral).

As they start to move up the mountain towards Spiral, the Circle person will still retain their Heart connection to other people, but they will feel less and less of a need for community. They will start to become more focused on their own inner journey and less focused on connecting with others who share their Heart values. It will become more important to them to know themselves at a deeper, cosmic level, and to discover their higher purpose is in this lifetime.

Their 'feeling' body will start to take less of their attention. They will start to increasingly explore following their higher knowing, listening to their intuition and connecting with their higher Self. Their choices will start to be made more and more from this higher knowing, rather than in response to the pull of their Heart and the impulses of their body.

While still holding on to their Heart values, they will become less attached to them and less identified with them. They will start to see the issues in the world that they once fought so hard for in shades of grey rather than in black and white. They will begin to develop the ability to have compassion for people who share different values from their tribe.

The person at Circle moving to Spiral will start to increasingly take responsibility for the reality that is showing up in their lives. They will start to work less on healing their emotional wounding and more on forgiveness, compassion and Self Love.

Their focus will start to shift from the Earth, the body, sexuality, the emotions and the Feminine onto subtler things beyond the 3D world, like energies, other dimensions, spirit beings, past lives, etc. As the person at Circle moves up the mountain and down the other side towards Spiral, their Infinite Self will give them more and more multidimensional experiences, to deepen their awareness of the invisible realms, preparing them for the jump to Spiral.

Such a person who is on the move to Spiral will look back at their time when they were stationary in the valley of Circle and feel that they have changed a great deal. They will probably have changed the activities they do and the lifestyle they live. They will probably have altered the way they interact with their community, such that their community is starting to look at them more as a free spirit and less as a member of their tribe.

Indeed, if reading this book, the person at Circle who is approaching the jump to Spiral might even mistakenly feel that they have already shifted into Spiral, so far do they seem to have come from their old self. However, until they actually cross the Event Horizon into Spiral this person at Circle on the move is still fundamentally living in the 3D world and is still primarily guided by their Heart and their Heart values. This will be the case until the moment when they cross the Event Horizon into Spiral and become connected with the cosmic world beyond 3D in a fully embodied way, when the invisible realms become their daily reality.

HISTORICAL FIGURES AT CIRCLE

A few famous historical figures who were at the Connection-Based Terrain are Henry David Thoreau, Chief Seattle and John Lennon in the later stages of his life. To see a full list of famous historical figures who were at the Connection-Based Terrain, make sure to get your free eBook *The Terrains Of Famous People In History*. It includes names of naturalists, shamans, druids, indigenous leaders, environmental campaigners, animal rights activists, social workers, musicians, painters, poets, writers, philosophers, healers, health pioneers and therapists, all of whom were at Circle.

MOVIES, TV & BOOKS AT CIRCLE

There are a growing number of works of fiction that celebrate aspects of life at Circle and characters at Circle, such as the movies 'Gorillas In The Mist', 'ET: The Extraterrestrial' and the huge hit 'Avatar'; and the books 'The Fifth Sacred Thing' by Starhawk, 'The Horse Whisperer' by Nicholas Evans, 'The Mists Of Avalon' by Marion Zimmer Bradley, and the 'Ringing Cedars' Anastasia series by Vladimir Megre.

To discover other popular books, movies and TV shows at Circle, watch our entertaining free videos on the 'Ten Terrains' YouTube Channel.

BIGGER PICTURE OF CIRCLE

From the spiritual perspective of Infinite Consciousness as Self, the Connection-Based Terrain can be seen as 'The Journey Of Heart Connection'. The lesson a person is learning while at this Terrain is to fully open their Heart. The gifts this Terrain brings are Love and Service to the Web Of Life. The challenge it brings is how to keep your Heart open to people outside your own community, and to those who hold different values to you.

If you are at this Terrain, we suggest that you read the '*Guidebook For The Circle Terrain*', available at www.tenterrains.com. In this booklet we go into far more detail about the lessons you are here to learn on 'The Journey Of Heart Connection'. We explain much more about the unique gifts and challenges of Circle. We also give you invaluable tips and strategies to help you navigate life at this Terrain.

THE COHERENCE-BASED TERRAIN (SPIRAL)

THE COHERENCE-BASED TERRAIN OF CONSCIOUSNESS (Spiral) is the next evolutionary stage on the Continuum Of Terrains. A person at this Terrain is experiencing 'The Journey Of Inner Truth'. As of 2015, we estimate that approximately 2.5% of people in the Developed World are living at the Coherence-Based Terrain.

The Event Horizon Into Spiral

As a person crosses the Event Horizon Of Perception into the Coherence-Based Terrain, the big shift that happens is that their sense of connectedness expands out beyond the Web Of Life on planet Earth to the entire 'Cosmic Tapestry', an interconnected circuit consisting of all other planets, galaxies, universes and dimensions.

In addition, as a person crosses into Spiral, they realize that they have a *unique place* in the Cosmic Tapestry that only they can fill; a specific energetic and vibrational signature that no other person born on Earth has ever had. This is different from the sense of unique identity that a person has at the Reflection-Based Terrain (Diamond). At Diamond, a person's sense of uniqueness is based on what they are 'doing'; at Spiral, it is based on who they are 'Being'. This is a shift from identity to true essence.

The Story At Spiral

For those at Spiral the subtle realms exist as a real, felt, daily experience. People at Spiral can often sense energy, frequency, resonance, vibration and the other subtle dynamics that are happening in the invisible realms beyond what is showing up in the physical reality screen of our 3D world. Essentially, the Story at Spiral is *"I am part of an unseen multidimensional intelligence greater than the visible 3D world"*.

The Strategy At Spiral

The Thrival Strategy of people at the Coherence-Based Terrain is to understand their unique place in the Cosmic Tapestry so as to fully radiate as their true Self. Therefore, people at Spiral seek to fully *know* their Self at all levels.

At Diamond, we saw that the central question was *"Who am I?"* and that this led to a deep search for one's identity. At Spiral, we are at the next evolution of this central question. Now the question becomes *"Who am I as a Self?"* The Spiral person seeks to know who they are at their core, in their essential nature, beyond their conditioning and programming, beyond their thoughts and emotional patterns, beyond their ego identity, beyond being a product of their environment, and beyond any inter-dimensional interference that may be running them.

The person at Spiral also seeks to recognize when they are being their true Self—that is coming from true free choice—versus when they are simply acting out of programming, wounding and reaction. If they discover that they have been triggered out of being aligned in their true Self, then they will seek to bring themselves immediately back into alignment.

CORE FEATURES & DRIVERS OF SPIRAL

Coherence

People at Spiral strive for internal coherence in all ways. They will only carry out an action if that action is in integrity for them and in alignment at *all* levels of their Being; that is if it aligns with their gut, their Heart, their ego, their thinking mind, their values, their body, and the higher knowing coming from their Infinite Consciousness as Self. They seek to hold their energy in every moment in alignment with their true nature.

Authenticity

Another aspect of the drive for coherence is that those at Spiral seek to live in full authenticity. They seek to discover their own true authentic way for every thing they do, such as their own authentic way of thinking, speaking, eating, moving, living, behaving and being. These many authenticities add up to their own unique energetic thread in the Cosmic Tapestry.

Self Love

As part of the drive to coherence, people at Spiral start to re-integrate the darkest parts of themselves that they had previously judged, condemned, denied and disowned. As more and more work is done by the Spiral person to forgive and love all parts of themselves—and to clear their programming and limiting beliefs about themselves, their emotional wounding, their body's toxicity, their past life traumas and anything inter-dimensionally that is distorting their view of themselves—the person starts to come to a place of greater

Self-acceptance, Self-worth and ultimately Self Love. This is one of the greatest gifts of the Spiral Journey.

True Life Purpose

People at Spiral are generally not interested in fame, recognition or personal glory; they instead seek to do work that aligns with their true nature, their Higher Self and their life path. At Spiral, a person is not searching to discover their unique contribution to the world, as happens at Diamond, but to find out what is the 'higher purpose' for which they incarnated in this lifetime.

Integrity

People at Spiral strive to be fully in integrity at all times. They tend to be ruthless with themselves to make sure that they do not compromise their own truth or sell themselves out. They generally seek to keep all aspects of their public and private life in coherence and harmony so that they can act with full integrity at all times.

Given that people at Spiral often have honed abilities with reading and sensing energy, they can often sense when other people are out of alignment with themselves, out of integrity, or have a hidden agenda. Because of this, they are less susceptible to propaganda and manipulation than people at the previous Terrains.

Integrated Decision-Making

People at Spiral are also fully internally-referenced in their decision-making. As a person at Spiral comes to fully embody this Terrain, they will stop referencing the outside world when making their decisions. They will stop being influenced by cultural norms, societal expectations and external opinions. As they come to embody Spiral more and more, they will factor in the needs of other people and their community less and less, preferring to base their decisions on their own internal truth and connection to their own higher Self. If they have a history as a people-pleaser, their Self will give them plenty of opportunities to shift this while they are at Spiral!

The person at Spiral understands that following their own truth is not selfish, it is the highest form of Service they can do. They understand that *their deepest inner truth will always be in line with the highest good of all*. This is a multidimensional form of decision-making, integrated at all levels.

Being fully internally-referenced also means that in making their choices, those at Spiral tune into their Self moment to moment to see what's right for them right *now*, rather than falling back onto some pre-existing identity or role they have—with all its attendant beliefs—to decide that for them. For example, when handed a beef burger, instead of automatically replying *"No thanks, I'm a Vegan, I don't eat any animal products"* or *"Thanks, I'm Paleo, so this is perfect for me"*, as one might at a previous Terrain, at Spiral one is likely to say *"hmmm, let me feel into this burger I'm being offered in this moment and see if my body wants to eat it right now"*.

Internally Referenced

In coming to know their Self, people at Spiral are fully internally-referenced. This means that in coming to know their own heart, mind, body, drivers, life purpose, tastes, desires, talents, etc. they do *not* reference other people, cultural norms, family pressures, fashions, dictates from authority, advertising, peer group pressure, popularity, public opinion or anything else outside themselves. To determine their own specific nature, they simply spend time with themselves, feeling into themselves, being ruthlessly honest with themselves in every moment, until they slowly unveil who they truly are behind all the conditioning that has been layered upon them over the course of their life.

Input

Simply because people at Spiral are internally-referenced does not mean that they are closed to input from others. Indeed, people at Spiral are generally willing to listen to opinions and advice from people of all backgrounds, and all Terrains. However, they are not able to be bullied in the way that people at Pyramid are or 'influenced' the way those at Diamond are. Nor will they be pressured by the consensus of the majority as are people at Square or swayed by the feelings of their community as are those at Circle. People at Spiral will always place their own higher knowing over the influence, input, opinions and feelings of others. They will take on board anything that feels like 'truth' for them or that feels 'right' for them, yet will throw out anything that they sense is coming from manipulation, agenda, fear or other shadow aspects.

Indeed, people at Spiral often seek input not only from other people but also from sources beyond the 3D dimension, in the form of channelings, divination, consulting the Akashic records, connecting with spirit guides, etc. However, if they do seek input from multidimensional sources outside of themselves this is not done to ask this outer source to make their decision for them, but merely to seek information. They will always ultimately make the decision themselves according to their own inner knowing. This 'taking ownership' and being Self-responsible is one of the main differences between people who seek advice from the higher realms at the previous Terrains and those who do it at Spiral.

Inner Power

As a person spends time at the Coherence-Based Terrain, they begin to come increasingly into alignment with their own specific thread in the Cosmic Tapestry, and they thereby start to step into their own authentic inner *Power*. By this, we mean that they are moving away from their own inner resistance and are becoming increasingly able to act from true choice, with the full force of the Universe on their side, because they are more in alignment with their Self. However, while people at Spiral are starting to come into their own individual Power, they are not yet fully in true Universal Power, for that requires a person to come into alignment with Infinite Consciousness, which happens at the Fractal-Based Terrain (Toroid).

Inner Approval

At the Terrains we have looked at so far people tend to need the approval or admiration of others in order to feel comfortable carrying out an action. At Spiral, a person no longer needs any kind of earthly approval or admiration from any other person or group. The only kind of green light they need now in order to act is that coming from their own Infinite Self, whether they see that as their Higher Self, their Intuition, their Spirit or have some other language to describe it. The only kind of approval sought now is *inner* approval. The question asked is: *"does this feel right to me at all levels of my Being?"*

Not Identifiable

As a result of their internal referencing, those at Spiral are not generally as identifiable outwardly as people at the previous Terrains, for they don't tend to use external means to build affinity or display their identity. At Spiral, people choose the kinds of clothes they wear, the products they buy and the way they decorate their houses based solely on what aligns most closely with their true Self in that moment and what resonates with them the most deeply. They are not trying to show allegiance to any group, fit into any kind of culture, display any kind of identity, make any kind of political point, or win the respect or admiration of anyone. They are simply being themselves.

The Now

People at Spiral always tune into the rightness of any action in that specific moment in time. They are very 'reversible'. They feel free to change their course of action mid way, if it feels right for them to do so. From the outside, their decisions can seem to be ad hoc, without any discernible pattern, but this is simply a reflection of the deeply authentic nature of their decision-making. Their commitment is not to other people's opinions or to societal expectations, but to their own truth and to the moment itself. This is what life is like living in the Now.

Acceptance Of Change

A fundamental corollary to this idea of living in the Now is that people at Spiral are comfortable with change. They understand that they are living in a complex world that is dynamic and always evolving. They do not resist change like at Square, feed on change like at Diamond or fight for change like at Circle, instead they embrace change if and when it comes into their lives and will always seek to find the lesson under it. They will generally ask *"why is this happening"* and *"what can I learn from it?"*

Synchronicity

People at The Coherence-Based Terrain are acutely aware of the phenomenon known as 'synchronicity'. Life for people at Spiral is a conversation between their 3D self and the realms beyond, and synchronicity is the language of this conversation. It is as if they realize that the Universe or their Higher Self or something infinitely wise is trying to reach them through simple everyday happenings, at every moment.

People at Spiral are always on the alert for hints, messages and signs; for example, in spoken conversations they overhear, chance meetings, songs, billboards, things flashing across TV screens, etc.. If they see a pattern repeat in their lives, they will know there is a message in it for them. Rather than deciding from their thinking mind where they should be heading in their life, as happens at Diamond, or following their Heart, as happens at Circle, the Spiral person allows the signs and markers of synchronicity to reveal to them where their Infinite Self wants them to be.

It is not that people at Spiral are making meaning out of nothing or creating these synchronicities, they are simply noticing the synchronicities and messages that are already there. They now have eyes to see the signs that people at the previous Terrains do not see. People at Spiral examine everything that happens around them for both its surface 3D meaning and also for its symbolic other worldly meaning. This awareness of the double meaning of things is an inevitable consequence of their sense of connectedness to the Cosmic Tapestry.

Frequency And Resonance

Frequency and resonance are primary drivers for action at Spiral. People at Spiral make their choices of who to befriend, where to live, what products to buy, and what work to do, based not on an alignment of values like at Circle, but on a *resonance match*. If the friend or place or event or job feels like it resonates with their own personal energetic frequency, the Spiral person will be drawn to it.

People at Spiral also innately understand that words, images and even thoughts have a resonance and frequency, and they thus strive to be very conscious and intentional about what they say, think and watch. They understand that people, food and environments have a particular frequency that can impact upon them energetically, so they tend to be very conscious about who they spend time with, what they eat and where they go, making sure the frequency of the things in their outside world resonates with them as much as possible.

When The Student Is Ready The Teacher Will Come

People at Spiral have a very different relationship to teachers than those of the previous Terrains. They do not look at the teacher as an 'authority figure', as an 'expert' or as a 'guru', instead they see that person as a fellow human seeker who is simply showing them something about themselves that they need to see. Indeed, at this Terrain, almost anything and anyone will be seen as a 'teacher' if it mirrors something back to the Spiral person about themselves.

People at Spiral, being powerfully aware of synchronicity, also know that when the student is ready the teacher will come. Those at Spiral follow their internal pulls to different teachers at different times, whether these 'teachers' be people or situations, trusting that the pulls they are feeling are coming at the right time towards the right person or situation. They do not feel the need to remain loyal to a particular teaching or identified with a particular school of thought, as happens at the previous Terrains. They know that their outside world mirrors their inner world and that different people and situations will show up at times in their life to reflect where they are at internally at that time.

Self-Responsibility

People at the Coherence-Based Terrain know that they *create their own reality* by the way they think, the way they behave, their emotional field, their vibration, their intention and the way they use their energy. They do their best not to blame others for their lot and instead seek to 'own' their part in the situations that arise in their life.

Many people at Spiral work very hard to erase any 'victim scripts' about perceived wrongs that they acquired in childhood and to replace these with understanding and compassion for all the people involved. They seek to let go of judgments about others and instead to take responsibility for projections they are making onto others. When difficult or painful events happen in the life of the Spiral person, they do not feel 'hard done by'; instead they know that it is all happening for their higher learning.

Inner Change Agents

Part of the quantum shift that happens at Spiral is that people stop trying to change other people and stop trying to change the world around them. They realize that everything is 'an inside job'. If they wish to shift something or someone in the world around them, they do not go out and actively campaign against the issue or try to change the other person; instead they go inside themselves and clear whatever lies within them that has a charge around that issue or person, and this diffusion of the charge force is what changes the world around them.

People at Spiral operate by *entrainment* rather than influence. By simply Being their true coherent Self and holding their vibration high, they shift those around them without even trying to.

Leading By Example

At the Coherence-Based Terrain, a person leads by example. They model the world they are choosing to create by embodying it in their own actions and deeds. People at Spiral generally have no interest in converting others to their cause, in leading others or in leaving any kind of legacy of principles or teachings or rules behind them. They tend to gain followers without meaning to do so. They simply live their life and follow their own convictions and their very Being inspires others to follow them.

Inner Pioneers

People at Spiral are often explorers and seekers who like to find new ways to be and new ways to do things, yet this is different to the Diamond urge to innovate. At Diamond, a person wants to discover or invent something new in order to make a unique contribution and to leave their mark on the world. Their sense of self depends upon the degree of influence they have and the admiration they receive. Therefore it is hugely important to them that their idea, product or vision be adopted and celebrated by others.

In contrast, people at Spiral like to explore different ways of living and being, simply for the sake of the exploration itself. They have no burning need to share their discoveries with the world, although they may offer these to people as an expression of their joy at having discovered them. This is a humble, quiet way to be in the world, yet its potential for change is powerful.

Service To Self As Service To Other

At Spiral, we are back to an individual-focused Terrain, yet at this more expanded consciousness, Service-to-Self becomes Service-to-Other. The needs of the truly integrated Spiral individual who is listening to their own highest truth will always align with the collective good of all.

Knowing this, instead of giving of their time and energy directly to others in a way that drains them, those at Spiral instead give to others by giving to themselves. They know that when they are filled to the brim with joy, abundance and nourishment then that fullness will radiate out to everyone around them, and that they will affect and uplift others by their shining essence.

Empathy

The Coherence-Based Terrain is the first Terrain where a person is able to hold multiple frames of perception. People at Spiral do not think in terms of right and wrong, and they therefore do not think that theirs is the only way to see the world. They see that every perspective is valid, and that every person is of value and has unique gifts to offer. This allows people at Spiral to accept others *without judgment*, and to treat them with true empathy and compassion, not just at a mental level, but as a fully embodied way of relating.

Harmony

People at Spiral are motivated above all else by finding coherence and harmony—within themselves, in their interpersonal interactions, and in society. They seek to love the differences and inconsistencies within their own Self, bringing these into harmony and coherence, and they seek to love the differences and inconsistencies in other people and in groups, and to bring them into harmony and coherence with each other. Their ability to perceive multiple frames of reference and operate with empathy, as well as their choice to be aware of their own judgments and projections, can make those at Spiral excellent mediators and peacemakers.

Multidimensional Sense Of Self

As a result of the Event Horizon of Spiral, where a person can feel their own unique energetic signature in the Cosmic Tapestry, *the sense of self now becomes multidimensional*. At Spiral a person can often feel their connection to other parts of their own Self beyond their current human form: such as their Self in previous lifetimes and future time-lines, in other dimensions or planetary systems and other iterations of their Self throughout the multiverse.

Know Thyself

Self-awareness is the number one goal of the Coherence-Based Terrain and underlies everything that happens here. At Spiral, the drive to 'know thyself' takes place at a cosmic level. The Spiral person seeks to know their Self in as many of its iterations as possible. They seek to know their own physical body, their etheric body, their astral body and the bodies beyond these. They seek to know their Self in past lives, in parallel universes, in different dimensions and on different planets. This is far beyond the quest for self knowledge that we see at the previous Terrains. It seeks to understand the deepest Essence of a person, in the totality of its cosmic expression.

In the case of the very few people at Spiral who have a spiritually-closed orientation, these people will still have a strong pull to cultivate deep Self-awareness, to come to know their own true nature, to recognize when they are being triggered out of their true nature, and to be fully unified within themselves in how they speak, act, move, think, and in all aspects of their doing and Being in the world.

The Subtle Realms

People at Spiral generally strive to master the discernment of subtle energies and different frequencies in the spirit world. They intuitively know that the more they strengthen their subtle perceptual inner senses the better they will be able to navigate their world, and find their unique energetic place in it, relative to the multidimensional whole. Therefore people at Spiral are often seeking to hone their ability to sense subtle energies, such as the flow of life force energy through their body, the energetic bodies beyond their physical 3D body, the presence of multidimensional beings, and other subtle energies such as sound vibrations, light frequencies, planetary energies, etc.

Actually, for many people at Spiral, the subtle energies and the world of the unseen can become more real than the 3D physical world. Staying grounded in the body, on the Earth and in the 3D reality is therefore one of the major challenges of this Terrain.

It is at Spiral that people often open up their senses beyond the five standard physical senses of seeing, hearing, smelling, tasting and touching, in order to be able to feel and tune into subtle energies in different ways. However, it should be noted that the Coherence-Based Terrain is *not about being psychic*. Many people at the previous Terrains also have psychic abilities and use them actively. The difference is that at Spiral these abilities are deliberately developed as a tool of Self-empowerment and Self-responsibility.

Energetic Boundaries

Being able to sense energies, both within their own auric field and in the world around them, people at Spiral need to learn where their expanded Self in fact ends and where another's begins. This lesson is crucial to ensure that the Spiral person does not either take on other people's 'stuff' or have their own energy drained or manipulated by others. Therefore many people at Spiral spend time learning to recognize different frequencies of energy around them, learning to set energetic boundaries around themselves to keep others out, and learning to sense the energetic boundaries of others so as not to transgress them.

Multidimensional Experiences

It is at Spiral that one can truly open not only to subtle energies, but also to multidimensional experiences, such as past lives, connecting with one's Higher Self, remote-viewing, telepathy, inter-dimensional interactions, channeling, and out-of-body experiences. These are not just ideas or occasional experiences at Spiral, as they are at the previous Terrains, but are a normal part of daily life. This is because one of the core features of Spiral is the ability to live in a fully embodied state of cosmic awareness at all times.

For people who have recently shifted from Circle to Spiral, they can sometimes worry that they are going mad. The people around them can reinforce this fear, because from the perspective of someone at a more contracted Terrain, the experiences of someone at Spiral can seem delusional. This is reinforced by the fact that the mainstream scientific world does not allow for the existence of multidimensional phenomena. Indeed, we are trained since childhood—by books, television and movies—to believe that such phenomena are 'fiction', and we are taught that any energies or Beings we sense are merely 'imaginary friends'.

One of the great acts of Service that people can do who are already anchored comfortably in The Coherence-Based Terrain is to help people newly arrived at this Terrain to realize that the expansion of their awareness beyond the physical 3D human experience is real, to help them understand why it is happening and help them feel more at ease with it.

Individuation And Specificity

The Coherence-Based Terrain is a Terrain of 'specificity'. People at Spiral make their choices in life based on specific moments in time; they understand innately that their own energy signature is utterly specific to them; and they are able to tune into the specific frequencies of other people.

This idea of specificity also extends to the multidimensional realms. Much like light can be divided into color and sound into frequency, people at Spiral see the Infinity of Consciousness as appearing divided up into many different kinds of Beings, whether they are angels, spirit guides, alien species, intergalactic councils, levels of light, or planetary energies, etc., all of whom have their own unique, specific frequencies, as well as their own unique offerings, powers, information, knowledge and purposes. Those at Spiral are able to tune into specific frequencies in the spirit world, just like they can tune into specific people in the 3D world.

Energetic Discernment

Often when people first arrive at Spiral they are so excited by the new world of subtle energies and multiple dimensions that are opening up to them that they naively start connecting with every kind of Being they can, and they suffer great harm as a result. As they spend more time at this Terrain, they learn that when working with energies, with the spirit world and with the multidimensional realms it is very important to pinpoint specifically where the guidance, information, energy or interference is coming from so that they can make empowered, discerning choices about who or what to connect with.[12]

Finding Neutral

In order to know when one has been affected by energies outside oneself, one has to be familiar with oneself in 'neutral'. This is another reason why there is such a huge focus at the Coherence-Based Terrain on Self knowledge and Self discovery. As the Spiral person becomes more coherent within themselves and more Self-aware, they will come to experience their true Self at neutral, that is, when they have not been triggered out of their Heart and out of their center, when they are not being run by their conditioning and their programming, and when they are not being influenced by anything 'other-dimensional' keeping them from Self-Sovereignty. As they learn to stay neutral, stay centered, and in martial arts terms to hold their 'One Point' or their Dan Tien, they will be able to feel the moment when they are knocked out of it and can then practice coming back to their Self.

Inner Growth

There is a huge pull towards inner growth at Spiral, driven by the need to deeply and fully understand and integrate one's own Self. This builds on the process of personal development which began at Diamond, yet takes it much deeper, for those at Spiral bring a much more Self-Responsible and ruthlessly honest approach to self-inquiry than do those at Diamond. At Spiral, inner work goes beyond even the emotional work done at Circle where one allows oneself to feels one's wounding and one's pain and to express ones grief, and steps into the next phase: *forgiveness*, both of others and of one's Self. This involves the healing and clearing of internal programs, beliefs, stories, emotional patterns, body-movement patterns, past life traumas and inter-dimensional interference, and the forgiveness and integration of one's shadow self until one comes to a place of Self Love. Spiral is therefore a Terrain of deep healing.

In choosing their path to growth, the Spiral person will of course be fully internally self-referenced. Being able to tune into exactly what is needed for their highest growth in any moment, the person at Spiral will not get attached to any one approach. They will draw on mentally-focused Diamond processes and emotional and body-centered Circle processes where needed, however they will also draw on specifically Spiral modalities that work on the energetic and multidimensional levels of one's Being.

KEY ELEMENTS OF SPIRAL

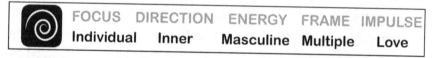

	FOCUS	DIRECTION	ENERGY	FRAME	IMPULSE
	Individual	Inner	Masculine	Multiple	Love

The Coherence-Based Terrain is an individual-focused Terrain, for people at Spiral are driven by the search to know their own unique Essence, their true inner nature, and they are focused on their own internal coherence, internal growth and internal integration.

The Coherence-Based Terrain is a more inner-directed Terrain than Circle, for people at Spiral go to great lengths to discover and accept who they truly are at their Essence—beyond any conditioning, programming, ego-identity, beliefs, or other interference—and to forgive themselves and clear themselves until they come to a place of Self-acceptance, Self-worth and ultimately Self Love.

The Coherence-Based Terrain is a more expanded version of the masculine than Diamond, for people at Spiral also use vision, focus and dedication in pursuit of growth and expansion, however they are doing this on an inner plane, with all parts of their Being in harmony.

The Coherence-Based Terrain is the first multiple-frame Terrain on the Continuum. Because those at Spiral are able to hold multiple parts of themselves in alignment as an integral whole in internal unity, this projects out onto the world as the ability to hold multiple perspectives of reality and to truly see things through another person's eyes. However, while people at Spiral are able to see the Terrains of others, they often have to work to be able to see their own, as it is the water they swim in.

The Coherence-Based Terrain is a love-responsive Terrain, for people at Spiral are connected to the Cosmic Tapestry and this gives them a sense of safety in the world that allows them to trust life and indeed to celebrate it. While, like everybody, there are times when they can be triggered into fear, those at Spiral can clearly feel it when this happens and can therefore choose to come back to Love.

SYMBOL OF SPIRAL

The symbol of the 'spiral' best describes the Coherence-Based Terrain because a spiral visually represents the movement of a journey of expansion. Starting from the broader arc of the circle—connected to one's Heart—this journey spirals inward toward the core of one's Being. However, this journey is an ever expanding arc that reaches both inwards towards coherence and outwards towards the full expanse of its cosmic Self. This is reflected in the ever expanding arc of the spiral shape, that moves in both directions.

The Coherence-Based Terrain also begins the journey beyond the 3D dimension of the outer five senses into the multi-sensorial realms of the Self. The drawing of the Spiral symbol reflects this, for it is the first shape on the Continuum that is drawn in three dimensions (x/y/z axis) with calligraphic lines that taper and swell, in contrast to the previous 6 shapes, which were flat and two dimensional (x/y axis). The variegated thickness in the lines of the Spiral, Toroid and Infinity symbols represents the expansion beyond the flat 3D perception of the first six Terrains to a multidimensional perception that perceives realms beyond our five senses.

EXAMPLES OF SPIRAL

Typical examples of people at Spiral might include:

- ◆ a martial arts master expert at moving chi or life force energy;
- ◆ a past-life regression practitioner;
- ◆ an energy healer who works with spirit guides;
- ◆ a sound vibration healer;
- ◆ a humble personal growth teacher who does not seek fame yet touches the lives of thousands of people;
- ◆ a nutritionist who teaches intuitive eating;
- ◆ a shaman who journeys into the spirit world for lessons and learnings;
- ◆ a channeler of beings from the spirit world;
- ◆ a person who teaches how to manage energy and set energetic boundaries;
- ◆ a Feldenkrais Practitioner who helps people get in touch with their own authentic way of moving;
- ◆ someone who connects regularly with their Higher Self and teaches other how to do the same;

- ◆ a person who specializes in identifying different energies and frequencies in the spirit world; and
- ◆ a mentor who teaches Self Love and Self-responsibility.

Once again, we remind you that the above examples are simplified stereotypes of people at the Coherence-Based Terrain, designed to give you a feel for this Terrain. There will be many people at Spiral who do not resemble the above examples at all; and you may meet people who fit the above descriptions yet who are not at Spiral. Accurate analysis of someone's Terrain requires extensive training in the Ten Terrains Model and must never be assumed based solely on what someone does for a living or their external behaviors.

SPIRAL MOVING TO TOROID

From Inner Truth To Universal Truth

The examples we've just provided are most likely to describe someone who is *stationary* at Spiral. Once a person is fully embodying all the lessons, gifts and experiences of Spiral, their Infinite Self will start them on the long journey up the mountain to the Fractal-Based Terrain (Toroid).

As a person at Spiral starts to move up the mountain towards Toroid, their focus will start to move from wanting to know *themselves* to wanting to know the deeper truths that apply to all Beings and the universal truths that apply throughout the Universe. They may start to think more in terms of general principles, metaphors and parables, and to see the fractal patterns playing out around them.

They will become less interested in the specific, individuated details of the Spirit world—such as which energy, spirit being, frequency, alien race, past life, etc. they are sensing—and they will start to focus more on the general principles that operate across all dimensions.

They will start to become increasingly aware of the multidimensionality of things at a macro level. For example, they may start to observe things happening politically in the world through an understanding of energies and entities and interplanetary agendas.

In terms of their personal growth, the focus of the Spiral person moving to Toroid will start to move from forgiveness, healing and Self Love, to practicing deeper and deeper levels of *trust*. They will begin to be tested more and more by life on their ability to trust in the flow. Indeed this stage of the evolutionary journey can become one big trust walk.

As the Spiral person approaches the jump to Toroid, they will start to feel the pull towards Universal Power, which comes about when you are in alignment with Infinite Consciousness and allow the wave to surf you, rather than you surfing the wave.

As the Spiral person moves closer and closer to Toroid, their sense of Self and energetic boundaries become clearer and clearer, their childhood and cultural conditioning and programming have less hold over them, their own thought patterns and emotional habits become less ingrained, and inter-dimensional beings become more respectful of their boundaries, realizing this person is a sovereign Being who cannot be interfered with. By the time the Spiral person arrives at Toroid, this Self-awareness will have grown to the point where the person is rarely being knocked off their center or taken over by anything outside themselves. And if they ever do, they will have enough mastery to clear themselves and snap straight back to neutral.

Such a person who is on the move to Toroid will look back at their time when they were stationary in the valley of Spiral and feel that they have changed a great deal. They may even feel like a completely different person. Indeed, if reading this book, they might even mistakenly feel that they have already shifted into Toroid. However, until they actually cross the Event Horizon into Toroid this person at Spiral on the move is still operating from their awareness of themselves as a multidimensional being who is part of a diverse Cosmic Tapestry. This will be the case until the moment when they cross the Event Horizon into Toroid and now have a direct sense of the intelligent Field of Oneness that is all life.

HISTORICAL FIGURES AT SPIRAL

A few famous historical figures who were at the Coherence-Based Terrain are Mahatma Gandhi, Carl Jung, and Rudolf Steiner. To see a full list of famous historical figures who were at the Coherence-Based Terrain, make sure to get your free eBook *The Terrains Of Famous People In History*. It includes names of consciousness pioneers, spiritual teachers, personal growth mentors, philosophers, monks, prophets, religious leaders, saints, peacemakers, spiritual healers, gnostics, taoists, past life experts, cosmologists, energy researchers and martial artists, all of whom were at Spiral.

MOVIES, TV & BOOKS AT SPIRAL

A few works of fiction that celebrate aspects of life at Spiral, characters at Spiral or Spiral themes are movies 'The Green Mile', 'La Belle Verte' (the Green Beautiful), and the comedy 'Groundhog Day'; the part fiction / part documentary movie 'What The Bleep Do We Know'; and books 'The Celestine Prophecy' by James Redfield, 'Jonathan Livingston Seagull' by Richard Bach, and 'The Prophet' by Kahlil Gibran.

BIGGER PICTURE OF SPIRAL

From the spiritual perspective of Infinite Consciousness as Self, the Coherence-Based Terrain can be seen as 'The Journey Of Inner Truth'. The lesson a person is learning while at this Terrain is how to be Sovereign over their own energy field by fully knowing and being coherent with their Self. The gift this Terrain brings is Self Love. The challenges it brings are how to discern between different multidimensional frequencies, and how to stay grounded in this 3D realm.

If you are at this Terrain, we suggest that you read the '*Guidebook For The Spiral Terrain*', available at www.tenterrains.com. In this booklet we go into far more detail about the lessons you are here to learn on 'The Journey Of Inner Truth'. We explain much more about the unique gifts and challenges of Spiral. We also give you invaluable tips and strategies to help you navigate life at this Terrain.

THE FRACTAL-BASED TERRAIN (TOROID)

THE FRACTAL-BASED TERRAIN OF CONSCIOUSNESS (TOROID) is the next evolutionary stage on the Continuum Of Terrains. A person at this Terrain is experiencing 'The Journey Of Universal Truth'. As of 2015, we estimate that approximately 0.4% of people in the Developed World are living at the Fractal-Based Terrain.

The Event Horizon Into Toroid

As a person crosses the Event Horizon Of Perception into the Fractal-Based Terrain, the big shift is that they now have a direct perception of and relationship with the infinite dimensionality of 'the Field'. The Field is not a concept or an idea to people at this Terrain; rather, it is something that they can actually feel, sense and intuit, even if they don't have the language to describe it. Beyond sensing the Web of Life, as people do at Circle, and beyond having an awareness of themselves as a cosmic Being, as people do at Spiral, the person at Toroid now has a direct sense of the intelligent Field of Oneness that is all life.

The Story At Toroid

The person at Toroid innately knows that the entirety of Creation is alive, intelligent and co-creative as one unified whole Field that operates as a closed-loop toroidal fractal of infinite dimensionality. They may not be scientifically minded or understand words like 'fractal' or 'Field', yet they can *feel* that this entire reality is an illusion, a collective hologram created moment to moment by each person. This is the Story at Toroid.

People at this Terrain innately understand how each of us affects and creates the collective Field. They know that they themselves are a multidimensional Being who creates anew not only their own reality, but the entire reality of everything, in every moment.

The Strategy At Toroid

As a result of being able to feel the Field, people at this Terrain have a profound trust in the living intelligence of the Universe, in life itself. This leads them to want to work together *with* life, in collaboration and co-creation (Power), rather than to fight against it or try to control it by will or mind (force). The Thrival Strategy of the person at Toroid is therefore to trust in life and cooperate with it in every moment. Those at Toroid are therefore experts at what the martial arts masters call 'Wu Wei', or effortless manifestation. They let the universe do the work, and live in a state of flow.

CORE FEATURES & DRIVERS OF TOROID

Collective Self

Their innate understanding of the Field means that people at Toroid accept that we are all part of one Collective Self; that I am a part of you and you are a part of me. They understand that each Being is simply expressing their unique piece in the fractal pattern, and each event is an expression of the tapestry of Consciousness.

For example, if a country has a tyrannical leader, the Toroid observer understands that this leader is a personification of the disowned 'shadow' of the collective Field of that nation's population. This awareness enables them to have much less angst, frustration and judgment over things that they see happening in the world around them, both at a personal level, a social level and a political level.

Trust

At Toroid, a person is starting to understand that everything is one Infinite Consciousness and that they themselves are part of the greater I AM. This gives them a great sense of trust in life.

Trusting the mechanics of the Field as a closed-loop recursive system, people at Toroid know that what goes around comes around. They know that if they give, they will receive, not necessarily directly from the person they gave to but indirectly via the toroidal workings of the Field, which some people call 'karma' or 'reciprocal balance'. They know that as long as they love their Self, Life loves them and has their back.

Guidance

As a result of this deep trust in life, the way a person lives at Toroid is by being guided moment to moment by the impulses of Life through their intuitive inner knowing. Those at Toroid begin to walk a path of complete trust in their Infinite Consciousness as Self which, if it ever reaches the point of complete Surrender will allow them to jump to the Unity-Based Terrain.

Fracticality

People at Toroid innately understand, even if they don't have the scientific language to describe this, that the universal structure is of a quantum, holistic nature, infinite in its dimensionality while being all one Self-similar fractal. They immediately recognize that something is a Truth because it is 'on fractal'; that is, fitting the larger pattern of everything and applying at all levels. They see the patterns and quantum interrelationships that are built into the multiverses of Infinite Consciousness, whether that be mathematical fibonacci sequences showing up in nature, or behavioral patterns showing up in people.

Their pattern recognition being fractal in nature, those at Toroid understand that the microcosm always reflects and informs the macrocosm (and vice versa). For example, seeing a child fight with another child over a toy in a playpen will inform them about how two nations negotiate with each other in the political arena.

More importantly, those at Toroid can always see the Principle under the pattern. They tend to think in metaphors and archetypes. The ancients at Toroid were masters at understanding these Principles, and this enabled them to create works of great Beauty, such as is found in sacred geometry or harmonic musical scales.

At Toroid, it is the beauty of the fractal that provides Divine law and order, not the systems created by man.

Universal Principles

As a result of their ability to directly perceive the Field, the person at Toroid has an innate knowing of Universal Truth—the laws and lore that govern this hologram-like fractal of our present reality. Unlike thinkers at Diamond, a person at Toroid does not need to use deduction, observation, experiments, research or 'trial and error' to solve problems; nor do they need to spend years studying in order to understand Universal Truths. From the time they first cross the Event Horizon into Toroid, everything they encounter begins to teach them these Truths. Every flower, every child, every brick reveals to them the workings of the Universe. Simple situations in daily life become parables of wisdom to them. As they spend more time at this Terrain, they come to see the fundamental Laws and Principles of our world as clearly and simply as other people see that the sky is blue.

Field vs. Ground

People at Toroid solve problems at the level of the Field, rather than dealing with symptoms at the level of the ground. Those at Toroid know that the quickest way to clean up the state of a person, an organization, a nation or a planet is to lift its 'frequency' or raise it's 'vibration'.[13]

This is why those at Toroid are usually working on lifting their own frequency by living in a super health-conscious way, keeping themselves joyful and maintaining positive loving thoughts. They understand the effect this has on the entire collective Field. They also understand that the more expanded is a person's awareness, the greater an impact they will have on the collective Field. As a result, they feel their responsibility to the Field keenly.

Induction

The Toroid person realizes that all things are happening simultaneously—past, present, and future—and that Universal Truth can therefore be tapped into at any time from anywhere. They know that there is nothing new to be invented or discovered; all that is required is to be able to 'tune in' to what is already there in the quantum Field of Infinite Consciousness. The great skill of those at Toroid is their ability to tap into the collective Field to 're-member' (rejoin with) what we already know, and to receive answers, direction, guidance, ideas, information and clarity.

When tapping into the quantum Field, those at Toroid are using the instant process of 'induction' to directly access universal all-knowing, rather than the slow, painstaking methods of deduction, trial-and-error, observation and experimentation used at the less expanded Terrains. At Toroid, a person immediately knows, through intuitive inner knowing, whether information is 'on fractal' or not.

Asking The Right Question

People at Toroid understand the importance of asking the right question. In the comic novel 'The Hitchhikers Guide To The Galaxy' by Douglas Adams, an entire civilization is disappointed when a supercomputer tells them that the 'Answer to the Ultimate Question of Life, The Universe, and Everything' is... '42.' They realize they need to build an even more advanced computer to find out what the question is! People at Toroid know that the greatest wisdom lies not in the answer, but in asking the exact right question. Some of the most important skills developed while someone is at the Fractal-Based Terrain is learning what questions to ask, how to ask questions with precision and how to recognize when an answer is coming from Truth or is being distorted.

Divination

The various ancient, time-tested systems of the divinatory arts such as the Tarot were crafted by adepts at the Fractal-Based Terrain. Similarly, their ability to tap directly into the quantum Field means that modern people at Toroid are often highly intuitive and skilled at a wide range of divination techniques like dowsing with a pendulum, reading Tarot Cards, Rune Stones, I Ching, animal telepathy, psychic readings, visualization or kinesiological approaches, etc., as these all require tapping into the collective Infinite quantum Field of all knowing. They are also often skilled at quantum healing and distance healing because they know and understand quantum non-locality.

There are, of course, many people at more contracted Terrains who have skill in these areas of divination. However, at Toroid divination is done without even a hint of fear or doubt, and without any giving up of one's power to a perceived wiser being or force outside oneself. It is at this Terrain that we find the Masters in the divinatory arts.

Genius

Because of their ability to ask original questions and draw precise answers from the Field, the Fractal-Based Terrain is often the Terrain at which we see true 'genius', such as that found in a Nikola Tesla or a Walter Russell. However, people at Toroid who bring new ideas and technologies to the world know that they have not 'discovered' or 'invented' anything, they have merely accessed (downloaded) existing information from the Field, which contains 'all knowing'. In contrast to the Diamond Innovators, pioneers at Toroid have no identity-attachment to what comes through them, and therefore do not seek fame or acclaim. They see themselves as conduits, bringing information through in Service to the whole.

Quantum Decision-Making

At Toroid, decisions tend to be made by tapping into the collective Field and asking which decision at that moment is in the highest good of all sentient Beings and indeed all life, in all dimensions. For example, the choice by someone at the Fractal-Based Terrain of embarking upon a career or starting a project is determined not just by how much it aligns with their own innate Gifts and resonates with their own Being, as would be important at Spiral, but by how it fits into the existing tapestry of human activity, how meaningful it is for the collective whole, and how 'on fractal' it is with the entire Geometry of the person's life and everything they have ever experienced. Those at Toroid intuitively know that if their choice is 'on fractal', that is if it fits the pattern of their life and serves the highest good of all, then it will receive the full support of the Universe, doors will open for them and life will flow effortlessly for them in all that they embark upon.

Service

People at Toroid intuitively understand that we are all facets of the same infinite holographic intelligence, and that, as such, we each have a unique Gift and purpose in the tapestry of the whole. They know that it is this unique Gift, this unique purpose we each have that we are to give back to life in return for the gift of life that has been given us. This giving our Gift back, to our fullest ability, without an agenda or strings attached, is what is understood as Service with a capital 'S'.

It is at Toroid that a person can take their Gift to the level of mastery and genius, by so fully being their true Self that they are the highest possible expression of the trajectory that they set up for themselves for this lifetime before they were even born. The person at Toroid knows that by giving their Gift in this full way, they are being an instrument of Divine Will in Service to the entire collective Field.

Quantum Self-Responsibility

At Toroid, we go beyond the Spiral idea of 'creating your own reality'. Here at Toroid a person knows that every single choice they make has a quantum ripple effect on the entire Field, creating a new trajectory or a new Geometry in the fabric of existence. They fully own that their current lifetime is showing up as a perfect mirror of the sum total of their Geometry across the parallel universes of time and space.

Therefore, people at Toroid live in a state of advanced Self-responsibility. Here at Toroid—and even more at the next Terrain of Infinity—people tend to explore much more deeply the behaviors, blocks, inter-dimensional interferences, karmic debts, and unconscious charge forces that are getting in the way of their true life flow, keeping them apart from fully BEING; and they seek to clear these as much as possible so they can live their Gift to the fullest and be of the highest Service.

However, clearing at Toroid has a very different quality than it did at Spiral. At Toroid, people know that this world is a hologram of our creation. They choose not to give energy to any stories, for they know that by doing that they would be reinforcing them as they recreate the hologram. At Toroid, clearing is done 'implosively' to neutralize charge, with much less attachment to or identification with the stories. This is very different from the approach we see at Spiral, where a person is honing in on specific beliefs, emotions, energies, beings, dimensions—and the stories that they contain—in order to shift them.

KEY ELEMENTS OF TOROID

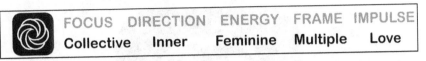

	FOCUS	DIRECTION	ENERGY	FRAME	IMPULSE
	Collective	Inner	Feminine	Multiple	Love

The Fractal-Based Terrain is a collective-focused Terrain, yet at this very expanded awareness the concept of 'group' or 'collective' no longer refers to clan or community or nation, it no longer even refers to a human group of any kind, it now refers to the collective Field of Consciousness.

The Fractal-Based Terrain is an inner-directed Terrain because it is based on 100% Self-responsibility. At Toroid a person knows that every single choice they make has a quantum ripple effect on the entire Field.

The Fractal-Based Terrain has a feminine energy, because it is about receiving Infinite Consciousness, allowing the information of 'Truth' to enter one's awareness, and being fully in alignment with Universal Laws and Principles rather than imposing anything onto life.

The Fractal-Based Terrain is a multiple-frame Terrain, as people at Toroid can see how all the different perceptions of reality fit together as a multidimensional fractal whole, and can see their own place in that. A person at Toroid is able to perceive the Universal Principles that govern the entire hologram-like, non-local quantum Field that gives rise to space and time as a whole, to act from these principles and live by them.

The Fractal-Based Terrain is a love-responsive Terrain, for people at Toroid know that the Love that is reflected back from outside of them is directly proportional to the Love they hold within for their own Self—their body, heart, mind and spirit—on infinite dimensions across infinite timelines—past, present and future. They know that the version of their life that is showing up in this place and time is simply a composite hologram of all these ways in which they are loving and not loving their Self.

SYMBOL OF TOROID

The symbol of the 'toroid' best describes the Fractal-Based Terrain because once the Event Horizon of this Terrain is crossed, it is like arriving in a new land where all the ever enfolding matrices of energy and matter, information and Spirit are now seen fully. It is much like opening the back of a giant clock and seeing all the many gears moving, where before all that was seen was the clock's hands moving externally upon its faceplate.

The shape of a toroid represents recursion from the point of infinity to the whole of the circle and from the whole of the circle to the point of infinity. This symbol therefore represents the continuation of the inner journey that started at Circle and continued into Spiral, as each arc of the shape moves from the outer circle into one of the toroid's enfolding spirals. Only, at the Fractal-Based Terrain, you now see where the journey to the unknown is leading: to the singularity of Infinity. The toroid shape shows that there is no place to run or hide, as all enfolds back onto its Self. As the principles of cause and effect are now seen interoperating together in unison, trust in the intelligence of Infinite Consciousness inevitably unfolds.

EXAMPLES OF TOROID

Typical examples of people at Toroid might include:

- A skilled dowser who is able to divine the answer to any question he asks without influencing it from his ego or mind;
- a master in earth grids and the harmonic code;
- a profound poet who shares Universal Truths in his writing;
- a spiritual teacher who teaches the pure laws of Dharma;
- a gnostic master unattached to his teachings;
- a physicist who innately understands the mystical laws of the Universe;
- a pioneer in inter-dimensional clearing techniques;
- a master of sound harmonics or sacred geometry;
- someone living the daily practice of Karma Yoga;
- someone who teaches the deeper laws of unconditional Love and self healing.

Once again, we remind you that the above examples are simplified stereotypes of people at the Fractal-Based Terrain, designed to give you a feel for this Terrain. There will be many people at Toroid who do not resemble the above examples at all; and you may meet people who fit the above descriptions yet who are not at Toroid. Accurate analysis of someone's Terrain requires extensive training in the Ten Terrains Model and must never be assumed based solely on what someone knows and understands or on their external behaviors.

TOROID MOVING TO INFINITY

From Universal Truth To Oneness

The examples we've just provided are most likely to describe someone who is *stationary* at Toroid. Once a person is fully embodying all the lessons, gifts and experiences of Toroid, their Infinite Self will start them on the long journey up the mountain to the Unity-Based Terrain (Infinity).

As a person at Toroid starts to move up the mountain towards Infinity, their sense of the interrelatedness of everything in the universal Field will start to sink in at an even deeper level. They will start to realize more and more that separation is merely an illusion, and that in reality everything is ONE.

They will become increasingly aware of their own blocks, filters and areas of charge force that are distorting their perception of Unity and keeping them in the illusion of separation, and they will choose to clear these.

As they start to understand more deeply that there is only One of us here, they will start to see that they have created the infinite dimensions of entanglements, trauma and challenge that make up their hologram. They will start to become aware that all things are infinitely possible and that where they put their attention creates what shows up.

They will increasing start to let go of their identity as a separate individual. They will start to see that the forces playing out in the world are all in fact expressions of their own I AM Self. Even so-called enemies will start to be seen as unloved parts of their greater Self as the Field.

As the person at Toroid moves towards Infinity, they will find themselves tuning into the Field to ask questions less and less, as they start to have longer and more frequent periods of direct perception of Infinite Consciousness. They will most likely pay much more attention to keeping their body/mind/heart vehicle clear and tuned, so as to be able to stay more permanently connected to this instant knowing.

Most importantly, as they approach Infinity, the Toroid person will be tested more and more on their ability to *surrender* to their Infinite Self, knowing that it has their back. They will increasingly be able to see the perfection in the things that are happening to them and that are unfolding in their world. They will become less and less attached to the things they do and will start to feel more and more at peace.

Such a person who is on the move to Infinity will look back at their time when they were stationary in the valley of Toroid and feel that they have changed a great deal. They may even feel like a completely different person. Indeed, if reading this book, they might even mistakenly feel that they have already shifted into Infinity. However, until they actually cross the Event Horizon into Infinity this person at Toroid on the move is not yet fully One with All That Is. They are slowly starting to understand this and to have more experiences of it, but it will not become a fully embodied state of Being for them until they cross the Event Horizon into Infinity.

HISTORICAL FIGURES AT TOROID

A few famous historical figures who were at the Fractal-Based Terrain are Confucius, Rumi and Nikola Tesla. To see a full list of famous historical figures who were at the Fractal-Based Terrain, make sure to get your free eBook *The Terrains Of Famous People In History*, available at www.tenterrains.com. It includes names of inventors, mathematicians, alchemists, physicists, philosophers, occultists, psychologists, spiritual pioneers, mystics, sages and spiritual gurus, all of whom were at Toroid.

MOVIES, TV & BOOKS AT TOROID

Many ancient esoteric teachings include Toroid Principles, such as the Gnostic teachings, the I Ching and the Mystical Kabbala.

There are not many works of fiction that depict life at the Fractal-Based Terrain. One popular example that has a Toroid element in it is the 'Star Wars' movies , for 'The Force' is a Toroid idea.

BIGGER PICTURE OF TOROID

From the spiritual perspective of Infinite Consciousness as Self, the Fractal-Based Terrain can be seen as 'The Journey Of Universal Truth'. The lesson a person is learning while at this Terrain is to have full trust in Infinite Consciousness. The gift this Terrain brings is an even greater experience of the 'Self', yielding now a deep trust in and receptivity to life. The challenge it brings is how to distinguish between what is 'on fractal' and what is false perception.

If you are at this Terrain, we suggest that you read the 'Guidebook For The Toroid Terrain'. In this booklet we go into far more detail about the lessons you are here to learn on 'The Journey Of Universal Truth'. We explain much more about the unique gifts and challenges of Toroid. We also give you invaluable tips and strategies to help you navigate life at this Terrain.

THE UNITY-BASED TERRAIN (INFINITY)

T HE UNITY-BASED TERRAIN OF CONSCIOUSNESS (INFINITY) is the next evolutionary stage on the Continuum Of Terrains. A person at this Terrain is experiencing 'The Journey Of Oneness'. As of 2015, we estimate that approximately 0.02% of people in the Developed World are living at the Unity-Based Terrain.

The Event Horizon Into Infinity

The Unity-Based Terrain is the first Terrain that is truly non-dualistic. As a person crosses the Event Horizon Of Perception into the Unity-Based Terrain, the big shift that happens is that they no longer experience separation at any level of their Being. They now know—from firsthand experience—that Consciousness is indivisible. Far beyond simply feeling themselves to be connected to the Web Of Life;

they experience themselves *as* the Web Of Life. They are not merely perceiving Infinite Consciousness; they *are* Infinite Consciousness. They are living Oneness, in a fully embodied way.

The Story At Infinity

A person at this Terrain believes that they ARE every thing—every person, every animal, every plant, every object and every single molecule in the multiverse—and that every thing is them. The Story at the Unity-Based Terrain is that 'it's all me!' Another way to sum up this Story is: *"I AM Infinite Consciousness I AM"*.

The Strategy At Infinity

People at Infinity know that the only things that show up in their life out of the pool of infinite possibility of 'every thing' are those things that they have put a 'charge' to. Every time they get triggered—by a person, a situation or a dimension—out of being 100% neutral and centered, they know that there is some place in their Being that is holding a charge force keeping that place apart from their Infinite I AM Self. Another way of saying this is that they realize they have a Story about it that is activating emotion and thus creating their reality to be as it is.

The Thrival Strategy at the Unity-Based Terrain is therefore to completely let go of any charge you are holding in your Self that is keeping you from a neutral Sovereign state of Being, that is keeping you in separation from your Self in any way. The paradox of this Terrain is that people at Infinity seek to clean up the entire trajectory of their morphogenic field, while simultaneously knowing and trusting that they are already *perfect* as they are.

CORE FEATURES & DRIVERS OF INFINITY

No More Identity

At the Unity-Based Terrain, identity falls away and is replaced by the unitary knowing I AM that I AM. A person at Infinity sees that there is NOTHING that is not them. They lose the reference points that typically 'hook' others into an identity—such as a particular set of religious or nation-state beliefs, one's economic, familial or relationship status, etc. They see their Self as infinite possibility, and are fully free in their Knowing of their Self.

No More Judgment

One of the key features of the Unity-Based Terrain is that people at this Terrain accept every 'thing' as being part of their infinite I AM. This means that they accept not just the so-called 'good' aspects of life as being them, but ALL aspects. People at Infinity do not judge others, for they known that I AM you and you are me. They see all so called acts of 'wrongdoing' or 'evil' in the world as the expression of an unloved aspect of their own Self.

If a person at Infinity finds that they are unable to accept some person or thing as being THEM, then they realize that there is some charge there within them that is keeping them from being fully in Unity, and they set about clearing it.

Perfection

Those at the Unity-Based Terrain see every thing as being of equal value. Given that they see the entire pool of infinite possibility, they do not give any greater weight to one expression of Infinity over another. They see that everything and everyone in this world is perfect—exactly as it is meant to be right now.

Understanding that everything is one Infinite Consciousness and everything is perfect, people at Infinity move through the world as a Witness, without getting attached to the dramas of human existence. They do not feel the urge to resist what is happening to them, to fight against life, or to seek to change themselves, others or the world around them. They surrender to accepting fully who they are and work to clear any stories or other charge that is keeping them from fully being their true Self.

Beingness

At Infinity, a person is still engaged in the world, yet because they can see the perfection of all things, they are not attached to anything they do. Their doing is more a kind of 'BEING'. They do not push and strain to achieve things, rather they know that if they just stay connected to Infinite Consciousness and act for the joy of acting, then the might of the Universe will be magnetized to them to make all tasks effortless.

No More Ego

Those at Infinity have completely surrendered their egoic small 's' self and therefore do not operate from individuated self-interest in any way. They act as an unfiltered expression of Infinite Consciousness. If you ever spend time with such a person, you will sense a deep calmness at their core, and a state of surrendered acceptance of the perfection of life that infuses their every moment. You will sense their humility, for they do not see themselves as a separate individual with an ego and will, but as an instrument of the great All. This is the deepest form of Service.

Surrender

The only way to cross the Event Horizon from Toroid to Infinity is through completely surrendering. People at Infinity surrender to the Infinite Knowing of Infinite Consciousness, and trust that with every fiber of their Being. They have let go of trying to control their life, trying to control others or trying to control the world around them. They trust that things will unfold as they are meant to, both in their life and in the world. This brings about a deep state of inner peace.

Infinite Knowing

People at the Unity-Based Terrain have immediate, direct and permanent access to All That Is. They no longer need to 'channel' information from the higher realms (as at Spiral) or 'tune into' the Field to ask questions (as at Toroid). This kind of direct Knowing is simultaneously experienced by the body, felt through the Heart, witnessed by the mind and seen through the inner eye.

To use a computer analogy, think of the human brain as a local computer and Infinite Consciousness as the internet. Instead of living offline, limited to the knowledge stored in their standalone computer (their thinking brain) with only occasional connection to the vast knowledge of the internet, at the Unity-Based Terrain people are now permanently online. The antenna that is the human body/heart/mind vehicle is tuned to Infinite Consciousness and it is now clearly receiving continuous Knowing, without any blocks or distortion.

No More Decisions

People at Infinity operate without needing to think, plan ahead or seek guidance, guided as they are in every moment by their direct connection to the Infinite Knowing of All That Is. Living at Infinity means living in a state of supreme trust, knowing that you will always be shown the way in the exact moment when you need to know it and not a moment before. At Infinity, a person has surrendered so completely that they can have a bullet coming at them and they will trust that at the exact right moment they will duck, if they are meant to survive; or they won't, if they are meant to die. People at Infinity always trust that at the exact right moment they will know what to do. This is a state of full surrender.

Cleaning The Temple

Those at Infinity intuitively know they need to keep their body/mind/heart instrument 'super tuned' so they can continue to receive Infinite Knowing without any distortion. They tend to be drawn to people, foods, situations and energies that fill them with Love, joy, bliss, energy and vitality, thereby keeping their Being resonating at a high vibration, so that their antenna to the Infinite can operate effectively.

If they do encounter so-called 'toxic' substances, people or situations, many people at this Terrain also have the ability to transmute these energies, so that they are not affected by them. Part of their ability to do this comes from their lack of judgment or criticism of these energies. The person at Infinity accepts the energies as they are and thereby is able to transmute them with their Love.

Inner Sovereignty

At Infinity a person is choosing to be 100% Self-responsible in every moment and to be the sole Self-governing Creator of their life. Sovereignty at this expanded Terrain of Infinity essentially means being able to hold your 'One Point' or your 'center' (also known as your Dan Tien), regardless of what is happening around you. It means staying neutral at all times, so as to be able to respond from full choice, rather than coming from compulsion, programming or reaction. It means being able to keep your energy field stable and the boundaries of your field strong, in the face of anything.

People at Infinity tend to use every means at their disposal to address every possible 'filter' that could be causing them to be triggered out of neutral: their conditioned fears, negative thoughts, limiting beliefs, social programming, cultural conditioning, emotional wounding, physical toxicity, inner child hurts, dysfunctional movement patterns, habitual reactions, ego desires, conditioned behavioral habits, energetic wounding, negative judgments, karmic imbalances, lack of Self Love, multidimensional traumas, inter-dimensional interference, genetic programming, ancestral conditioning, etc...

Creator Being

At Infinity, there is no separation between you and a 'supreme Being' or a 'supreme Power', as we saw at Radial on the other end of the Continuum of Terrains. At Infinity, a person knows *themselves* to be a Creator, with full Power to imagine into reality anything they choose.

At this Terrain, a person sees the 'hologram' they are projecting outward from the infinite possibilities of Infinite Consciousness. Rather than living inside the matrix created by others, they energize and manifest their own universe as a fully realized, Self-responsible Creator Being, with full consciousness of each choice. They know that if they are unhappy with what they see, it is time to look into how they are imagining their Self into Being.

Imagination

From the perspective of those at the Unity-Based Terrain, all of Creation that you perceive about you with your five senses, from the infinitely small to the infinitely large—across the infinite fractal of multi-verses and the multi-dimensions of time and space—is all here as a result of being imagined into existence by your larger Infinite Consciousness as Self.

When a person expands to the Unity-Based Terrain they realize that it is their responsibility to consciously image and re-image the hologram that is their life. Thus, at Infinity people learn to actively, consciously and responsibly focus their imagination and their visioning, knowing that this gives rise to the thoughts and forms that evolve out from them.

This is a very different kind of visioning than the mental one that happens at Diamond, sourced from the 'offline' thinking mind. Being permanently connected to Infinite Consciousness, at the Unity-Based Terrain one's visions, ideas and imaginings are coming directly from Infinite Consciousness.

Instant Manifestation

At Infinity there is no opposition between one's ego and one's Spirit, so there is nothing that can block the process of manifestation. At this Terrain, a person is so plugged into the Universal Field, so aligned with their own true Heart's desires and the highest good of all, and so surrendered to the unfolding of Infinite Consciousness that their visions manifest quickly and powerfully. Indeed, the more they do the work of clearing their personal filters, then the more and more quickly they will be able to manifest those visions until, as they come closer to the Void-Based Terrain, they are able to manifest in real time.

Seeing The Illusion

Some people at Infinity are so aware of the hologram that is their continual creation that they can feel as if life itself is an illusion. They no longer prioritize the sensory information that their everyday eyes and ears seek to convey to them, for they now see their 3D experience for what it is: a moment-by-moment co-creation. To understand this, think of the final scene in the movie 'The Matrix', when the character Neo is suddenly is able to see the flickering binary code that is creating the illusory experience of reality inside the Matrix

This idea that our 3D reality is an illusion is well known in spiritual circles; however for those at Infinity, this is a lived, felt experience. For many people at this Terrain, their dream time is more real than their awake time.

Honoring The Vehicle

Despite their awareness of the illusion that is life, people at Infinity are not 'off in the clouds' living in the abstract realms of Spirit, neither are they trying to 'ascend' out of their body; but rather they are very grounded in the physical. They understand that the process of Creation requires the weaving together of both vision and emotion. They know that in order to Create we draw on our greater Self to give us our vision and use our individual body to energize that vision with the emotion of joy.

Therefore people at Infinity do not scorn the fact that they are in a body, nor do they take it for granted. They celebrate their body as an instrument of Creation. They treat their body as the Sacred Temple that houses their Divinity, giving it honor, respect, care and great Love.

LAGGING BEHAVIOR

It is important to understand that people at Infinity are not saints, nor are they 'perfect enlightened beings'. They are still real flesh and blood people who have their issues, their fears and their idiosyncrasies. It is very important not to put them up on a pedestal. They are simply people who have a very expanded perception.

We mentioned earlier in this book that there are situations where a person's behavior can 'lag' behind their internal Terrain. This kind of discrepancy can happen even at the Unity-Based Terrain, because people at this Terrain have usually expanded very far from the Terrain in which they grew up, from the Terrain of their family and friends, and from the Terrain of their entire culture. Therefore, the pull on them from not only their early conditioning but indeed from the entire quantum Field of the culture they live in can be extremely strong.

It is easy to condemn people at Infinity who still have an old conditioned behavior—such as in the area of money or sexuality— that is out of alignment with their internal Terrain. It is easy to call them 'hypocrites' or 'fakes'. However, they are not. They are truly people at Infinity who know deeply in their Being that they are indivisibly One with everything, who know the truth behind the illusion of separation, who have access to direct and instant knowing and who have a potent ability to manifest their reality. They simply have some charge remaining in their field that they need to discharge in a particular area, some filters that they need to clear. That is all.

Fortunately, the degree of incongruity that one can find in the behaviors of people at Spiral, Toroid or Infinity in those few areas where they still have old conditioning is matched by the degree to which they are fully Self-responsible and proactively working on getting these last vestiges cleaned up and the incredible speed with which they can shift things once they become aware of them.

So we must always remember that even people at these most expanded Terrains are human. They have their 'bad hair days', just like the rest of us! It's how they handle these that distinguishes them from everybody else.

KEY ELEMENTS OF INFINITY

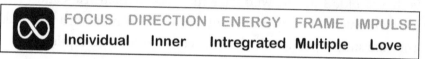

∞	FOCUS	DIRECTION	ENERGY	FRAME	IMPULSE
	Individual	Inner	Intregrated	Multiple	Love

The Unity-Based Terrain is the last of the individual-focused Terrains; however, the individual focus is no longer on 'me' separate and apart from others, but on 'I' as one indivisible unity with All That Is.

The Unity-Based Terrain is the most inner-directed of all the Terrains we have seen thus far, for the core belief of people at Infinity is 'I AM Every Thing'. Therefore anything the person at Infinity turns their attention to, even in the outside world, is by definition something inside them.

The Unity-Based Terrain is the first Terrain to have a fully integrated masculine and feminine energy. In this balanced state of integration, the doing energy of the masculine is driven from the deep internal 'Being' energy of the feminine.

The Unity-Based Terrain is a multiple-frame Terrain, for Infinity is pure infinite possibility, therefore here perceptions exist in simultaneous potential. Each perception can be conceived of as a thought or program waiting to be activated, with no charge yet put to any one perception to distinguish it from the others. People at Infinity see themselves as cause and creator of the entire Continuum of perception.

The Unity-Based Terrain is technically a love-responsive Terrain, because Love is the expressed aspect of the Self-healing principle of Infinite Consciousness. Yet here at Infinity you can't be 'responsive' to this outer force of Love pulling you toward Unity because now at Infinity you ARE Unity—and Love just 'is'. It is unconditional and therefore it can not be perceived as being apart from itself. At Infinity, you are truly 'inside' of Love.

SYMBOL OF INFINITY

The shape of the 'infinity-symbol' (otherwise known as a 'figure8' or 'lemniscate') best describes the Unity-Based Terrain because now we have arrived at the point of seeing perfection in the eternity of time and space as a never ending loop, and the Unity of all of Creation as one Infinite Consciousness forever expanding and contracting, giving and receiving, etc. All polarity is simply the opposite point on Infinity's great wheel. Because in Unity-Based Infinity all points are the same point, resistance to one's Self is seen for its futility and folly, and surrender is the only option unless you want to be once again carried around the wheel of cause and effect. This is represented by the timeless, looping, endlessly recursive shape of the infinity symbol.

EXAMPLES OF INFINITY

Typical examples of people at Infinity include:

- a person who has had a near-death experience and now has no fear of death;
- a spiritual master who is able to sit on the road in the middle of a war zone without being affected by the bullets flying past his head;
- someone who is able to stay neutral and fully surrendered no matter what the challenge;
- a person whose state of knowingness is such that they can answer questions in the moment the question is merely being contemplated;
- someone who acts in complete faith and trust at all times, knowing "I AM that I AM";
- a mystic who expresses unconditional Love by who they are simply Being; and
- a shaman who is a master of the imaginal realms of the Unity-Based Terrain and communicates telepathically with all the infinite possibilities moving around a person or situation.

Once again, we remind you that the above examples are simplified stereotypes of people at the Unity-Based Terrain, designed to give you a feel for this Terrain. There will be many people at Infinity who do not resemble the above examples at all; and you may meet people who fit the above descriptions yet who are not at Infinity. Accurate analysis of someone's Terrain requires extensive training in the Ten Terrains Model and must never be assumed based solely on what someone calls themselves or their external behaviors.

INFINITY MOVING TO NO-THING

From Oneness To Being

The examples we've just provided are most likely to describe someone who is *stationary* at the Unity-Based Terrain. Given that the work required at this Terrain is the deepest work on the entire Continuum, it is likely that a person will spend many lifetimes in the valley of Infinity, before beginning the journey up the mountain to No-Thing. Yet eventually, once they are fully embodying all the lessons, gifts and experiences of Infinity, their Infinite Self will then start them on the long journey up the mountain to the Void-Based Terrain (No-Thing).

As the person at Infinity starts to move up the mountain towards No-Thing, life will start to show them their deepest beliefs, their most core emotional wounding, their most formative holographic traumas and their most foundational inter-dimensional blocks, so that even those things that have caused their most basic karmic 'Geometry' can now be cleared and their charge force dissolved.

As the person becomes even more and more Self-responsible, they will no longer be taking on any *new* charge force, any new wounding or any new beliefs. They will become even less attached to the world around them, and the daily stuff of life will no longer stick to them.

They will find it easier and easier to stay neutral in all situations and to hold their center in the densest environments. As a result, they will find themselves able to be more and more Present.

As the person at Infinity continues to move up the mountain towards No-Thing, they will begin to be able to access and embody almost any possibility. They will start to be able to imagine into reality and manifest anything they choose, faster and faster, until they are able to do it in *real time*.

They will find that they are increasingly able to *transmute* anything around them that is not resonating at their frequency. They will no longer need to take care of the Sacred Temple of their body as much, and their attachment to it will lessen.

In the final stages of their journey down the other side of the mountain towards No-Thing, even those beliefs most deeply anchored into the collective consciousness will be discharged, such as the need to eat, to drink, to breathe, to age and to die.

A loop will begin to develop between expanding and BEING that causes progressive de-materialization and they will know that soon they will have the ability to step free of even the bounds of time and space.

At the threshold of the jump to No-Thing, they will be on the point of mastering what is known in the Hindu traditions as the Siddhic realms and to be able to perform acts of seeming impossibility. Those around them, perceiving them to be 'enlightened', may think that this person has jumped across to No-Thing.

However, until they actually cross the Event Horizon into No-Thing this person at Infinity on the move is still held by the bounds of time and space and the light of Infinite Knowing. This will be the case until the moment when they cross the Event Horizon into No-Thing and enter the realm of pure and absolute BEING, where you *are* every 'where', at once all the infinite universes and able to be in connection with every atom therein.

HISTORICAL FIGURES AT INFINITY

A few famous historical figures who were at the Unity-Based Terrain are Buddha, Paramahansa Yogananda and Black Elk. To see a full list of famous historical figures who were at the Unity-Based Terrain, make sure to get your free eBook *The Terrains Of Famous People In History*. It includes names of sages, mystics, spiritual masters, saints, medicine men, gurus, seers, alchemists and yogis, all of whom were at Infinity.

MOVIES, TV & BOOKS AT INFINITY

There are very few fictional works that portray characters at the Unity-Based Terrain. One beautiful movie with a central character at Infinity is 'August Rush'. And, as we have seen earlier, the characters of Obi-Wan Kenobi and Yoda in the Star Wars movies are at this Terrain.

However, there are many autobiographical works about near-death experiences that illustrate the jump to Infinity, such as 'Saved By The Light' by Dannion Brinkley and Paul Perry, and 'Beyond The Light' by P.M.H. Atwater. In these documented cases, the person returns to their body after the near-death experience—often spontaneously healed from the terminal illness that had caused them to 'die'- with a dramatically more expanded perception of reality than they had before. Oftentimes they have passed through several Terrains in an instant and jumped to Infinity.

BIGGER PICTURE OF INFINITY

From the spiritual perspective of Infinite Consciousness as Self, the Unity-Based Terrain can be seen as 'The Journey Of Oneness'. The lesson a person is learning while at this Terrain is how to hold themselves 'Sovereign' in all situations, having no 'charge' at all in their field. The gift this Terrain brings is inner peace. The challenge it brings is how to remain in the state of Unity at all times, despite the constant pull back to separation.

If you are at this Terrain, we suggest that you read the 'Guidebook For The Infinity Terrain'. In this booklet we go into far more detail about the lessons you are here to learn on 'The Journey Of Oneness'. We explain much more about the unique gifts and challenges of Infinity. We also give you invaluable tips and strategies to help you navigate life at this Terrain.

THE VOID-BASED TERRAIN (NO-THING)

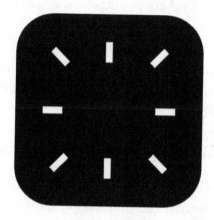

THE VOID-BASED TERRAIN OF CONSCIOUSNESS (NO-THING) is the final evolutionary stage on the Continuum Of Terrains. A person at this Terrain is experiencing 'The Journey Of Being'. The number of people in the Developed World living at the Void-Based Terrain is uncertain at this time, as such people do not register in the collective Field of Humanity. However, the numbers of people living at this Terrain are likely to be infinitesimal.

What Is The Void?

The Void is virtually an impossible concept to get our human mind around. This is the stuff of deep esoteric learning in the Mystery Schools.

The Void is the *context* that gives rise to Infinite Consciousness. The emptiness—the 'No-Thing'-ness—of the Void creates a condition that allows its opposite to manifest: *everything*. The very first polarity is created between the emptiness of the Void and the fullness of Infinite Consciousness, and this polarity (and all other polarities emanating thereafter) plays out in the infinite fractal of the Field that is then begotten by Infinite Consciousness.

Many of you reading this book may be thinking that the Void is somewhere to get to. No, the Void is not the so called holy grail of 'ascension'. It is not 'heaven'; nor is it 'paradise'. All of these are notions that come from Terrains of much more limited perception than No-Thing. The Void is not a place to get to, it is the place that we all come from. The Void is the womb of Infinite Consciousness.

The Event Horizon Into No-Thing

Beyond time and space, the Void-Based Terrain is the most expanded of all the Terrains on the Continuum. It is the Terrain of absolute Mastery. The Event Horizon that is crossed as someone expands into the Void-Based Terrain is that *the Self is now dissolved.*

As impossible as this is to conceive, at the Void-Based Terrain there is no 'person' at all. There is no Self (the Spirit that animates our life path). There is no Soul (the cellular genetic memory that records all our experiences). There is no Body (the vessel that holds our light). All of these are 'things', and at the Void-Based Terrain there is *no thing*. All these illusions and holograms have fallen away. At this Terrain, a Being is completely free of any 'thing' forever. They are simply Presence.

No Story

At the Void-Based Terrain there is no Story. When you have no beliefs left, when you are free of all 'charge' on every level of your Being, you are left in a pure state of Presence.

No Strategy

There is also no Thrival Strategy at the Void-Based Terrain. At No-Thing you have neutralized every charge on every level to become as still as the mirror upon which Infinity's imagination reflects its Self. There is nothing to do. There is no thrival to seek. All strategy is left behind and you are pure BEING.

CORE FEATURES & DRIVERS OF NO-THING

No Charge

A Being can only cross into the Void-Based Terrain when they have experienced a final, complete and absolute dissolution of every 'charge' at every point in their Field; whether that is along their genetic line, in their past life Geometry, in their emotional body, cellular memory, genetic memory, unconscious, belief structures, thoughts, etc. There is nothing (no thing) in any timeline or dimension of their Being that is creating any 'Thing'.

It takes countless lifetimes of dedicated refinement, clearing one's filters and surrender at The Unity-Based Terrain (Infinity) to come to this state of No-Thing.

Siddhic State

When a Being gets to this level of Mastery, they are so clear of charge force that nothing sticks, not even the notions of aging, disease or death. They are immortal. They may appear as a pure 'apparition' of light if they choose to make their presence known to others.

So called 'impossibilities' such as levitation, omni-location and walking through walls are simply some of the many Siddhic realms available to them, for there is no charge in their field to hook them into illusory concepts such as gravity, solid matter, etc.

Empty

There is no thing in the Void. There is not even light, for light requires a charge force, or Field. Even the concept of Consciousness is now passive and receptive more so than active and potent as it is at Infinity. As we have seen, the Void is truly empty. All concepts of 'Infinite Consciousness', 'Spirit', 'Mind', 'I AM', 'All That Is', 'God-force', 'Source', etc. have been left behind. A Being at No-Thing lives in an absolute state of emptiness.

Meaningless

At the Void-Based Terrain, there are no stories or meanings attached to events and happenings, they are simply observed and experienced without any attachment or charge. This is the opposite of the meaninglessness we saw at the Matter-Based Terrain. What is terrifying randomness at Particle is blissful formlessness at No-Thing.

Being

At Infinity you are 'doing' Being; at No-Thing you are 'being' BEING. No-Thing is the absolute journey because at this Terrain you are beyond any form of doing. At No-Thing you are no longer even doing 'the light' of Infinite Consciousness. You are beyond the doing of 'Love'. You are beyond the doing of even 'life' itself—the cycles of life and death, the doing of air, food, water, gravity and such.

After you have left even the infinite possibilities of Infinity behind, what are you left with? From what the Masters at Void have shown us, it is the pure Presence of BEING.

KEY ELEMENTS OF NO-THING

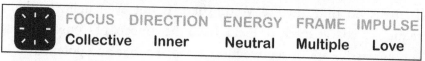

	FOCUS	DIRECTION	ENERGY	FRAME	IMPULSE
	Collective	Inner	Neutral	Multiple	Love

The Void-Based Terrain is a collective-focused Terrain, but only in the very broad sense that No-Thing may be conceived as the collective context that allows the individual organism of Infinite Consciousness infinite expression. In addition, in order to cross the Event Horizon of No-Thing, a Being has to be clear of all 'charge-force' including their collective ancestral lineage that exists in the morphogenic Field. Thus, strictly speaking, this Terrain has a Collective Focus—not in the sense of assemblage, but in the sense of dis-assemblage.

The Void-Based Terrain is an inner-directed Terrain, for one can only find stillness by going within, and a Being at No-Thing lives in the still, dis-charged state of 'non-doing'.

The Void-Based Terrain has a neutral energy. The Void is neither feminine nor masculine as it is in fact no thing at all.

The Void-Based Terrain is a multiple-frame Terrain, for the Being at No-Thing exists as a possibility from which multiple universes of perception can arise. These will arise at the Unity-Based Terrain, if given focus there by a charge force.

The Void-Based Terrain is technically among the five love-responsive Terrains, if one follows the pattern of the Continuum of Terrains to its conclusion. However, at No-Thing, even Love—unconditional or otherwise—doesn't exist! Nevertheless, just like a mother's womb provides the context for the organism of a developing fetus to grow, thus does the Void provide the context for Infinite Consciousness. So in that relationship it may be conceived of as Love.

SYMBOL OF NO-THING

The symbol of the dispersed dashes used to illustrate No-Thing best describes the Void-Based Terrain because literally in the Void there is no 'thing'. The Void is empty and beyond time and space as we perceive them. There is no thing because in the Void there is no charge applied to create any thing. The Void's emptiness is the great cosmic womb that provides context for the singularity of Unity to birth the Infinity of Creation. This is represented by the dashes in the symbol that convey the nothingness inside the space.

EXAMPLES OF NO-THING

It is difficult to find examples of Beings at the Void-Based Terrain, as they do not usually make themselves known to the visible world, so you are unlikely to have ever seen or met one. They are immortal and are not subject to any of the basic laws that the rest of humanity subscribes to, such as gravity, time or space. They are beyond gender, race or age, beyond even Unity or light and beyond Infinite Consciousness. They are simply Presence, without any Self or body.

Note: Such Beings have often been described as 'ascended masters' in the new-age literature and are popularly thought to have 'ascended to the fifth dimension' or beyond. Neither of these notions are being held here.

BIGGER PICTURE OF NO-THING

From the spiritual perspective of Infinite Consciousness as Self, the Void-Based Terrain can be seen as 'The Journey Of Being'. The gifts this Terrain brings are Presence, Being and pure bliss. There is no lesson to learn here, nor are there any challenges.

4

COLLECTIVE TERRAINS

THE TERRAINS OF CIVILIZATIONS

IT IS NOT JUST individual people who have a Terrain Of Consciousness. Groups of people have a *collective* Terrain Of Consciousness too. This applies to nations and, indeed, to entire civilizations.

The collective Terrain of a civilization is known as the 'Prevailing Terrain' of the day. It shapes life in that civilization at that time—at a social, economic, political and cultural level. The Prevailing Terrain is the Terrain that holds the most gravity in the civilization and tends to create the behaviors and beliefs that characterize a particular era.

The Prevailing Terrain sets the perceptual 'lens' that creates all the present cultural norms, values and social practices, as well as the legal system, art, and other collective behaviors in that civilization. When we talk about, for example, 'the Prevailing Terrain of Ancient Rome', we are talking about the Terrain that was the prevailing influence over the entire sphere of life in Rome at that time.

COLLECTIVE GROWTH

Our Collective Self is also on a spiritual journey of expansion through the Ten Terrains, from separation to Unity, just as your individual Self is. Therefore, all cultures and civilizations are moving slowly across the Continuum of Terrains, just as individual people are.

A civilization can move along the Continuum of Terrains through the course of its history, just like a person can move along the Continuum through the course of their life. This happens as the numbers of people at each Terrain change over time. The numbers of people at some Terrains will shrink as people at that Terrain either expand into the next Terrain or die off and are not replaced as fewer people are born into that Terrain. Other Terrains may grow in size as living people expand along the Continuum into these other Terrains, and as more babies are born into these Terrains. This shifting change in the numbers of people at each Terrain combined with the relative impact of each Terrain over the quantum Field will cause the collective awareness of the entire civilization to expand over time, until the Prevailing Terrain actually shifts.

The effect of this expansion by a civilization from one Terrain to the next is similar to the expansion of an individual from one Terrain to the next. Just as an individual expands their individual awareness as they move along the Continuum, so too does a culture or civilization expand its awareness and its consensus reality as it evolves along the Continuum. As the population of that civilization 'awakens' over time, the collective perception expands and the Prevailing Terrain shifts along the Continuum always toward No-Thing's emptiness and Presence.

Therefore at all times, in all ways, humanity is on the move.

WHICH DIRECTION?

During a civilization's lifecycle, its Prevailing Terrain cannot become more constrained, it can only expand. Just like in the case of individuals, once a culture or civilization becomes aware *it cannot become unaware*. Therefore, generally a culture will expand over time across the Continuum of Terrains towards No-Thing.

However, while a particular culture cannot itself devolve or go backwards, it can be replaced or taken over by another culture that is less evolved (such as an indigenous civilization at Circle being conquered and killed off by imperialists at Pyramid). In such a case, a more contracted Terrain will thereafter be prevailing in the same geographical area where the more expanded Terrain once was.

Even without interference, a civilization will inevitably run to the end of its lifecycle, just as a person lives to the end of their life, and then it will either perish completely or morph into a new civilization. The new civilization or culture can have a more contracted Prevailing Terrain than the one that it superseded, just like a person can be reborn at a more contracted Terrain than they lived at in their last lifetime[14]. Therefore at any given point in time, the Terrain in a region may indeed be more contracted than at earlier periods in that region's history, simply because a new, more contracted civilization has arisen in place of a previously more expanded one.

The rise and fall of cultures and civilizations is part of the unfolding play of humanity being written by Infinite Consciousness for the benefit of all Beings here in classroom Earth. Where a culture is at on the Continuum of Terrains at any time is perfect, just as where an individual is at is perfect.

THE INTERSECTION OF THE INDIVIDUAL & THE COLLECTIVE

In any era, there will be some people whose individual Terrain is the same as that of the Prevailing Terrain of the society they are living in, and there will be other people who are less expanded or more expanded than their society.

People who are at the same Terrain as the prevailing culture will always feel themselves to be very 'modern' and on the pulse. To these people who are in sync with the Prevailing Terrain, other people whose Terrains are much more constrained can seem primitive or barbarian. People whose Terrains are a little more constrained can seem to them conservative, old-fashioned and reactionary. People whose Terrain is just ahead of the curve can seem quite progressive and 'counter culture'. People at very expanded Terrains who are far ahead of the curve can seem totally 'out there'.

This has always been the case throughout human history. Terrain is always relative and people always tend to assess the Terrains of others relative to their own and relative to the Prevailing Terrain of that time. For example, when the Prevailing Terrain of Western Europe was shifting from Radial to Pyramid in the 1500s, the people at Square bringing in systems of reserve banking seemed highly innovative and the Renaissance artists and philosophers at Diamond seemed incredibly advanced.

(See *Mastering The Ten Terrains Of Consciousness* for a more thorough discussion of the history of the Western World as it has moved across the Continuum of Terrains. Also see your free eBook *The Terrains Of Famous People In History* to discover the Terrains of individual historical figures in each of those eras.)

WHAT IS OUR SOCIETY'S CURRENT TERRAIN?

Based on our demographic and intuitive research, we estimate that the distribution of people by Terrain in the 'Developed' or 'Western' World as of 2015 is approximately as is set out in the chart on the following page.

As a Western culture as a whole, we made the collective jump from Square to Diamond in approximately 1969. Since then Western society has undergone profound transformation in almost every aspect. There are still many aspects of life in the developed Western World operating under Square systems, such as in the spheres of public education and government; however, these are slowly changing to reflect the new Diamond Terrain.

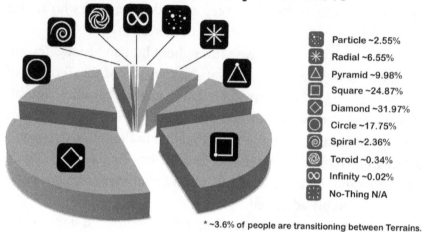

THE DEVELOPED WORLD
Population Distribution By Terrain 2015

Particle ~2.55%
Radial ~6.55%
Pyramid ~9.98%
Square ~24.87%
Diamond ~31.97%
Circle ~17.75%
Spiral ~2.36%
Toroid ~0.34%
Infinity ~0.02%
No-Thing N/A

* ~3.6% of people are transitioning between Terrains.

The Impact Of Our Diamond Prevailing Terrain On Our Western World

Since our collective shift to Diamond, no longer do we in the Western World live in the cookie-cutter world of Square where people work in the same one job for life, where the husband goes to work while the wife stays at home, and where father knows best. People in our Diamond world are now encouraged to think for themselves and follow their dreams, and children are taught that they can grow up to be President or a rock star or anything they want to be.

The 'American Dream' of the 'self made man' (or woman) is a Diamond concept. It is seen today in employees climbing the corporate ladder, in individuals striving to move up the socio-economic ladder, and in entrepreneurial ventures motivated by dreams of wealth, success and fame.

The Diamond success drive fuels the desire in our modern society to continually accumulate 'more', with individuals seeking to amass more personal possessions, corporations striving to increase their 'bottom line', and nations seeking economic growth as an end in itself.

The Diamond desire for freedom has created much of what is great about our Western World. It has brought about huge advances in human rights and social equality. It has created freedom of opportunity and of travel. It allowed sweeping social changes such as the sexual revolution and women's liberation.

One of the biggest game changers of the modern era—the Internet—could only have come about in a Prevailing Terrain of Diamond. People at Diamond inherently resist the mass distribution of information and products from a single centralized, controlled source that exists at Square, preferring widespread access to information and products, individual customization and personal optimization. This has created the modern info-era.

The generic, mass-produced products coming from the production lines of the Square industrial era are starting to be replaced by more personalized, individualized products. We are moving from a world where everyone drives the same T-Model Ford, to a world where people can request their own fully customized car that meets their individual requirements. This move away from standardization to customization is happening in other areas too. Medicine is becoming more individualized, with tests now available to determine a person's exact genetic makeup and blood chemistry so that a personalized treatment plan can be designed. Even in education, that most mass-produced of sectors, people are now able to design their own learning plans online and learn at their own pace.

The power of Diamond visioning combined with the driving Diamond need to be successful and to be celebrated is what has enabled so many cutting edge innovations to sweep our world in recent decades. With the rising numbers of people at Diamond, this re-visioning and re-creation of our world through innovation will continue and continue, until the tide finally turns and the Prevailing Terrain shifts to Circle, at which time the urge for innovation will start to shift towards reconnection, and a return to simpler, more traditional ways of being.

The Diamond Survival Strategy to influence and control the world with the intellect has led to some of the greatest scientific, technological, social and cultural advancements in human history, many of these taking place in the past 50 years. However this same Survival Strategy has also tended to create new technologies—such as GMO foods and nuclear energy—without taking into account moral, health or ecological consequences. The Diamond urge to technologically manipulate and dominate the natural world in the name of 'progress' has had devastating consequences for the environment, food supplies, animal species, human health and the wellbeing of future generations.

One of the reasons why such short-sighted decisions are able to be made by Innovators at Diamond is that, as we saw in the earlier chapter about the Reflection-Based Terrain, 82% of people at Diamond have a 'spiritually-closed orientation'; that is, they only believe in things that they can see with their own eyes and measure with scientific instruments. Lacking a spiritual perspective, their actions are unchecked by any sense of a higher purpose or by any belief in the interconnectedness of all beings.

The *mental* nature of the Reflection-Based Terrain has had many consequences for our modern world. The Diamond need to take in as much information as possible in order to make mental decisions has led to the development of powerful Diamond technologies for mass distribution of information such as the printing press, the telephone, the internet, cell phones and more recent innovations such as YouTube, TED Talks, etc.

On the other hand, the Diamond head-driven way of living is necessarily fast paced, complex and very busy, with activity driven by mental schedules rather than by natural cycles or by the tuning into each moment that comes at the more expanded Terrains. This has created a very hectic, stressful modern world. In addition, the huge need for mental stimulation at Diamond has created a hyper-developed entertainment industry providing infinite methods of mental busy-ness.

The driving Diamond need for one's identity to be reflected en masse has led to a cult of personality and an obsession with celebrity in our Western World. Celebrities have more power and influence than ever before, and are compelling mouthpieces for the 'Powers That Be'. Their daily lives are followed in excessive minutia by both the public and the press. People are no longer just celebrated for their achievements, now they are also famous for simply being famous. Ordinary people dream of being 'discovered' in talent shows and reality TV shows, and of having instant fame and celebrity, even if only for 15 minutes.

The Diamond person's need to influence their world combined with their identification with their convictions means that we have a battle for mindshare taking place today in the Western World. In the Diamond 'marketplace of ideas', the person who is the most persuasive with their opinions wins the most followers, the most acclaim, the biggest market share, the greatest influence and the largest place in the history books.

This also causes the modern phenomenon of the 'guru', that highly influential Diamond Innovator who is so charismatic and certain of his opinion that his magnetism and certainty compels multitudes of Diamond Adopters to follow him. In our modern world, such guru figures—whether personal growth experts, financial thought leaders, fashion icons or spiritual teachers—are taking over the role that 'authority figures' played in the Square world, that tyrannical leaders played in the Pyramid world, and that gods and deities played in the Radial world; giving the large numbers of people at Diamond someone outside themselves to follow.

There are many many more ways that the Prevailing Diamond Terrain has shaped and forged our modern Western culture. We explain these at length in *Mastering The Ten Terrains Of Consciousness*.

BEING OUT OF SYNC

It must be remembered that even though Diamond is our current Prevailing Terrain in the Western World, only approximately 32% of people are actually at Diamond. This means that approximately 68% of people living in the Western World are at Terrains *other than* Diamond. This creates major challenges for the vast majority of people in our world, for they are trying to live in a culture that they are not suited to on the deepest level of their Being.

There are fairly large numbers of people in the Western World at Radial (~6.5%), Pyramid (~10%), Square (~25%), Circle (~18%) and Spiral (~2.5%), whose entire way of seeing reality is out of sync with the prevailing culture they are living in. None of these people sit well with the fast-paced, progress-driven, individualist, urban, technological, consumerist, influence-based and hype-driven culture that surrounds them. Yet this is the civilization they live in, so they must develop a strategy to survive in this world.

The strategy they choose will depend on their Terrain. In today's Diamond world we see people at Radial railing against the decadent, 'ungodly' ways of our modern culture; people at Pyramid trying to exploit the current culture for profit; people at Square trying to find a way to regulate the modern world, and if that doesn't work, to fit into it, even though they feel overwhelmed by it; people at Circle either escaping from or rebelling against the culture; and people at Spiral and beyond sidestepping the culture entirely to create amongst themselves a parallel sandbox to play in.

To find out if YOU are one of these people living out of sync with our modern culture, fill in your Terrain Analysis Questionnaire. The questionnaire results will tell you which Terrain you are at right now. If it turns out that you are at a Terrain other than Diamond, we recommend you read the *Guidebook* for your specific Terrain. Your *Guidebook* will give you strategies to help you live in the Diamond world with less stress and greater ease.

WHAT IS THE GLOBAL TERRAIN?

Interestingly, the distribution of Terrains in the so called 'Developing World'—that is, the world outside our Western commercialized realm—is quite different than here in the Western World, as you will see in the following chart of the estimated percentages at each Terrain:

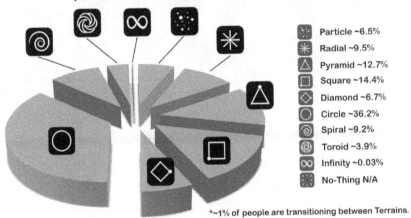

THE DEVELOPING WORLD
Population Distribution By Terrain 2015

Particle ~6.5%
Radial ~9.5%
Pyramid ~12.7%
Square ~14.4%
Diamond ~6.7%
Circle ~36.2%
Spiral ~9.2%
Toroid ~3.9%
Infinity ~0.03%
No-Thing N/A

*~1% of people are transitioning between Terrains.

Taking into account the raw numbers of people at each Terrain, as well as the *power* of each Terrain over the collective quantum Field, relative to the power of all the other Terrains, the Prevailing Terrain in the Developing World is currently the Connection-Based Terrain (Circle).

Given that the Prevailing Terrain of the Developed World is at Diamond, and the prevailing Terrain of the Developing World is at Circle, *where does this leave us as a planet?* The next chart shows the estimated distribution of people by Terrain worldwide.

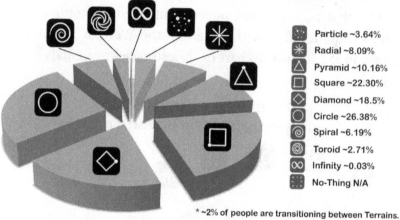

WORLDWIDE
Population Distribution By Terrain 2015

Particle ~3.64%
Radial ~8.09%
Pyramid ~10.16%
Square ~22.30%
Diamond ~18.5%
Circle ~26.38%
Spiral ~6.19%
Toroid ~2.71%
Infinity ~0.03%
No-Thing N/A

* ~2% of people are transitioning between Terrains.

Taking into account the distribution of the entire human population[15] around the world, as well as the power of each Terrain over the collective quantum Field, relative to the power of all the other Terrains, the Prevailing Terrain on planet Earth right now is Circle.

So those of you who are despairing at the state of the planet and worried that we will destroy ourselves... take heart. Infinite Consciousness has things well in hand. The overall collective Field on this planet is at a love-responsive Terrain; therefore, even if those at the fear-reactive Terrains harm Mother Earth in their unconscious pursuit of 'safety', the planet as a whole is in Circle hands energetically and will survive. Life will always win out here in the end, for Love's unity is always more coherent than fear's divisiveness.

HISTORICAL ARROGANCE

What is interesting is that in any civilization, when the enormous shift to a new Prevailing Terrain first happens, people in that society feel like their civilization has become incredibly 'modern', and they cannot imagine a society being any more advanced than theirs is at that time.

For example, when Western Europe shifted from the Will-Based Terrain of the Renaissance to the Order-Based Terrain of the Industrial Revolution, the people of the day thought themselves wonderfully modern and clever, and couldn't imagine anything more advanced than their culture. Similarly, since our culture has shifted recently from Square to Diamond, many people feel that we are the most advanced modern culture ever, and cannot imagine any civilization more advanced than ours. This fallacy causes our modern world to overlook much of the ancient wisdom of previous civilizations.

This kind of historical arrogance is merely a symptom of the fact that neither a person nor a society can see the reality that lies beyond the next evolutionary Event Horizon on the Continuum of Terrains, and therefore will mistakenly assume that their way of being is the most advanced.

CHANGE IS IN THE AIR

There is another phenomenon that happens in any culture as the evolution of Consciousness inevitably continues, as the numbers of people at the more contracted Terrains continue to dwindle and the numbers of people at the more expanded Terrains continue to grow. As the time approaches for the next big Terrain Shift, people in that culture can sense the huge collective Event Horizon that is approaching. It is as if the collective culture becomes restless. There is change in the air and those who are sensitive can feel it.

A similar sense of restlessness can hit a culture as it prepares to leave the comfortable valley of its current Terrain and begin its long journey up the mountain towards the next Terrain. It is this second type of restlessness that many people are feeling right now in our Western culture, for as a collective we are currently in the valley of the Reflection-Based Terrain (Diamond) and are gearing up to begin the long evolutionary trek towards the Connection-Based Terrain (Circle).

While some cities and countries in the Western World are already on the move up the mountain from Diamond to Circle, others are firmly ensconced in the valley of Diamond and yet others are still moving from Square to Diamond. When looked at as a whole, the Prevailing Terrain of our Western World is currently *stationary* in the valley of Diamond, as is illustrated in the diagram on the next page.

Many people in spiritual and new age circles feel that we are currently experiencing a 'Shift' or 'Great Turning'. Yet what they are picking up on is not the shift to Circle. The collective 'Shift' they are sensing is the exciting first stirrings around the edges of our Collective Self as it readies itself to start to move along the Continuum once again, once it has finished having this rich, juicy experience of life at Diamond. Our research anticipates that the Western World will begin its journey up the mountain to Circle within the next 10 years, as more and more children come in[16] at that Terrain. The journey will likely take several decades.

Many of you, who are ahead of the curve, may already be at Circle or may even be at a Terrain beyond that. It is important to be patient and hold space while the rest of the world is going through this important developmental phase at Diamond. As a culture, we cannot shift to the next Terrain until we have completed our collective learning at our current Terrain. All Terrain Shifts happen when they are meant to.

Eventually, we will indeed make the collective jump to the Connection-Based Terrain. This is is the next shift in store for our Western World. This will not be the first great shift in consciousness that we have faced as a society, nor will it be the last. The jump from Diamond to Circle is simply *one* of the huge quantum shifts that all societies face as they journey along the Continuum of Terrains. Yet it is a major shift, for it is the shift from the head to the Heart. As such, it will completely and radically transform our world.

WHAT WE CAN DO TO HELP

Those of you who are Diamond Cultural Creatives already moving towards Circle or who are at the Terrains beyond Diamond may be working hard to try to 'shift' the culture in order to try to force the next collective Terrain jump. This will be an especially strong urge for those of you who are at Circle and who are anxious to bring our civilization back into harmony with the Earth.

However, until the Collective Self of our civilization is ready to cross the next Event Horizon, all of this energy is futile. Just as you can't convince or persuade or otherwise make an individual person jump Terrains before their individual Self is ready to do so, you cannot make a culture jump Terrains until its Collective Self is ready to do so.

Yet... there is plenty you can do (and be) that is even MORE effective in the long run!

Instead of trying to destroy the existing institutions, another approach is to give gratitude to them, cradling them with Love as they inevitably pass away. For they will pass away. Remember that they are not evil—they have merely played their part in the unfolding story of Consciousness.

For those of you at Spiral and beyond it is easier for you to believe in the Infinite Intelligence of Consciousness and trust that it has the collective evolution of all the civilizations on this planet in hand, as it always has had and always will have. Those of you at Circle may find the waiting and trusting a little more challenging. However, there are things you can be actively 'doing' in the world, while our Collective Self is preparing our evolutionary way behind the scenes.

A fantastic thing to do is to stop trying to destroy the mainstream sandbox, and instead start building a new alternative sandbox and start playing a new game there. You can play a part in building heart-centered Circle communities and modeling what it is like to live a simple modern life in harmony with the Earth. You can play a part in developing new alternative money systems, food systems, collaborative resource pools, free energy devices, etc. Even more importantly, instead of wasting energy trying to change individuals in the mainstream who aren't yet ready to shift, you can spend your energy welcoming those who have newly arrived into Circle and helping them find their way.

But the most important point is to be PATIENT. Our research indicates that the Prevailing Terrain in the Developed World is most likely to shift from Diamond to Circle in the 2050s. That is still 40 years away. Do not be disheartened about this! This may feel like a long time to wait, but taking into account the broad sweep of human history, it is merely the blink of an eye.

Furthermore, what we must remember is that with every year that passes, there will be more and more people living at the Connection-Based Terrain. These rising numbers of people at Circle will need to be *supported*. Many of them will have been at Circle from childhood, yet they will find themselves living in a Diamond world. They will need guidance on how to stay true to themselves and to their Connection-Based values in a world that they are new to and may not yet fully understand. They will be looking to those at Circle or Spiral to provide a role model for this.

There will also be many people who in the course of their lifetime will make the epic jump across the Event Horizon from Diamond into Circle. These people too will need our support, as they struggle to understand what has happened to them, why their values have changed so radically, and why they no longer fit into the life they have built for themselves. These growing numbers of love-responsive people will need new networks and new systems to support them, as they move into a heart-centered, earth-friendly, community-focused lifestyle. The bottom-line is, the business and growth opportunities for the coming decades are ones focused on ushering people on the move from Diamond to Circle and supporting them in the transition once they arrive there.

So do not lose faith! There is much work to be done in the next few decades and much good that we can do now, if we set aside our urge to change the world by force of will and instead act as mentors and midwives to support those who are already shifting. Then when the Collective Self is ready to jump, those of us who are on the planet at that time will have the opportunity to individually and collectively take responsibility and seize the moment as we all collectively jump to a new paradigm.

EXPONENTIAL GROWTH

As a person or civilization shifts along the Continuum, the pace of change starts to speed up. This is because the Continuum of Terrains Of Consciousness itself plots along a Bell Curve. As we move along the Continuum, the progressively expanding nature of each Terrain creates an exponentially greater accelerating potential to shift to the next Terrain beyond it in a shorter span of time (because there is progressively less resistance as you approach Unity). This applies just as much to Collective Terrains as it does to Individual Terrains.

Therefore, the collective shift in the Western World from Diamond to Circle will happen much more quickly than did the shift from Square to Diamond, which was quicker than the shift from Pyramid to Square, which was quicker than the shift from Radial to Pyramid. Yet it will still take as long as it will take. We cannot speed it up by force of will.

In *Mastering The Ten Terrains Of Consciousness* we include a much longer discussion of Collective Terrains. Among other things, we discuss how the Prevailing Terrain of a civilization is calculated and determined; the complex correlation between the Prevailing Terrain and the power distribution in the civilization; the mechanics by which the Prevailing Terrain can change, as the civilization evolves and expands its awareness; and much more. Make sure to study this full body of work, if the collective aspect of the Ten Terrains Of Consciousness fascinates you.

COLLECTIVE SYSTEMS

WHEN ENOUGH PEOPLE gather at the same Terrain, particular kinds of systems start to emerge amongst those people. We see this playing out in nations and civilizations at different Terrains, particularly in the kinds of political systems that emerge.

The following chapter will briefly discuss the kinds of systems that tend to emerge at each Terrain, as a collective expression of its fundamental perception of Consciousness. We explore these systems more deeply in *Mastering The Ten Terrains Of Consciousness*.

MATTER-BASED SYSTEMS

There is *no* collective expression of the Matter-Based Terrain. Indeed, there is no government or system at all governing life at this Terrain.

This lack of a collective system is not the same as the kind of anarchy and lawlessness that occurs when societies collapse and everything reverts for a time to a kind of chaotic, dog-eat-dog behavior. The lack of a collective system at Particle is not a temporary dissolution of government in response to an emergency situation; it is a way of life.

At Particle, everyone is out for his own survival, with no alliances, allegiances, laws, groups or agreements of any kind. There is no underlying longing for order or even a belief that any kind of system will be helpful. Remember, at Particle, man doesn't even believe it is possible to survive. There is no strategy or solution here other than a moment-to-moment reaction to life.

In short, there is no collective system at Particle, as such a system simply cannot form with this kind of relationship to reality.

FAITH-BASED SYSTEMS

The collective expression of Radial can be seen in the system of 'ecclesiocracy'.

Ecclesiocracy is a form of government in which a man or body of men rule over the people in the name of a particular deity. In an ecclesiocracy we either have rule by people who claim to have been given divine authority to interpret, apply and enforce laws given to them by their 'god' or 'gods', or rule by people who see themselves as being divine rulers in their own right and thereby having unlimited power and superiority over the masses.

The first of these two kinds of Radial rule tends to lead to large religious organizations administered by clergy who claim themselves to be keepers of the doctrine of the god(s) they follow. Early Judaism and the Roman Catholic church provide well known examples of this. The second type of Radial rule tends to lead to cult leaders who claim to be divinely ordained and gain large numbers of adherents who wholly devote themselves to their dogma. Historical examples of deified Radial leaders include many pharaohs in ancient Egypt, such as Pharaoh Ramesses II The Great.

The population at Radial is living collectively in a state of fear of the world around them, and perceive that their safety will be gained by pleasing supernatural forces. Thus, the Radial system of ecclesiocracy aims to maintain a favorable relationship with these forces or gods, or at least to *look like* it is doing so. One of the chief ways it does this is to institute regular ceremonies, ritual and rites, which have ranged throughout history from the most benign all the way through to animal and human sacrifice. Such rituals and ceremonies are necessary to keep up the appearance of pleasing the gods, and to thereby assure the congregation of their continued safety and good graces. This keeps the system of ecclesiocracy functioning.

WILL-BASED SYSTEMS

Collective systems that we have identified as being Will-Based at their core are systems like dictatorship, tyranny, feudalism, monarchy and empire, all of which place one person—a dictator, tyrant, Lord, King or Emperor—in a position of power, able to exert their will over their subjects at their own capricious whim. They are not subject to law or to other checks and balances, but instead have total power over their dominion. Even when the ruler is overthrown, he will be replaced by another equally power-hungry or power-wielding leader. This kind of regime was best satirized in George Orwell's famous book 'Animal Farm', where the Square communist ideals of the characters are slowly corrupted over time into pure Pyramid tyranny.

As we have already said, another collective system that will often emerge in a Pyramid culture is that of slavery. Here, those at the base of the pyramid are exploited and treated as sub-human, to force them to serve the masters at the top. The entire system of slavery is a hierarchical structure ruled by fear, and it cannot survive once a civilization shifts to Square.

Another, more insidious, collective expression of Pyramid is the system known as Oligarchy: the ruling of a civilization by a small group, a 'hidden hand' of powerful elites. This is the league of the most powerful men and families who pull the strings behind the scenes and orchestrate and manipulate much of what is currently happening on our planet. The hidden system of Oligarchy is running, manipulating and profiting from all the other systems of government in operation around the world, be they Radial, Square, Diamond or Circle. This is the most pervasive system of government on this planet, and always has been.

ORDER-BASED SYSTEMS

The Order-Based Terrain is the Terrain of *'the system'*, therefore there are more points to discuss here in relation to collective systems than at the other nine Terrains.

Keeping The System Running

The Order-Based Terrain is the most highly organized of all the 10 Terrains at a collective level. It is at Square that we see both the organization of the masses and things organized en masse. It is here that we find mass administration, mass bureaucracy, mass education systems and mass armies.

At Square, those running 'the system' need to control everyone in it in order to keep the system running smoothly. Strategies such as codification, regulation, centralization, administration, homogenization, standardization, replication, mass distribution, globalization, institutionalization and bureaucracy are used to ensure that everyone in the system acts the same way, so that they will function together smoothly like cogs in a machine.

The Order-Based Terrain is all about *the State*. Here we see the emergence of State institutions and State systems of distribution. At Square we find things such as a central body of law, a central Constitution, a central Government, central banks, central power generation, central reservoirs of water and central control of public utilities.

Everyone is subject to the same rules in the Square world. Punishment is seen to be metered out fairly—whether by the legal system, church, corporation, or parent—and justice must always be seen to be done. This ensures that the citizens do not rebel and that the system continues to run smoothly. While the system may be strict, it also must project itself to be fair. This is farm management, not dictatorship.

Policing and law enforcement keep the Square system functioning. Enforcement of Square order is fairly easy amongst the large numbers of people who are themselves at the Order-Based Terrain, for a number of reasons. Those at Square are generally self-monitoring and self-policing; they tend to feel guilty when they break the law or stray from social norms; they are obedient and follow authority without question; and they are easily influenced by central propaganda, especially when a climate of fear is created to make them look to their government to feel safe.

However, enforcement of Square order amongst people at the other nine Terrains is not so easy. Keeping them under control requires more extreme measures. This tension is the source of the classic Square policing and enforcement bodies that range from the hall monitor and the neighborhood watch through to the police force, the border patrol, the national security agencies, the National Guard, all branches of the military, NATO, and the United Nations Peace Keepers, etc. Regardless of their scope, all of these policing bodies generally play the same role in keeping people who are not at Square in line with the Square system.

Political Systems

Politically, the systems that are collective expressions of the Order-Based Terrain are those that are set up to organize large numbers of people according to consistently applied rules—such as the constitutional republic, two-party representative democracy, classic communism[17], and state capitalism.

While the nature of the distribution of wealth and the decision-making processes may be different in each of the above systems, they are all coming from the fundamental perception that we need a well-organized mass system of government that operates consistently for everyone in our wider group. In each of these cases, all citizens have tacitly consented by social contract to allow 'the system' to govern them in return for protection from that system. In all these systems, the people have given their power for policy decision-making over to authority figures, rather than taking direct responsibility for it themselves.

When enforcement of any of the above systems is taken to the extreme, the shadow side of Square takes over. This is collectively expressed in the systems of totalitarianism and fascism.

Leadership

Political leadership is different at Square than at the Terrains next to it. Leaders at Square generally believe themselves to be working for the highest good of the majority. This is the Terrain of chivalry and knights of the round table. It is the Terrain of the gentleman and the statesman. And it is above all the Terrain of the public servant or civil servant.

This is in contrast to Pyramid, where those in political office are there to accumulate their own personal power, or are minions put in place to fearfully carry out the dictates of those behind them who are accumulating power. It is also in contrast to Diamond, where we find the career politician who is in office for his own fame and glory, delighting in the use of his talents and genius, pushing himself to excel and grow. At Square the leader is not there for power nor for glory or growth, but to serve his country.

REFLECTION-BASED SYSTEMS

An example of a Square system on the move to Diamond is the multi-party democracy found in many European countries, where representatives are elected by Proportional Representation, and there are no electorates. Here, small parties who would never have the financial power to get a member elected in a two party ('duocratic') system now have a chance to get their members elected and to be part of a government, albeit usually a coalition of multiple parties. This is a much more level playing field, with more freedom and greater opportunity all around, than is the duocracy that is a closed shop to all but the highest paying special interest groups. Therefore it is an example of a Square collective system on the move to Diamond.

However, a multi-party democracy is still a representative form of government, and as such it is still at Square. A truly Diamond system would be a 'Direct Democracy', where every person is able to vote on every issue at every stage, such as was found in Ancient Greece. Such systems are starting to appear in other areas of the modern world outside the political sphere, such as in the direct decision-making styles emerging in the corporate world, vertical marketing in the consumer sphere and even the real time voting via apps by viewers during reality television shows. Now that the Prevailing Terrain in the Western World is at Diamond, there is a greater scope for such systems to begin to appear in our political arena too.

A truly Diamond process of this kind would require people to take greater responsibility than happens at Square, for in order for people to be able to have a meaningful say on all issues, they would need to make sure they were educated and up to date on all issues. As you will start to realize as you read through this chapter, each Terrain on the Continuum requires a greater degree of Self-responsibility than the last, as governance moves from disempowerment to empowerment.

CONNECTION-BASED SYSTEMS

A simple way to describe the collective system of The Connection-Based Terrain is to call it 'Heart Community'. This is in contrast to 'communalism', which is a collective system used by groups of people who have not yet expanded to Circle, one based in shared ownership, rather than in Love.

In the Circle system of 'Heart Community' there is a focus on relationships and collaboration, and people treat each other from a place of honor, respect and Love. The system is based not on shared ownership, but on 'resource pooling', which means putting together the available resources of every participant to yield a greater synergy; a whole greater than the sum of the parts. For such a community to work it requires that each member deeply value and honor each other's offerings.

The focus in Heart Community is not on individual achievement, competition or supporting the vision of an individual person, like at Diamond, but on collaboration and cooperation towards a common vision. Those at Circle intuitively know that the synergy of collaboration brings about greater results than striving towards something by oneself.

As we have seen, the Circle way of relating is built on dialogue, cooperation and building relationships. Organizations and projects at this Terrain are therefore structured laterally rather than hierarchically. Where there are leaders at Circle, they operate more as facilitators than as rulers or law makers. Decisions are made by the community or group as a whole by consensus, with everyone given a chance to speak and be heard.

The greater whole created by a Circle Heart Community creates a collective 'Field', and that Field is one of Love that feeds back and infuses the members of the community to generate even more synergy and Love. Such communities are popping up all over the world now among pockets of conscious people, and are providing a new model for civilization that will serve well as we in the Developed World collectively start to move from the current Prevailing Terrain of Diamond towards Circle.

COHERENCE-BASED SYSTEMS

The collective expression of the Coherence-Based Terrain is the system known as 'synarchy'. In contrast to hierarchy, in synarchy everyone's role is distinct and equally valuable, and everyone works together for a higher purpose. Think of an orchestra, where each participant performs the role best suited to them, whether that be violinist, flautist, or cymbal player, with no one being considered more valuable than anyone else. People follow the conductor not because he is considered superior to them or because he is in a position of authority, but because conducting is his true talent, just like playing the cello is the true talent of the cellist. He leads in Service to the whole.

The system of synarchy is indeed like a philharmonic orchestra. More than the 'all for one and one for all' refrain at Circle, at Spiral each person is 'in tune' with the part they play best. Because each person at Spiral is in coherence with their own individual unique truth, the value they bring to the group is more potent, for each person is a 'prodigy' in their own right. With everybody working together in synarchy, all towards a shared purpose, here the sum is vastly greater than its parts.

Awakening at Spiral to one's coherence in the overall fractal of Creation involves the death of the illusion of one's individuality separate from all others. The moment a person gives up their egoic individuation for the betterment of the whole, that is when true synergy is created. Therefore, a true system of synarchy will only flourish on this planet when there are large numbers of people living at the Coherence-Based Terrain, all of them Self-responsible and Self-loving enough to recognize their own unique energetic contribution and with enough awareness of Unity to be able to participate in a oneness of purpose and a oneness of action that allows their individuality to start to dissolve.

FRACTAL-BASED SYSTEMS

What might a collective system look like at the Fractal-Based Terrain? There are no examples of this yet living and flourishing in our world, so here we have to turn to our imagination and extrapolate out from what we know of Toroid, based on Universal Principles.

We know that such a system would be based on trust, on full Self-responsibility, on the interrelatedness of the quantum Field, on being in full co-creative collaboration with life, and on each person offering their unique Gift in true Service.

A likely expression of this would be a global gifting system where gifts would be given freely, with no expectation of return or recompense at any future point. Gifts of talents, services and money would be given simply for the joy of giving and for the joy of being in Service, without any thought as to how or when or even *if* they would ever be reciprocated.

In this system, not only would gifts be absolutely freely given with no strings attached, but they would also be freely *received* with no guilt or obligation felt to give in return. The recipients of the gifts would need to be equally Self-loving and giving. The loop would self-perpetuate, for everyone in the system would be coming from the same joyful, Self-loving, freely-giving place of trust in Infinite Consciousness I AM.

For such a system to work, all the participants would need to be at the Fractal-Based Terrain, for they would each have to be able to genuinely let go of all expectations, limiting beliefs and scarcity consciousness. They would also have to be able to let go of hoping or praying for recompense, and of micro-managing Infinite Consciousness in any way (each of which puts a charge force into the Field, thus blocking free flow). Only those at Toroid or beyond can truly do this: let go of every shred or speck of doubt or expectation, knowing the Universal Truth that the Field is a closed loop system.

It will only be when a global network of people at Toroid emerges, who honestly can walk the talk of reciprocal Self Love by giving of their Self with no expectation of recompense and receiving with a fully open Heart, that we will see a real Toroid collective system on this planet. Given that, at this point, only 0.4% of people in the Western World are at Toroid and most of these people are not yet connected to each other, that day is likely to be far off.

UNITY-BASED SYSTEMS

The core Infinity principles of being in complete Unity and coherence throughout all dimensions with one's Self as Infinite Consciousness have not yet emerged into a collective expression in our world. This is because at this time in history, the numbers of people living at the Unity-Based Terrain are so low (only 0.02% of people in the Developed World) as to make it unfeasible.

But what kind of collective system would emerge if the Prevailing Terrain were at Infinity? In an Infinity society all people would experience themselves as One with everybody else. There would be no separation of any kind in interactions. Each person would see all life as being his own Self. Each person would be fully Self-responsible, Self-loving and Sovereign.

In an Infinity society there would be no need for any form of external 'governance'. Like the cells in our body all working together to reach out our arm or think a thought, a society at Infinity would be a fully 'Self-healing' system. In such a system each person would be a node and all nodes would be intermeshed as one Consciousness, thereby always and immediately responding in whatever way is required to bring the Field into infinite wholeness, meaning there are no 'charge force' points that 'poke out from' the collective fabric. In other words, everything would smooth itself out automatically, as a reflex. If any point of contention were to temporarily develop—such as two people getting into an argument and polarizing into 'us vs them'—the event would quickly soften and each person would recognize and pull back their energy (the charge force they each have put toward the other on the matter) and would 'Self-heal' the shadow aspect within themselves that created the flare-up in the first place.

In the collective systems currently in place in our world there are the police, the judge and the jury enforcing the law; the social workers doing rehabilitation; and the anger management trainings and other self-help approaches enabling people to reach forgiveness of others and of themselves. In a Prevailing Terrain at Infinity, that whole cycle of outer events would happen automatically and instantaneously within each of us.

In an Infinity society, there would be no need for any of the outer bureaucracy we see now. There would be no need for licensing of any kind, nor for permits, taxes or any other form of outer government 'privilege', for all privilege would be given to oneself from within, with the attendant responsibility that goes with such privilege. Thus, you would not need a fishing license to fish, as you would never over-fish the rivers or oceans enough to cause an undue ecological imbalance, because the ocean and river are YOU. The same would apply in regards to global warming. The entire collective of humanity would each and equally pare back their consumption to yield the net result of our global system being kept in balance.

This kind of system that would emerge collectively on our planet in a Prevailing Terrain of Infinity can best be described by the word 'Beinghood'. Beinghood represents what life would be like if we were all living at the Unity-Based Terrain. If everyone stepped into their Beinghood, all coming together as one Beinghood, we would have a world based on Unity, unconditional Love, Heart connection, higher Knowing, true freedom, Sovereignty and Self-responsibility.

'Beinghood' is a word that was coined by Allen David Reed and Tahnee Woolf in early 2012. You can read the full definition of the word 'Beinghood' at www.beinghood.com. And to help you visualize what life as a Beinghood might be like, read the inspiring 'Proclamation of Beinghood', also at www.beinghood.com.

VOID-BASED SYSTEMS

Collective Systems are not applicable at the Void-Based Terrain, as this is the realm of immortals and they are beyond needing the collective systems of humanity.

This is the polar opposite of what we see at Particle down at the other end of the Continuum of Terrains, where there is a lack of government because people are not yet at an evolutionary point where they can even conceive of a collective strategy with which to organize their lives. Here at No-Thing, there is no collective system because there is simply no need for one. There is no 'thing' to be managed or controlled or organized. There is only BEING.

5

FIND OUT MORE

LEARN MORE

AFTER EVERYTHING you have read in this introductory book, you must be eager to find out your own Terrain!

You may already have a *sense* of which Terrain you are at from what you have read here. Or perhaps you are trying to choose between two different Terrains, that both seem to apply to you. Completing your Terrain Analysis Questionnaire will help you confirm which Terrain truly is your current Terrain.

Finding out your Terrain will help you to understand so much about yourself. You will finally know:

- ♦ WHY you are living the life you are living.
- ♦ WHY you are drawn to the things and people you are drawn to.
- ♦ WHY you are facing the challenges you are facing.
- ♦ WHY you are making the choices you are making.
- ♦ WHY you get along with some people and not others.
- ♦ WHERE you are on your spiritual evolutionary journey and where you will be heading next.

You can fill out the Terrain Analysis Questionnaire right now on your computer, at www.tenterrains.com. After you complete your Terrain Analysis Questionnaire, you will receive a report with an assessment of which Terrain you are at. You will then be able to get the specific *Guidebook* for your Terrain, which contains crucial material to help you navigate life at your Terrain.

Once you have done your Terrain Analysis Questionnaire, we will also tell you how you can connect with *other people* at your Terrain, around the world. We let you know about Terrain-specific groups on social media and in online forums, so that you can meet people who see the world the way *you* do.

So go and fill out your Terrain Analysis Questionnaire right now! See how many pieces start falling into place for you once you have this crucial information about yourself.

FREE OFFERINGS

If you would like to learn more about the Ten Terrains Of Consciousness, we explain this Model in many live and online presentations, articles, videos, interviews, workshops and other spoken and visual media. You can find out more about these at www.tenterrains.com.

In addition, make sure to check out the 'Ten Terrains' YouTube Channel, where we post many short entertaining videos explaining this Model. We share a range of different types of videos there, including: profound interviews with thought leaders from the different Terrains; fascinating discussions about how the Terrains apply to current events and politics; fun animations teaching the Ten Terrains concepts; entertaining presentations about the Terrains in famous movies, books and TV shows; in depth Q&As where we answer YOUR questions; and much more... This is a fun way to learn about the Terrains!

The more of this material you absorb, the more thoroughly you will come to understand the Ten Terrains Model and the better you will be able to use it to navigate the world you live in.

GUIDEBOOKS

For those of you who wish to learn more about your specific Terrain than the basic points we have covered in this introductory book, we have written a detailed 'Terrain Guidebook' for each Terrain. These are available at www.tenterrains.com. Once you have done the Terrain Analysis Questionnaire and found out your Terrain, we suggest that you read the specific Guidebook for your Terrain, as it contains invaluable material for you.

Each of the Terrain Guidebooks contain very different material, as they are designed specially for people at their target Terrain. Each Guidebook has been written from the perspective of that Terrain, with concepts explained in the way that is easiest to understand at that Terrain, using the language of that Terrain.

In your Guidebook we give you many tips and strategies to help you navigate life at your current Terrain. We go into far more detail about the unique challenges and gifts of your Terrain and the lessons you are here to learn at this point in your spiritual journey. We go through the different stages of the evolutionary journey up the mountain from your Terrain to the next one, so that you can recognize exactly where you are at right now. We give you strategies to help you get along better with people at the other 9 Terrains. We help you understand how your Terrain fits into the modern Western culture so that you can feel more at home in our world. And much more!

Your Terrain Guidebook is an invaluable resource for you, so make the most of it! It is offered to you from our Heart in the hope that it will both make your life easier and bring greater harmony to our world.

PRACTICAL PAMPHLETS

We will soon be offering a series of *Terrain Mapping Pamphlets*. In these short pamphlets, we will list the Terrains of different health, healing and medical modalities; relationship and sexuality modalities; personal growth modalities; spiritual traditions and approaches; exercise and body movement modalities; nutritional and diet approaches; and popular songs and music styles.

These practical pamphlets will help you find products, services, approaches and modalities at YOUR Terrain so that they will be right for YOU at this point in your life.

It is always best to use modalities and processes that are coming from your specific Terrain and that are designed for people at your Terrain. However, if you are are already moving towards the next Terrain, then it can also be helpful to explore approaches and modalities from the Terrain you are approaching, in order to help prepare you for your next big evolutionary leap. So you might also choose to take a look at the *Terrain Mapping Pamphlets* for the Terrain immediately beyond your own.

Although it can sometimes be helpful to explore approaches and techniques that are at Terrains far from your own, there is usually a more powerful impact when they are coming from your own Terrain or the next Terrain you are approaching, as they will be more in alignment with where you are at now and with the life teachings you are to experience here.

If you would like to be notified when the *Terrain Mapping Pamphlets* are available, please go to the following webpage and put your name down: www.tenterrains.com/notify-me.

GOING DEEPER

This entire Model is set out very comprehensively in our groundbreaking, deeper body of work, *Mastering The Ten Terrains Of Consciousness*. This is the foundational material you need to study in order to fully understand this model. It explains everything we have hinted at in this introductory book in far more detail, covering over 1000 pages of content.

In *Mastering The Ten Terrains Of Consciousness* you will learn *much more* about the things we have covered in this book. We discuss each of the 10 Terrains in far greater detail, exploring many additional aspects of them that we did not cover here. You will develop a much deeper understand of exactly what differentiates each Terrain from the other, and the evolutionary purpose of each one.

In *Mastering The Ten Terrains*, we also cover in much greater detail how each Terrain plays out in people of different spiritual orientations and with different sets of cultural values such as 'Cultural Creatives', 'Traditional' and 'Moderns'. We look much more deeply at how each Terrain plays out in collective and political systems. We set out more thoroughly the kinds of instances where someone appears to be at one Terrain but really is at a different Terrain and instances where someone really is at one Terrain but displays behaviors from another Terrain. We also look at the challenges a person can face when they shift from one Terrain to the next and the difficulties that people at each Terrain can face when interacting with people of other Terrains.

Mastering The Ten Terrains Of Consciousness also covers deeper topics that we have not touched on in this introductory book, such as the mechanics of how a person changes Terrain; the relative 'bleed through' that happens between Terrains; the details of collective evolution through the Continuum; and many other factors that can influence a person's evolutionary journey. We also share a lot more about the symbology of the Ten Terrains.

Mastering The Ten Terrains Of Consciousness provides a comprehensive grounding in the Ten Terrains Model. Studying this material will enable you to clearly recognize each Terrain of Consciousness when you see them playing out in the people and situations around you, to spot them playing out in the political sphere and on the world stage, and to have a profound understanding of your own Terrain and how it influences every aspect of your life. It is a very deep study, perfect for those of you who are true *seekers*, wanting to really understand life on this planet at a profound level.

We will be releasing *Mastering The Ten Terrains Of Consciousness* as an online course in the coming year. If you would like to be notified when this course is available, please put your name down here: www.tenterrains.com/notify-me.

ADVANCED LEARNING

For those who have studied *Mastering The Ten Terrains Of Consciousness*, we will soon be offering a series of advanced booklets: *The Ten Terrains Of Consciousness Applied*. These booklets will illustrate how the Ten Terrains play out in specific areas of human life, such as health, relationships, sex, money, politics, personal growth, science, the environment, art, pop culture, and death.

We are also in the process of writing two additional full-length books that provide further information and learning about the Ten Terrains for those who have studied *Mastering The Ten Terrains Of Consciousness*. In the first of these advanced books, *Resolve Conflict—Using The 10 Terrains Of Consciousness*, we explain how so much of the conflict in our world—both interpersonal and political conflict—is caused by differences in Terrain. We explore how people at the different Terrains handle conflict. And we share with you how you can better resolve conflict, from whatever Terrain you are at, so as to create both a peaceful life for yourself and a more peaceful world.

In the second of these advanced books, *Understand Evolution—Using The 10 Terrains Of Consciousness*, we explain the more esoteric principles that underlie the Ten Terrains Of Consciousness Model. This book is essentially a journey into the deep mysteries. We explain in far greater detail the mechanics of the evolution of Consciousness, both at an individual and collective level. We discuss such things as the pole shift in perception of Consciousness that lies at the heart of this Model, the spiritual trajectory of Consciousness towards Unity, and the nature of contraction and expansion of Consciousness. We also discuss how babies come into this world and 'settle' at a particular Terrain, and the complex of factors including karma, genetic lineage, past life history and more that contributes to a person's unique 'Geometry' in this lifetime and which sets them on their own particular 'train ride' through the Continuum of Terrains.

If you would like to be notified when the *The Ten Terrains Of Consciousness Applied* series of booklets or the advanced books *Resolve Conflict—Using The 10 Terrains Of Consciousness* and *Understand Evolution—Using The 10 Terrains Of Consciousness* are available, please go to the following webpage and put your name down: www.tenterrains.com/notify-me. We will let you know as soon as these books are released.

TERRAIN MAPPING™

We have given a name to the process of identifying the Terrains of people, groups and phenomena. We call it Terrain Mapping™. Terrain Mapping is the method used to assess which Terrain Of Consciousness someone or something is at, at a particular point in time, and then to analyze the implications of that for people and for our world.

Terrain Mapping can be used for many different things. As we have already shared, you can map your own Terrain by completing your Terrain Analysis Questionnaire. Your family and friends can also map their Terrains using the questionnaire. Terrain Mapping can also be used to accurately pinpoint the Terrains of world leaders, celebrities and other public figures. In addition, Terrain Mapping can be used to pinpoint the Prevailing Terrains of different kinds of groups, such as families, communities, cultures, organizations, companies and civilizations. Finally, Terrain Mapping can be used to map the Terrain of conceptual phenomena, such as ideas, political systems, products, books, movies, works of art, historical events, cultural trends, etc.

In order to *accurately* do Terrain Mapping you need to have a deep understanding of the Ten Terrains Of Consciousness Model. Simply reading this introductory book is NOT enough.

Of course, the more you read about the Ten Terrains Of Consciousness, the more videos you watch about it, the more you think about it, and the more you play with applying it to the world around you, the more you will come to understand the Ten Terrains Model. Over time, you will start to get a feel for which Terrain other people around you are coming from, and you will begin to get a rough idea of the Terrains of people, groups, current events, situations and more subtle phenomena.

However, for *real accuracy* in mapping Terrains, you will need to study the full foundational material contained in *Mastering The Ten Terrains Of Consciousness*. That comprehensive body of work explains each of the Ten Terrains in great detail and also explains all the evolutionary principles underlying the entire Ten Terrains Model.

If you are not inclined to study the Ten Terrains Model in great detail yourself, you will soon be able to engage the services of a certified Terrain Mapper™ and ask them to map the Terrain of the person, situation, idea, or group that you are interested in. Terrain Mappers have completed extensive training in the Ten Terrains Of Consciousness Model and are deeply learned in the full foundational material. They will not only be able to tell you which Terrain is operating in the case you are interested in, but also how it is expressing itself in behaviors, choices, dynamics, conflict and other implications. In addition, they will be able to help you *use* this knowledge of Terrains to improve the situation that concerns you, whether that is your relationship, your business, your health, or your projects, etc.

Whether you yourself come to learn how to map the Terrains playing out in the world around you by studying the full foundational material, or you hire a Terrain Mapper to help you with that, the knowledge you will gain from mapping the Terrains of the world around you is *invaluable*. You can use that knowledge to enhance your relationships, your business success, your health, your understanding of the world, your personal growth, your spiritual evolution, your global impact, and much much more.

You can read more about the many applications of Terrain Mapping at www.tenterrains.com. Terrain Mapping is a powerful tool that, when applied, can help you come to deeply understand, navigate and master your world. Use it wisely!

Terrain Mapping Training

For those of you who wish to go even further with this Model and *use it in your own work*, you may wish to complete the 'Terrain Mapping Certification Program'.

This training program will certify you as a Terrain Mapper™, allow you to advertise yourself as an expert in the Ten Terrains Of Consciousness Model and will qualify you to use the Terrain Analysis Questionnaire with your clients.

The training program will immerse you thoroughly in the deep teachings found in *Mastering The Ten Terrains Of Consciousness* and will give you an incredibly profound understanding of the Model. It will train you in how to apply the Model to people, groups, political events, situations, interpersonal dynamics, ideas, products, and systems, etc., so that you can advise your clients in every aspect of their lives and their business.

This training program is invaluable for anyone who is a coach, counselor, analyst, strategic adviser, teacher, journalist, marketer, researcher, psychologist, writer, artist, health professional, mediator, change agent, activist, or anyone who is simply a passionate student of human nature! You can read more about the Terrain Mapping Certification Program at www.tenterrains.com.

If you would like to be notified when the Programs are starting, please put your name down here: www.tenterrains.com/notify-me.

CHECK IN

As you can see, we have many new educational offerings in the pipelines, all designed to help you understand the Ten Terrains Model more completely and to apply it to your life more fully. We will be rolling out the above-mentioned booklets, pamphlets, advanced books, online courses and training programs over the next few years, with some of them coming out very soon.

So please check in regularly at www.tenterrains.com to see what is newly available. And if anything in particular interests you *now*, make sure to go to the following webpage and put your name down: www.tenterrains.com/notify-me. We will notify you as soon as that offering is available.

BE PART OF THE TEN TERRAINS CONVERSATION

A S MORE AND MORE PEOPLE are learning about the Ten Terrains Of Consciousness Model, a very exciting conversation is beginning to grow around the world. Here are some ways YOU can be part of it.

FOLLOW THE TEN TERRAINS ON SOCIAL MEDIA

We post lots of interesting examples and illustrations of the 10 Terrains on Twitter and on our Facebook page. This is a really easy, fun way to continue learning about the Terrains. So make sure to *like* and *follow* 'Ten Terrains'!

→ www.twitter.com/TenTerrains
→ www.facebook.com/TenTerrains

Social media is also a great place to share YOUR discoveries about the Ten Terrains and to find other people who are interested in these ideas. Tweet your thoughts and insights about the Terrains on Twitter; post your realizations about the Terrains on your Facebook page; leave comments and share pics. Soon you will be part of fascinating conversations with like minded, like-hearted people from around the world!

Make sure to include the hashtag #TenTerrains in all your posts on social media, so that your posts become part of the online conversation and others can read them who are interested in the Ten Terrains.

SUBSCRIBE TO THE TEN TERRAINS YOUTUBE CHANNEL

Watch fascinating free videos, and take part in inspiring discussions!

→ www.youtube.com/c/TenTerrains

Go to our channel and click 'Subscribe', to make sure you see all our fascinating videos as soon as they are released. Our videos range from discussions, to Q&As, to animations, to interviews and much more! This is a fun, easy way to keep learning about the Ten Terrains.

JOIN OUR MAILING LIST

Our regular newsletter contains a selection of our best videos, articles and posts about the Ten Terrains.

Sign up below and we will include YOU when we send the newsletter out. This is a great way to learn more about the Ten Terrains, and stay up to date with everything happening in the Ten Terrains conversation.

→ www.tenterrains.com/mailinglist

CONNECT UP

Once a critical mass of people from around the world have completed their Terrain Analysis Questionnaire, people at each Terrain will be able to start *finding each other* and connecting up, both in their local areas and also globally.

People who always thought they were *alone* will now be able to find others who share their perspective on life. For example, people at Diamond will be able to find like-minded friends at Diamond, people at Circle will be able to connect with their Heart-tribe at

Circle, people at Spiral will be able to draw to them kindred spirits at Spiral, etc.

Not only will new 1:1 relationships be able to be formed based on having a shared Terrain, but *groups* of people will be able to come together who all share the same core perspective on life. Groups will be able to self-organize around their shared Terrain. Resource-pools will begin to be formed.

All these connections will be based on a shared core perception of reality. Can you imagine the kind of friendships, business partnerships and romantic relationships that could grow out of such deep core compatibility? Can you imagine the kinds of communities that could form? Can you imagine the kinds of gatherings, events, projects and innovations that could come out of the synergy of such like-minded and like-hearted people meeting each other?

But the first step is for everyone to find out what Terrain they are at. So play your part in making that happen. Tell everyone you know to go to www.tenterrains.com and complete their Terrain Analysis Questionnaire. You will be helping get the ball rolling on a major worldwide phenomenon—a new global network based in shared consciousness!

And if *you* are interested in meeting like minded people at *your* Terrain, make sure to go to www.tenterrains.com and do the 'Terrain Analysis' yourself. When we give you your Terrain results, we will let you know how to connect with other people around the world who are also at your Terrain, by joining Terrain-specific groups on social media, in online forums and more.

CHANGE THE WORLD

The Ten Terrains Of Consciousness is a ground-breaking new Model to help all of us understand our world. And YOU are one of the first people to learn about it!

YOU have the power to make a huge difference to our planet, by letting other people know about the Ten Terrains.

Think about how much this information could help all your friends and loved ones. It would help them understand where they are at on their own evolutionary journey, why they are living the kind of life they are living, why they are facing the challenges they are facing, why they are drawn to the people and things they are drawn to, and why they are having so much conflict with people who see the world differently from them.

Think about how much this knowledge could help people to make sense of the outside world, and to understand why historical events have played out as they have. It would help them see what is really going on beneath the surface of the political struggles on this planet and what is truly causing the environmental and social problems we are facing today as a species.

If everyone in the world had this knowledge, think of all the conflict that would be avoided. Think of how much better people would get along with each other. Think of how much clearer everyone would be on their spiritual journeys. Think of how much more Love and acceptance and peace there would be among human kind.

Simply by spreading the word about the Ten Terrains, you will be making a HUGE difference to life on this planet.

SPREAD THE WORD

A powerful way to spread the word about the Ten Terrains is to *leave a positive review of this book on Amazon.* Even a *two line* review by you could inspire someone out there to read this material and could completely change their life. If you have found this book helpful, then go to www.amazon.com right now and leave a review!

Here are some other quick, easy ways you can spread the word to your friends and loved ones:

1. Send them the Terrain Analysis Questionnaire, so they can to find out their own Terrain.

   → Share this link: www.tenterrains.com/map-yourself

2. Send them the free eBook *The Terrains Of Famous People In History*.

    → Share this link: www.tenterrains.com/people

3. Let them know about this book, *Introducing The Ten Terrains Of Consiousness*.

    → Share this link: www.tenterrains.com/book

4. Invite them to join the Ten Terrains mailing list, so they can learn more about the Ten Terrains.

    → Share this link: www.tenterrains.com/mailinglist

5. Encourage them to follow the Ten Terrains on Facebook and Twitter, so they can read our daily posts.

    → www.facebook.com/TenTerrains
    → www.twitter.com/TenTerrains

To make it even easier for you, we have pre-written some posts and tweets about the Ten Terrains that you can share on Facebook and Twitter with just one click! You can find them here:

→ www.tenterrains.com/spread-the-word

The more of the above steps you take, the more people who will learn about the Ten Terrains. Thank you so much for taking a few minutes to help spread the word. YOU are now a crucial part of this expanding global conversation!

GET INVOLVED

Finally, we love to hear from people who are passionate about the Ten Terrains Model. We always welcome new ideas, suggestions, talents, skills, connections, financial contributions and energetic support to help us get this work out to the world.

If you feel called to be part of the Ten Terrains in any way, do get in touch with us at support@tenterrains.com. We'd love to hear from you!

APPENDIX A:

CORE SPIRITUAL ASSUMPTIONS

1. LIFE IS AWARE

THE IDEAS written in this book all come from the fundamental presupposition that everything in the Universe is alive and conscious. As you have seen in the previous chapters, there are a great many consequences that flow from this fundamental presupposition, such as the expansion of human consciousness from fear to Love, the Continuum of awareness from the perception of separation to the knowing of Oneness, and the trajectory of evolution from duality to Unity as the Self-healing, Self-organizing nature of Infinite Consciousness. These principles are as fundamental in the world of Consciousness as gravity is in the world of matter.

In contrast, most other explanations you have read about our world come from a very particular way of thinking that we call 'spiritually-closed'. This is the perspective of much of modern science. It is materialistic, deductive, and rational. It only allows to be true what phenomena it can measure with limited, matter-based instrumentation. It sees the world as 'insentient'—meaning unconscious or inanimate. Inert atoms and molecules are seen to give rise to living organisms (of course, science is not entirely sure how this happens), and only the most advanced of these organisms are seen to have some awareness of themselves.

Along with this belief comes the belief that this inert world is made up from basic material building blocks—matter, energy, time and space—and nothing more. This way of thinking cannot explain a long list of phenomena such as intuition, awareness, telepathy, clairvoyance, distant healing, out of body and Near Death Experiences, remote viewing or dowsing, to name but a few. Furthermore, it cannot explain the existence of our own consciousness, other than explaining it as the mere chemical by-product of the working of our brains. Consciousness is seen by science as a *local* occurrence being a result of matter. According to this theory, it is believed that only humans have the sufficient chemical ability to generate consciousness; all other life is merely reacting from instinct at best.

Science coming from the spiritually-closed perspective is always collecting data and trying to find ways to explain life that fit within its core belief that the world is inert. This is not an easy task, particularly as mankind has developed more and more sophisticated devices to measure our universe, and as a result more complex and baffling data keeps coming in. Spiritually-closed scientists have been at greater and greater pains to explain that data in a way that fits with their core belief. Thus over the centuries, we have seen all manner of changing scientific theories to explain life on this planet, such as flat earth theory, geocentrism, Darwinian evolution, creationism, the big bang theory, quantum physics, string theory, genetic determinism, the human genome, etc. Scientific theory is constantly adapting to try to make sense of its latest observations with reference to a core belief that makes everything complicated. Nothing can ever be truly understood in the greater scheme of life or creation from the self-limiting point of view that consciousness arises from inert matter. Elaborate theories will always be needed to explain away new data, until the next lot of data comes in, requiring yet more complex theories to attempt to explain it.

However, if one were to make just one simple 180 degree shift in perception, suddenly everything that scientists are observing makes sense.[18] Suddenly all becomes *simple* and obvious. That 180 degree shift in perception is this: Our world—our universe—is not inert. It is ALIVE. Consciousness is not an accidental result of matter, it is the *cause* of matter. It is Consciousness with a capital 'C'; sometimes called 'Universal Intelligence' or 'God-force'. It is in every 'thing' and it creates everything in our world, including us. In scientific parlance, Consciousness is *non-local*!

Mystics and enlightened Beings throughout the ages the world over have all known this, as do people who spend time quietly in nature simply observing without any preconceptions; people who work closely with animals, plants and even crystals and minerals; and those who are deeply feeling and connected from their Hearts. For these people, the Universe is alive, from the smallest atoms to the most vast galaxies and beyond. They do not measure this with scientific devices and report it to the world in scientific journals, because it would not occur to them to do so. They are not looking for proof. They have no need to convince others of what they know; they simply know it—as can you.

The entire cosmos is conscious of itself. Although at every level this Consciousness presents itself differently—just like atoms present themselves differently than stars do—yet it all shares the same underlying principle of Self-awareness. This Self-awareness, with its infinite order and symmetry, gives rise to all we see. Nothing is an accident.

The great debate of logicians and their modern scientific ilk is the one often cast as 'evolution versus creation'. The creationists, with their religious notion of 'gods' having made the heavens and the earth, are only partly accurate. The scientific notion of chaos theory giving rise to life is only partly accurate. Both of these viewpoints are limited in their understanding, and thus flawed in their projections. Creation and evolution are in play simultaneously; they always have been and they always will be. Like modern scientists mixing and matching genetic sequences to see what new creations they can concoct, or master chefs in the kitchen testing different recipes to see what new culinary delights can be created, Consciousness is always tinkering and perfecting life. The proof of this is in the mirror! You are Consciousness. You are 'God Consciousness' looking back at its 'Self', and you are every moment of every day tinkering and perfecting your life, are you not?

What if we started with the presupposition that matter—and hence all life and all we see—is the *result* of Consciousness? That the quantum Field, the Zero Point Field, the Plenum, the Ether, the Vacuum, the Void, space—however you choose to relate to the workings of the Universe—is Self-aware and conscious. This notion puts everything into its proper order, its proper symmetry.

'Occam's Law', also known as 'the law of parsimony', states: 'The simplest explanation is usually the right one'. Seeing Consciousness as Non-Local provides a simple explanation that eliminates all the intricate dead-ends modern science constantly runs into. Like putting the Sun rather than the Earth at the center of the solar system, when you put Infinite Consciousness as the cause giving rise to matter rather than matter giving rise to consciousness, everything suddenly makes sense.

When we hold that all life is a result and an expression of Infinite Consciousness, an entirely new reality emerges. We step out of the victimhood, the suffering and the separation of materialism to embrace our Beinghood as Creator Beings. This is the first step to manifesting and realizing your freedom and liberation and your Self-actualization and Self-empowerment: realizing you are more than one with all that is, you ARE all that is—you have all of Consciousness within you!

It is therefore one of the core assumptions of the Ten Terrains Model that this is an intelligent, conscious, self-aware universe. You will find this assumption underlying all of the points in this book. It is inherent in every idea we share and every word we write. Only in an intelligent, conscious, self-aware universe can you have a spectrum of awareness ranging from matter to void. Only in an intelligent, conscious, self-aware universe can you have a Continuum of Consciousness that is self-healing everyone in it back to Unity.

As a result of this underlying assumption, any spiritually-closed scientist who picks this book up may well laugh out loud at it, because it is quite simply outside their paradigm of reality. Or... reading this book may be for them like the life-changing red pill in the movie 'The Matrix', the step that sends them down the rabbit hole into a new reality.

2. WE ARE SPIRITUAL BEINGS

WE, THE CO-WRITERS of this book, do not see ourselves as human beings having a spiritual experience, but as a spiritual Beings having a human experience.

The teachings in this book are based on the assumption that we are each cosmic Beings who come into a human body to experience 3D life. Some people explain this by the workings of 'reincarnation' or 'karma' (at Spiral), others see it as a holographic projection of the morphic Field (at Toroid). But these are just distinctions based on a person's Terrain. The point in common is that this human 3D life is not the be all and end all of our existence. We are in fact much more than a walking body/mind/ego. We have a cosmic nature beyond the current meat suit we are wearing.

The body/ego part of us that is showing up in the walking-talking 3D world is an expression of the choice of Infinite Consciousness to experience itself. Infinite Consciousness has chosen to experience itself in this moment in the vehicle of this particular body, with its own unique physique, coloring, emotional patterns, thinking style, skills, talents, parents, cultural environment, genetic history, and many other factors.

However, it is no longer Infinite Consciousness as pure Self, for once Infinite Consciousness incarnates into a body, it starts to be affected by the input from things outside itself; such as by mental conditioning, emotional trauma, physical toxins and inter-dimensional interference. It is no longer purely Self (Spirit); in addition, it now also has the sum total of all its filters.

Further, from the perspective of the Unity-Based Terrain (Infinity), just like the momentary white tips on the waves of the ocean are all expressions of the one ocean, at an even deeper level we are all different human expressions of *one* Spiritual Being. This one Spiritual Being as Infinite Consciousness exists beyond space and time, and is immortal, omniscient and omnipresent. And we are that.

As a singular Being, we are indivisible, unconditional Love. Yet as our human expressions endure traumas and conditioning, our individual and collective human perceptions experience the illusion of false separation away from our indivisible 'Unity'. Every person alive in this world is an expression of Infinite Consciousness that has become distorted to some degree or other, a watered down version of their true infinite Self. This is why the spiritual path is the path back to remembering who we truly Are.

This truth of our cosmic Oneness, of our true spiritual nature, is the second major assumption underlying the Ten Terrains Model. It is inherent in everything we have written in this book.

APPENDIX B:
TABLES

THE FIVE KEY ELEMENTS

	FOCUS	DIRECTION	ENERGY	FRAME	IMPULSE
	Individual	Outer	Masculine	Single	Fear
	Collective	Outer	Feminine	Single	Fear
	Individual	Outer	Masculine	Single	Fear
	Collective	Outer	Feminine	Single	Fear
	Individual	Outer	Masculine	Single	Fear
	Collective	Inner	Feminine	Single	Love
	Individual	Inner	Masculine	Multiple	Love
	Collective	Inner	Feminine	Multiple	Love
	Individual	Inner	Intregrated	Multiple	Love
	Collective	Inner	Neutral	Multiple	Love

THE 10 EVENT HORIZONS

	You incarnate into a body
	You realize events have patterns and meaning
	You realize you have power over your own destiny
	You realize your value as a human being comes from the part you play in something larger than yourself
	You realize you have your own unique identity
	You are able to feel the 'Web Of Life'
	You realize you are a unique thread in the Cosmic Tapestry with a specific energetic signature
	You are now aware of the infinite dimensionality of the quantum Field
	No more separation - you are One with everything
	The Self dissolves

THE 10 STORIES

	(No story)
	There is a supernatural force totally separate from you that has power over your life and death
	The world is a dangerous, dog-eat-dog place, where everyone is out to get you
	The order of 'the system' will protect you
	Human ingenuity will protect you
	All living things are interconnected
	You are part of an unseen multidimensional intelligence greater than the visible 3D world
	The entirety of Creation is alive, intelligent and co-creative as one unified whole Field
	It's all me!
	(No story)

THE 10 STRATEGIES

	No survival strategy, simply reacting moment to moment
	To please a supernatural force in order to gain its protection
	To gain as much earthly power (wealth, territory, domination) as possible
	To fit into 'the system'
	To influence the world using your mind
	To cooperate with the 'Web Of Life'
	To understand your unique place in the Cosmic Tapestry so as to fully radiate as your true Self
	To collaborate and co-create with the quantum Field
	To completely let go of any charge you are holding in your Self that is keeping you from a neutral Sovereign state of Being
	(No strategy)

THE 10 JOURNEYS

	The Journey Of Separation
	The Journey Of Faith
	The Journey Of Free Will
	The Journey Of Selfless Duty
	The Journey Of Unique Expression
	The Journey Of Heart Connection
	The Journey Of Inner Truth
	The Journey Of Universal Truth
	The Journey Of Oneness
	The Journey Of Being

THE 10 LESSONS

	Learning to experience the pain and suffering that comes from separation
	Learning to place hope and faith in something greater than yourself
	Learning to use your power of choice to further your own interests
	Learning to set aside your individual will and desires in order to fit into 'the system'
	Learning to march to the beat of your own drum
	Learning to fully open your Heart
	Learning to know your Self and manage your own energy field
	Learning to have full trust in Infinite Consciousness as Self
	Learning to hold yourself Sovereign in all situations
	(No lesson)

THE 10 GIFTS

	Staying present in the now
	Commitment to one's faith and beliefs
	Empowered action
	Stability, loyalty and steadfastness
	Intellect, vision and originality
	Love and Service
	Self-love
	Self-knowing, trust and receptivity
	Inner peace
	Presence, Being and bliss

THE 10 CHALLENGES

	Keeping overwhelming fear at bay in order to stay alive
	Ignoring temptation and following the dictates of your god
	Gaining power when other people are resisting you, within an ordered system that is regulating you
	Maintaining the status quo while the world is constantly changing around you
	Finding your own unique identity and standing out from the crowd
	Listening to your Heart and keeping your Heart open
	Discerning between multidimensional frequencies and taking responsibility for your projections
	Distinguishing between what is 'on fractal' and what is false perception
	Remaining in the state of Unity at all times, despite the constant pull back to separation
	(No challenge)

THE 10 DECISION STYLES

	Knee-Jerk Reaction
	Obedient
	Willful
	Duty-Bound
	Mental
	Heart-Guided
	Integrated
	Quantum
	Surrendered
	Neutral

COLLECTIVE SYSTEMS

	No Collective System
	Ecclesiocracy
	Dictatorships, Tyranny, Feudalism, Monarchy, Empire, Oligarchy
	The 'State', Constitutional Republic, Representative Democracy, Communism, Totalitarianism, Fascism
	Direct Democracy
	Heart Community
	Synarchy
	Global Gifting System
	Beinghood
	No Collective System Needed

SELF-GOVERNANCE APPROACH

	Chaos
	Submission
	Domination / Capitulation
	Consensus
	Revolution
	Evolution
	Involution
	Self-rule
	Beinghood
	Presence

Glossary

The 'Ten Terrains of Consciousness' Model is a map. It is a map of Infinite Consciousness as it is playing out in the human experience. Every map needs a legend to help the reader navigate by it. Here is the legend to help you read this map:

UNIQUE TERMINOLOGY

Collective Self

When we use the term 'Collective Self', this is referring to all the individual 'Selves' of humanity as a cluster or group together as one whole Being. Some traditions may use the term 'collective Soul' or 'over-Soul' to describe this notion of the sum total or cluster of humanity's spiritual Being. Collective Self here is being used to include all humanity as one Field.

The Continuum Of Terrains

The term 'The Continuum Of The Ten Terrains Of Consciousness' refers to the progression of increasingly expanding awareness spanning from the fullest resistance of matter out to the total emptiness of the Void, through which all people and civilizations are moving in their spiritual evolution.

Each of us views what we see as our reality from a specific Terrain along this Continuum, from what might be considered a very 'narrow' and potentially limiting viewpoint (Particle) to a perspective that is able to simultaneously see beyond the infinite whole (No-Thing). On the more limited end of the Continuum are fear-centered, separation-oriented tendencies. At the more expanded end of the Continuum are love-centered, unity-oriented tendencies.

The Cosmic Tapestry

'The Cosmic Tapestry' is a multidimensionally expanded perception of the Web Of Life. It extends beyond the seen world of planet Earth to the unseen realms and dimensions, both on and off planet. It includes Beings beyond humans, plants, animals and minerals—such as spirits, entities and other energies—as well as past and future lives and events. As multidimensional Beings each with our own unique bundle of energy 'charge', we each have a place in this grand Cosmic Tapestry as one of its threads, each equally important to the 'whole' of it; remove one thread and the entire fabric of life begins to unravel.

Evolutionary Phase

The term 'Evolutionary Phase' describes which stage of the journey from one Terrain to the next a person is in: 'Stationary' and 'On The Move'. A person who is Stationary at their Terrain has not yet started moving (in an evolutionary sense) to the next Terrain on the Continuum. They are fully immersed in the core lessons of their current Terrain and their behavior will tend to be very typical of that Terrain. A person who is On The Move has already mastered some of the main lessons of their current Terrain and thus their Infinite Self is starting to orchestrate the events in their life to slowly shift them towards the next Terrain. These two phases have a very different energy; one is more inert, settled and resistant and the other is more open, seeking and questing.

To describe where someone is at on their journey from one Terrain to the next, we use a metric out of 10. This number reflects the person's resistance to the natural pull back to Unity, the inertia that is keeping them in their current evolutionary position. A person who is Stationary at their Terrain is 10 out of 10, for they are experiencing the full force of evolutionary resistance and inertia which is keeping them firmly at their current Terrain. A person who is On The Move will have a score of decreasing resistance from 9 to 1, for as they move towards the next Terrain, their evolutionary resistance to the next Terrain starts to decrease, until they cross the Event Horizon of Perception into the next Terrain and are again at 10 at that new Terrain.

Evolutionary Role

The metric 'Evolutionary Role' indicates the role someone is here to play in the evolution of the collective Field of human consciousness. If someone has a high Evolutionary Role, they are here to grow and expand individually in order to expand the consciousness of the entire Field. If someone has a low Evolutionary Role, they are here to remain stable and not expand very much in their lifetime, in order to hold the consciousness of the entire Field stable so that Consciousness on this planet does not expand too fast and thus imbalance the Field. Both types of people are equally important for the timely evolution of human consciousness.

Focus & Filters

The terms 'Focus' and 'Filters' describe two pivotal factors that cause a person to show up in the world the way they do. 'Focus' refers to the degree to which a person is on their true path in this lifetime and is critical to how effectively they are using their life force. 'Filters' refers to how much a person's (conscious or unconscious) conditioning, programming, beliefs, habits and inter-dimensional distortions are getting in the way of them realizing their life's full potential.

Essentially, a person is like a slide projector. In order for their 'holographic image' to fully and brightly show up on the 'screen' that is life, they must both have a clear focus of their light and have cleaned any filters that may be obscuring or occluding the image that is showing up on their screen. In real terms, this means that in order for a person to truly thrive and live the purpose they are here to live, they must have both a high Focus, that is be clearly on their true life path, as well as have low Filters, as the result of clearing away any distortions, conditioning, programs and fears that are preventing them from being their true Self.

Geometry

A person's 'Geometry' refers to the current energy pattern held by the Self in the Field. This pattern is the sum total and nature of the charge forces of energy holding the tapestry of space-time in its present state. This pattern is in constant flux as new intentions create new charge, and as healing and clearing processes remove old charged energy patterns built up over time as a result of a myriad of factors such as traumas, stuck beliefs, etc.

Everyone comes into this life with a unique Geometry, made up of such factors as their time and place of birth, the family, culture and era they are born into, their genetic makeup and ancestral Soul history, the karma and agreements of their past lives, and lots more. All of this is part of the 'set up' that allows them to have the experiences, learn the lessons and contribute the specific gifts that their Self wishes them to express in this lifetime. People's personalities, talents and personal qualities are formed by all of these factors.

A person's Geometry sets up the trajectory where they will end up, assuming nothing comes along to knock them in a different direction. That Geometry, with its myriad of variables, forms the self-similar cycles repeating themselves over and over again until a person dissolves the charge forces holding them in place and creates a new Geometry.

Infinite Consciousness

We use the terms 'Infinite Consciousness' and 'Consciousness' as shorthand for the full title 'Infinite Consciousness as Unity.' See below.

INFINITE CONSCIOUSNESS AS UNITY

When we refer to 'Infinite Consciousness as Unity', we are referring to the infinitely self-aware intelligence that is everything in every universe in every dimension. It is the source of all true Knowing and all true Power. It is the Creator of everything that happens, for it chooses to experience itself in infinite ways.

This is sometimes referred to as 'Source', 'God', 'God-force', 'Universal Mind', 'Infinite Intelligence', 'I Am That I Am', 'Great Spirit' or 'Unconditional Love'. We are calling it 'Infinite Consciousness as Unity' because it is Infinite Consciousness in its full unified form; omnipresent, omniscient and omnipotent. It is infinite in space and time and includes all possibilities; it is aware of itself, is completely neutral and has no conditions; and it is unified in itself, indivisible and all One. It is immortal, because the cycles of time have not yet begun. Infinite Consciousness as Unity is what gives rise to universes and multiverses and infinite other forms of Creation.

Throughout the book, we either refer to this by its full name, 'Infinite Consciousness as Unity', as 'Infinite Consciousness I AM' or by the shorthand terms 'Infinite Consciousness' and 'Consciousness'.

INFINITE CONSCIOUSNESS AS SELF

When we refer to 'Infinite Consciousness as Self', we are referring to that same Infinite Consciousness that is self-aware, omniscient, omnipresent, omnipotent and immortal, only now it is expressing itself in an individuated way. It is the greater part of each of us, that part that is observing all of our choices, that is guiding us on our life path. It is our true self, the part of us that is not subject to conditioning, programming, toxicity or trauma. This is sometimes referred to as a person's 'Spirit', their 'Higher Self' or, in some cases, their 'Soul'.

We are calling this 'Infinite Consciousness as Self' because it is the fractalized expression of our divine Oneness into infinite individuated spiritual Beings each moving through cycles of space-time on their own multidimensional timeline on their own journey with their own unique Geometry.

Throughout the book, we either refer to this by its full name, 'Infinite Consciousness as Self' or by the shorthand terms 'Infinite Self' and 'Self'.

INFINITE CONSCIOUSNESS AS MATTER

When we refer to 'Infinite Consciousness as Matter', we are referring to that body/ego part of us that is showing up in the walking-talking 3D world as an expression of the choice of Infinite Consciousness to experience itself. Infinite Consciousness has chosen to experience itself in this moment in the vehicle of this particular body, with its own unique physique, coloring, emotional patterns, thinking style, skills, talents, parents, cultural environment, genetic history, and many other factors. However, it is no longer Infinite Consciousness as pure Self, for once Infinite Consciousness incarnates into a body, it starts to be tainted with the input from things outside itself; by mental conditioning, emotional trauma, physical toxins and inter-dimensional interference. It is no longer purely Self (Spirit); in addition it now also has the sum total of all its filters.

Every person alive in this world is an expression of Infinite Consciousness that has become distorted to some degree or other, a watered down version of their true Infinite Self. Therefore, when we are referring to any person, we are referring to 'Infinite Consciousness as Matter' not to 'Infinite Consciousness as Self'. Therefore, any time we mention a person by name or use a pronoun—such as 'I', 'you', 'him', 'her', 'us', 'we', or 'them'- we are referring to 'Infinite Consciousness as Matter'.

Reed's 180 Rule

'Reed's 180 Rule' is a maxim developed by co-writer Allen David Reed. It means that everything is the opposite of what you perceive it to be (until your awareness reaches a certain point where it is able to perceive Truth).

An example of Reed's 180 Rule is the expression "I'll believe it when I see it", which is the catch cry of those with the spiritually-closed orientation. The reality and truth is the opposite: "I'll see it when I believe it".

Spiritual Orientation

We have found that people tend to fall into two camps in their 'spiritual orientation' to the world: closed or open.

People with a 'spiritually-closed orientation' are only able to conceive as truth that which they can see with their own eyes and observe with their physical instruments (the gauges, dials and meters of science). These people believe in a materialistic universe, where consciousness is a local phenomenon that arises from the brain. This could also be described as the modern Western 'scientific' or 'atheistic' orientation.

People with a 'spiritually-open orientation' are able to accept as truth the possibility of things that are beyond what they can see with their own eyes and observe with physical instruments. These people are open to the possibility that this is a spiritual universe that is intelligent, in which invisible forces beyond the scope of our outer senses and instruments operate alongside visible ones, where Consciousness is a non-local phenomenon.

Terrain Of Consciousness

A 'Terrain of Consciousness' is the perceptual filter that a person places on the Oneness of Infinite Consciousness. It creates a person's core relationship with reality. It is the context in which all their thoughts, beliefs, values, actions and choices arise.

There are 10 Terrains of Consciousness, existing on a Continuum of awareness ranging from the fullest density of matter to the emptiness of the Void.

GENERAL TERMINOLOGY

The Field

Modern physics terminology defines 'the Field' as the backdrop of the entire Universe. In this sense, it is the container or context of space-time, energy and matter. The Field is also known by the terms 'the quantum Field', 'the collective Field', 'the non-local Field' and 'the morphic Field', and we also refer to it in these terms throughout this book.

However, the Field is much more than what is currently understood by the scientific community; it in fact spans infinite dimensions as the space-time expression of Infinite Consciousness. The Field has been likened to a hologram[19], yet it is much more than that. The Field is the fractal expression of Infinite Consciousness and is intelligent in its own right. It maintains the memory of the infinite dimensions of the cycles of time.

Frequency & Vibration

The terms 'frequency' and 'vibration' are often used somewhat simplistically in metaphysical and new-age literature, and very differently to the way these terms are used in electro-mechanical physics.

For the sake of common understanding we are using the expressions 'high frequency/vibration' and low frequency/vibration' in this book as a shorthand to express the degree of coherence, resonance, integration, unity and harmony that a person has at every dimension of their Being with their greater Infinite Self. The term 'high frequency/vibration' really expresses a greater degree of coherence with one's Infinite Self, and the expression 'low frequency/vibration' really expresses a greater degree of separation, dis-integration, polarization, chaos, and density of one's filters.

The Head

When we refer to the 'head', the 'intellect', the 'thinking mind' or the 'brain mind' we are referring to the thinking that arises from the human brain, as opposed to the *Knowing* that arises from connection with Infinite Consciousness. For most people, the ability to access infinite Knowing has been muted and blocked by mental programming and conditioning; by emotional stress and trauma; and by physical calcification of the pineal gland, clogging of the lymphatic system and desensitizing of the enteric brain in the endocrine system. When the ability to access infinite Knowing is muted, we are like a computer that has been taken offline and can no longer access the vast information on the internet (which in this case is Infinite Consciousness). We can only run ourselves with the small amount of local information that happens to be stored on our hard drive. This is the 'thinking mind'.

Many scientists refer to this small local intellect or thinking mind as 'consciousness'. This is not to be confused with what we are calling 'Consciousness' with a capital 'C', which is the Infinite Intelligence that is Everything. See above under Infinite Consciousness as Unity.

The Heart

We are using the term 'Heart' in this book as a shorthand for 'Energetic Heart Field'. The fact of being in a body means that our connection to Infinite Consciousness as Unity becomes inevitably distorted to some degree. As we have said, it becomes distorted by filters such as programming, conditioning, toxicity, trauma and inter-dimensional interference. Our 'Energetic Heart Field' (which we are shortening to 'Heart') is the part of us that feels this disconnection from Infinite Consciousness as Unity, the part of us that feels our division from unconditional Love, the part of us that suffers the pain of this separation.

Not only does our Energetic Heart Field monitor our connection to Infinite Consciousness and feels when it is disconnected, but our Heart keeps us protected from energetic invasion. When a person is traumatized or suffers great emotional pain, the coherence of our Heart can lower enough that we can be invaded by forces outside ourself. Yet when our Energetic Heart Field is strong and radiating at a high coherence, we can remain clear and Sovereign and in full command of our own vehicle at all times. This is why maintaining a state of Love over fear is important.

Synchronicity

'Synchronicity' is a term that was coined by psychologist Carl Jung, himself at the Coherence-Based Terrain. The term synchronicity means a significant coincidence—or coinciding—of physical and psychological phenomena that are acausally connected. Another way to explain it is that a synchronicity is an experience of two or more events as meaningfully related, where they are unlikely to be causally related.

The Void

When we refer to the 'Void', we are referring to the emptiness from which everything springs. In the pure Presence of the Void is BEING. It is that which sources Infinite Consciousness. It is beyond thought, beyond mortality, and beyond mind. It is beyond light and dark, beyond good and evil, and beyond masculine and feminine, for it is beyond polarity. It contains not even potential or possibility. It has no space or time. It is simply 'no thing'.

The Web Of Life

The 'Web Of Life' is the interconnected thread of mother nature that runs invisibly between all life on this planet. It includes humans, animals, plants and minerals. It includes past ancestors and unborn generations.

References

Here is a list of the works specifically mentioned in this book:

NON FICTION

Atwater, P. M. H. *Beyond The Light*. Transpersonal Publishing, 2009. Print.

Bohm, David. *Wholeness and the Implicate Order*. Routledge, 1980. Print.

Brinkley, Dannion and Paul Perry. *Saved By The Light*. Villard Books, 1994. Print.

Ferriss, Timothy. *The 4-Hour Workweek: Escape 9-5, Live Anywhere, and Join the New Rich*. Crown Publishing Group, 2007. Print.

Graves, Clare W. *The Never Ending Quest: A Treatise On An Emergent Cyclical Conception Of Adult Behavioral Systems And Their Development*. (Unfinished Manuscript edited together by Christopher Cowan and Natasha Todorovic). Santa Barbara, 2005. Print.

Hawkins, David R. *Power vs Force: The Hidden Determinants Of Human Behavior*. Hay House, 2002. Print.

Machiavelli, Niccolò. *The Prince. (Il Principe)*. Antonio Blado d'Asola, 1532. Print.

Ray, Paul. *The Cultural Creatives: How 50 Million People Are Changing The World*. Harmony Books, 2000. Print.

FICTION

Aesop. *Aesop's Fables*. Trans. L Gibbs. Oxford University Press, 2008. Print.

Atwood, Margaret. *The Handmaid's Tale*. McClelland and Stewart, 1985. Print.

Austen, Jane. *Pride and Prejudice*. T. Egerton, Whiltehall, 1813. Print.

Bach, Richard. *Jonathan Livingston Seagull*. Macmillan, 1970. Print.

Blyton, Enid. Various works for children. 1922-1975.

Bradley, Marion Zimmer. *The Mists Of Avalon*. Alfred A Knopf, 1983. Print.

Doyle, Sir Arthur Conan. Various works about Sherlock Holmes. 1887-1927.

Evans, Nicholas. *The Horse Whisperer*. Delacorte Press, 1995. Print.

Fitzgerald, F. Scott. *The Great Gatsby*. Charles Scribner's Sons, 1952. Print.

Gibran, Kahlil. *The Prophet*. Alfred A. Knopf, 1923. Print.

Golding, William. *Lord Of The Flies*. Faber & Faber, 1954. Print.

Golding, William. *The Inheritors*. Faber & Faber, 1955. Print.

Lewis, C. S. *The Chronicles of Narnia*. Series. HarperCollins, 1950-1956. Print.

Megre, Vladimir. *Anastasia* (The Ringing Cedars, 9 Vol. Set). Ringing Cedars Press, 2008. Print.

Montgomery, Lucy Maud. *Anne of Green Gables*. Series. L C Page & Co, 1908-1939. Print.

Orwell, George. *Animal Farm*. Secker & Warburg, 1945. Print.

Orwell, George. *1984*. Secker & Warburg, 1949. Print.

Redfield, James. *The Celestine Prophecy*. Warner Books, 1997. Print.

Rice, Anne. *The Vampire Chronicles*. Series. Knopf, 1976-2014. Print.

Rowling, J.K. *Harry Potter*. Series. Bloomsbury Publishing, 1997–2007. Print.

Seuss, Dr. *The Lorax*. Random House, 1971. Print.

Shelley, Mary Wollstonecraft. *Frankenstein*. Lackington, Hughes, Harding, Mavor & Jones, 1818. Print.

Starhawk. *The Fifth Sacred Thing*. Bantam, 1993. Print.

Tolkien, J. R. R. *The Lord Of The Rings*. George Allen & Unwin, 1954-1955. Print.

Vergil. Aen*eid*. Translated by John Dryden. Vol. XIII. The Harvard Classics. P.F. Collier & Son, 1909–14. Print.

Additional Resources

There are thousands of teachers and teachings that have informed and influenced the authors of the Ten Terrains Model over the course of our lives—far too many to list here. However, so that you can get a sense of the scope of the background to this work, here are some notable resources we feel you may wish to investigate further:

RECOMMENDED BOOKS

Bowman, Carol. *Children's Past Lives*. Bantam, 1998. Print.

Campbell, Joseph John. *The Hero with a Thousand Faces*. New World Library, 2008. Print.

Cathie, Bruce. *Harmonic 33*. A. Reed Ltd., 1972. Print.

Chittick, William C. *The Sufi Path of Knowledge*. State Univ. of N.Y. Press, 1989. Print.

Cohen, Alan. *A Course in Miracles Made Easy*. Hay House, 2015. Print.

Dollard, Eric P. *A Common Language for Electrical Engineering*. A. & P. Electronic Media, 2015. Print.

Easwaran, Eknath. *The Bhagavad Gita and The Upanishads*. Nilgiri Press, 2007. Print.

Everett, Alexander. *Cosmic Consciousness*. Holisys, 2005. eBook. (www.experienceinnerpeace.com)

Faulkner, Raymond. *The Egyptian Book of the Dead*. Chronicle Books; Rev. ed., 2015. Print.

Feldenkrais, Moshe. *The Potent Self*. Harper S.F., 1992. Print.

Fortune, Dion. *Mystical Qabalah*. Weiser Books, 2000. Print.

Fuller, R. Buckminster. *Intuition*. Doubleday, 1973. Print.

Gleiser, Marcelo. *The Island of Knowledge: The Limits of Science and the Search for Meaning*. Basic Books, 2015. Print.

Hagelin, John. *Is consciousness the unified field? A field theorist's perspective*. Modern Science and Vedic Science 1, 1987, pp 29–87.

Hall, Manly P. *The Secret Teachings of All Ages*. The Philos. Res. Soc. Inc., 2000. Print.

Hesse, Hermann. *Siddhartha*. Bantam, 1982. Print.

Hu, Ra Uru. *Human Design: The Definitive Book of Human Design, The Science of Differentiation*. HDC Publ., 2011. Print.

Huang, Alfred. *The Complete I Ching 10th Anniversary Ed*. Inner Traditions, 2010. Print.

Hurtak, J. J. *An Introduction to the Keys of Enoch*. The Academy for Fut. Sc.; 4th ed. 1997.

Jung, Carl G. *Synchronicity*. Princeton Univ. Press, 2010. Print.

Keirsey, David and Bates, Marilyn. *Please Understand Me*. Prometheus, 1984. Print.

Krishnamurti, Jiddu. *The Ending of Time*. HarperOne, 2014. Print.

Kroeger, Hanna. *God helps those who help themselves*. Hanna Kroeger Publ., 1984. Print.

Lao Tsu, *Tao de Ching*. Various Publishers, est. 600 b.c. Print.

Lipton, Bruce. *The Biology of Belief*. Hay House, Revised Ed. 2013. Print.

Lotterhand, Jason C. *The Thursday Night Tarot*. Newcastle Publ. Co., 1989. Print.

Malachi, Tau. *Gnosis of the Cosmic Christ*. Llewellyn Publications, 2005. Print.

Padmasambhava. *The Tibetan Book of the Dead*. N. Atlantic Books, 2013. Print.

Polari de Alverga, Alex. *Forest of Visions*. Park Street Press, 1999. Print.

Reich, Wilhelm. *Ether, God & Devil & Cosmic Superimposition*. Farrar, 1972. Print.

Rudd, Richard. *Gene Keys: Unlocking the Higher Purpose Hidden in Your DNA*. Watkins, 2013. Print.

Russell, Walter. *The Universal One*. Univ of Science & Philosophy, 1974. Print.

Sri Aurobindo. *Powers Within*. Lotus Press, 1999. Print.

Strassman, Rick. *DMT: The Spirit Molecule: A Doctor's Revolutionary Research into the Biology of Near-Death and Mystical Experiences*. Park Street Press, 2000. Print.

Szekely, Edmond B. *The Gospel of the Essenes*. C.W. Daniel Co Ltd., 1979. Print.

Targ, Russell and Katra, Jane. *Miracles of Mind: Exploring Nonlocal Consciousness and Spiritual Healing*. New World Library, 1999. Print.

Tesla, Nikola. *My Inventions: The Autobiography of Nikola Tesla*. SoHo Books, 2015. Print.

Yogananda, Paramahansa. *Autobiography of a Yogi*. Self-Realization Fellowship, 1998. Print.

RECOMMENDED ORGANIZATIONS

American Society of Dowsers:
www.dowsers.org

Foundation for Mind Being Research. Bill Gough, co-founder:
www.fmbr.org

HeartMath Institute:
www.heartmath.org

Holographic Kinetics. Steve Richards, Founder:
www.holographickinetics.com

Institute Of Noetic Sciences (IONS). Edgar Mitchell, Founder:
www.noetic.org

SRI International, VALS (Values and Lifestyles) Model:
www.sri.com

Taroscopes Mystery School. Michael Tsarion, Founder:
www.taroscopes.com

TimeGnosis Timing Calendar:
www.timegnosis.com

Notes

1. See the Glossary at the back of the book for the definition of 'Infinite Self', as well as definitions of all other original terms used in this book.
2. David R. Hawkins. *Power vs Force: The Hidden Determinants Of Human Behavior*. Hay House, 2002. Print.
3. Clare W. Graves. *The Never Ending Quest: A Treatise On An Emergent Cyclical Conception Of Adult Behavioral Systems And Their Development*. (Unfinished Manuscript edited together by Christopher Cowan and Natasha Todorovic). Santa Barbara, 2005. Print.
4. The vampire genre is a good example of Pyramid, as vampires by their very nature live off the life force of others and thus vampire characters are generally at the Will-Based Terrain.
5. Paul Ray. *The Cultural Creatives: How 50 Million People Are Changing The World*. Harmony Books, 2000. Print.
6. See the discussion of these Square political systems in Part 4.
7. See note 5 above.
8. Of course people at Diamond, like people at all Terrains, can have experiences of being tapped in to Infinite Consciousness—for example during an ecstatic experience or by deliberately tuning in through various means—and in those moments they are not limited to their thinking mind. As people expand further out over the Continuum of Terrains, they are able to tap into Infinite Consciousness more and more, until at Infinity they are permanently plugged in. At Diamond, these instances tend to be only occasional, and the predominant approach to life is still a mental one.
9. *The 4-Hour Workweek: Escape 9-5, Live Anywhere, and Join the New Rich* (2007) is a self-help book by Timothy Ferriss.
10. This is 180 degrees opposite the Infinity knowing of 'I AM that I AM'.
11. See the Glossary for a more detailed explanation of the Heart.
12. Once a person expands to Infinity, this perspective falls away and all these iterations of reality that are seen at Spiral as being outside of oneself are now seen as being aspects of one's own Self. Therefore there is no longer any need to 'protect' oneself, there is instead the opportunity to go within and heal one's shadow aspects at a deeper level.
13. The terms 'frequency' and 'vibration' are often used somewhat simplistically in metaphysical and new-age literature. See the Glossary for how we are using them.
14. This can happen if the person has accumulated unresolved trauma and charge force creating an altered Geometry to their forward motion.
15. Our statistical sample includes all people alive today in a human body who are past the age of infancy and therefore 'settled' into a Terrain and who are at least two thirds in charge of their own body vehicle. This is approximately 6.5 billion people. Note: we do not include Beings at No-Thing in our calculations as they are not strictly part of the collective Field of humanity.
16. In our advanced book *Understand Evolution—Using The 10 Terrains Of Consciousness*, we explain the process of how a child comes into their incarnation from the Void and then gradually 'settles' at a particular Terrain in their infancy based on multiple factors.
17. However, it should be noted that many forms of socialism are at Diamond.
18. This is a classic example of 'Reed's 180 Rule'. See Glossary.
19. See David Bohm. Wholeness and the Implicate Order. London: Routledge, 1980. Print.

Index

Terms Of Agreement

The Ten Terrains Of Consciousness is a Model co-created by Allen David Reed and Tahnee Woolf for the purposes of Self-learning, personal empowerment, expansion of Consciousness and global healing, for the highest good of all. It exists in its own dimension at the Unity-Based Terrain (Infinity) and is coming from Love.

This Model and the writings in this book are covered by standard laws of copyright and trademarks. In addition, and above and beyond human laws, by reading any passages in this book you are entering the laws of this dimension and are deemed to have agreed to the following terms and conditions:

1. You will not use any of the ideas or concepts in this book to manipulate, entrap, exploit, judge, exclude or otherwise harm another person.
2. When sharing the ideas in this book with others, you will not deliberately distort, modify, water down or in any other way alter them.

Should you breach the terms of this Agreement, you will find that any harm or distortion you cause will be experienced by yourself at a future point in your timeline, by the universal law of reciprocity.

Find out more
about the
Ten Terrains
Of Consciousness

<u>www.tenterrains.com</u>